Praise for *The New IT*

"*The New IT* taps directly into the current CIO mindset, regardless of industry. In a landscape of rapidly changing technologies and calls for greater innovation, Jill concisely articulates the IT organization imperative to closely collaborate with business counterparts to succeed. She provides clear templates, examples, and advice to start the important conversations and lay the groundwork for wholesale success, not mere incremental change."

—Gary A. King, Chief Information Officer, T-Mobile

"Jill has penned a Tocquevillian map of the digital world. *The New IT* should be a required text for every business leader in the country."

—Thornton May, futurist and author of *The New Know*

"Enterprise IT has reached an inflection point in how services are delivered and consumed, requiring our profession to undertake a transformation of our own. Jill Dyché describes well the challenges we face, how to assess them, and how to take action to complete the journey toward modern enterprise IT."

—Kimberly Stevenson, Vice President
and Chief Information Officer, Intel

"Jill Dyché's new book is the first book on IT that I've enjoyed in some time. Conversational, intuitive, and intelligent, Jill goes right to the heart of governance (control), innovation (change), identity (authority), relevance (alignment), and influence (strategy). It's a timely book that should be read by executives across organizations."

—Peter Marx, Chief Innovation
and Technology Officer, City of Los Angeles

THE NEW

How Technology Leaders Are Enabling Business Strategy in the Digital Age

Jill Dyché

Mc
Graw
Hill
Education

NEW YORK CHICAGO SAN FRANCISCO
ATHENS LONDON MADRID
MEXICO CITY MILAN NEW DELHI
SINGAPORE SYDNEY TORONTO

2 3 4 5 6 7 8 9 0 DOC/DOC 1 2 0 9 8 7 6 5

ISBN   978-0-07-184698-1
MHID   0-07-184698-0

e-ISBN 978-0-07-184699-8
e-MHID   0-07-184699-9

Library of Congress Cataloging-in-Publication Data
Dyché, Jill.
 The new IT : how technology leaders are enabling business strategy in the digital age / Jill Dyché.
    pages cm
 Includes bibliographical references and index.
 ISBN 978-0-07-184698-1 (hardback) — ISBN 0-07-184698-0 (hardback)
 1. Information technology—Management. 2. Strategic planning. I. Title.
 HD30.2.D93 2015
 658.4'012—dc23

                                                                    2015001179

Interior design by Mauna Eichner and Lee Fukui

McGraw-Hill Education books are available at special quantity discounts to use as premiums and sales promotions or for use in corporate training programs. To contact a representative, please visit the Contact Us pages at www.mhprofessional.com.

To Amy, who accompanied me
on the journey through Chapter 9,
then blessed me on my path.

Contents

part 3
Leadership in the New IT

Foreword

As you open this book, I can hear a voice in the back of your mind saying, "IT enabling business strategy? Since when?" The short answer is, "Starting now."

To be more precise, "enterprise IT" used to stand for a set of systems that transacted and recorded business operations—what we call "systems of record." These were designed around departmental processes, organized around databases, enabled by online transaction processing, and understood through business intelligence reporting and analytics. Accounting, human resources, order processing, procurement—you name it, there was (and still is) a system for it somewhere. And this system never captures what we do perfectly or how we do it—hence the incessant bickering.

Today, however, there is another IT. This one was born in the consumer sector, and it is more a type of media than computing. Communications and content are its anchor tenants, and *interactive* and *democratic* are its watchwords. Its iconic manifestation is the smartphone, the device that has toppled dictatorships, tanked careers, and turned etiquette and social protocol upside down. This device is omnipresent, and as such, it is restructuring not only commercial relationships but social, political, and cultural ones as well. Welcome to the world of *Systems of Engagement*.

Your enterprise still needs the old IT to function effectively and efficiently. But it simply cannot survive if it does not also adapt to the new IT. Sector after sector of our economy is capitulating to this realization. Media, financial services, education, travel and hospitality, retail—all are being upended by the new digital infrastructure, and real estate, healthcare, and government all know they are in the on-deck circle. So what does it take to get yourself into the game?

At the front end, it takes customer-facing systems that leverage the ubiquitous computing power we each carry in our pocket or purse. People still like to talk to people, but on their terms, not ours, so whenever self-service can be an option, it should be an option.

That said, it's at the back end that things are getting really interesting. Digital systems log everything we do—and I mean *everything*. Of course, they always have, but in an era of scarce computing resources, that didn't matter much because no one had the horsepower to scour those logs for patterns and insights. Now we do. These logs record the traces of every behavior on every device at every second. It is as if you were a store manager and could watch people's eyes to see what they are looking at, follow their footsteps to see where they are going, note where they are stopping and how long they are lingering. In short, it's as if you could see into all the behaviors that lead up to their going to the checkout line where a traditional system can capture what they are actually buying.

But this is not just about stores. We could be watching a student learn, or a heartbeat vary, a taxicab en route, or a story's viral spread. The point is, *we can see it!*

Or not. If your enterprise does not have this capability, if it cannot read the digital footprints in the sand, it needs to hire a guide—and quickly. The Wild West is a wonderful place to explore new territory in the hunt for riches, but it can be hard on a tenderfoot. The good news is that this market is developing so rapidly it is attracting attention from startups and established players alike, so wherever you are, there is likely to be talent nearby.

And that brings us to this book. Jill Dyché has been spending time with people on the frontier of the big data revolution and all the social, mobile, analytics, and cloud dynamics that go along with it, and she has a tale to tell. At the end of the day, it is a tale about forming a new social contract between IT and the lines of business, one that is more agile, more intimate, and more impactful than any before. It makes for great reading. I can only hope it will also be something you and your colleagues embrace to shape your own future.

Geoffrey A. Moore
Author, *Crossing the Chasm* and *Escape Velocity*

Acknowledgments

don't exactly remember why I had time on my hands in Waunakee, Wisconsin, or what I ordered at the independent coffee shop there. All I remember is that I was consulting with a company in Madison and the CIO had his particular brand of challenges. That little coffee shop on East Main is where I decided to write a book on how enterprise IT organizations needed to change in order to survive, and that CIO, who will remain anonymous, is the first of many people to whom I owe a debt for the writing of this book.

I'd also like to thank the hardy crew at SAS for supporting this project. My team of thought leaders—Kimberly Nevala, Anne Buff, Analise Polsky, Bree Baich, Lisa Loftis, and Rachel Alt-Simmons—never needed my management in the first place, so they didn't miss it on the occasions when it wasn't there. Jeannette Fino helped me with the myriad permissions I needed to take this book from anonymous "blended case studies" to complicated and often-messy real-life stories. David Rankell choreographed my calendar so that evenings and weekends stayed sacred. Tamara Dull took the draft manuscript and worked editorial miracles, for which the professional editors at McGraw-Hill would be grateful, if they only knew.

Thanks, too, to Mike Bright in SAS Marketing for putting up with me during the ideation process, and to Courtney Peters for taking the helm during delivery. Their honesty and perspective have been invaluable. Karen Day and Julie Platt gave me the rules of the road, and Julie Legeros kept offering me small gifts along the journey. Adele Sweetwood, Deb Orton, and Barb Anthony were enthusiastic cheerleaders, who continue doing me the favor of taking me seriously, sometimes at their peril. My boss, Jim Davis, astutely saw the opportunities for a book like this and gave me room. Thanks, Jim.

I humbly requested guidance from some expert reviewers along the way. Art Petty, ever on my informal board of advisors, worked the same magic on my strategy chapter that he did on our corporate strategy at Baseline Consulting. Thanks for both, Art. Donald Farmer is an acknowledged technology innovation expert. I never recognized his diplomacy skills until I read his comments on my chapter on innovation. I cherish every word of encouragement from him.

Thanks to my team at McGraw-Hill for their prowess in both vision and execution. Donya Dickerson was uber-patient and saw the potential of this topic early. Thanks to Cindi Howson and Wendy Rinaldi for making that connection.

They don't know it, but Scott Humphrey and Bob Eve helped seed the idea for this book. Bob's comments continue to resonate even now, and Scott's inspiration endures. Evan Levy, Mark Merritt, Paul Kautza, Tom Davenport, and Thornton May all helped to germinate crucial concepts.

I am so proud of the experts quoted and profiled in this book and thrilled that they allowed me to capture their voices. I interviewed over two dozen executives, and those that made the cut are the renegades who have shaken things up, so it's no surprise that their stories are at once compelling and fun. As diverse as their experiences are, a wicked sense of humor is the thread that connects them all.

Certainly in this constellation of stars, Geoffrey Moore, my Foreword author, shines luminously. I'm so honored that his name is on the book jacket (though it should be in a much bigger font).

Finally, I'm tempted not to give my colleague Dave Accampo a shout-out, but rather ply him with cash on the down-low and keep him a well-guarded secret. Dave IS the best graphic designer and rich media producer on the planet. The images in this book, roughly rendered by me, came to life through Dave's burnishing. If this book has in any way moved from good to great, it's due to Dave's lapidary handiwork.

Jill Dyché
Los Angeles, California
October 2014

Introduction: Why This Book Is Different

In 2001, I became a faculty member of The Data Warehousing Institute (TDWI) and began teaching a full-day workshop called *BI from Both Sides: Aligning Business and IT*. At an event where database administrators and IT architects comprised the majority of attendees, the workshop drew an immediate following. The IT audience wanted to understand how to work more effectively with businesspeople, whom they considered hard to reach. Disengaged. Barriers to progress. The list went on.

BI from Both Sides challenged some entrenched IT orthodoxies, piercing the veil of complex architectures and encouraging a technical crowd to get comfortable with business strategy. In class, we discussed how to engage more fully with the business, who should do what, and how best-practice companies were using analytics to drive collaboration.

Occasionally a stray project manager would find his or her way into my workshop. These project managers often represented lines of business, and they, too, were searching for clarity around work plans and organizational structures. They wouldn't admit it, but most of them were wondering how they could become more nimble by circumventing IT.

Despite the event's focus on business intelligence and data warehousing, workshop attendees asked questions that had nothing to do with technology:

- How do we know what to build when we have no insight into business planning?

- How do we keep executives' attention long enough to get their support—and funding?

- How do we find an executive sponsor for our projects?

- How do we effectively prioritize key initiatives and not alienate remaining stakeholders?

- Our vendors say they can help us deliver. What should they own relative to what we own?

- What does innovation look like in a corporate culture that's deadline driven?

- What should I outsource?

- What should I surrender?

The prevailing sentiment seemed to be: "If we don't know where the business is going, how the heck can we know where *we're* going?"

These professionals were aware of the well-worn platitudes coming from high-tech industry analysts. "Drive business value through IT" and "Become a data-driven company" and, increasingly, "Total digitization!" may as well have been tattooed on their foreheads. Few knew what those admonishments looked like, and fewer still had ever seen them in action.

Moreover, everyone seemed to be focused on the question of "Who?" irrespective of the "Why?" and "How?" My students were wrestling with mission statements, ownership debates, job descriptions, functional boundaries, and corporate politics. They were looking for org charts on which to base their delivery processes—never mind that those processes didn't exist.

The Ironic Shift

Then a weird thing happened. Businesspeople began attending my workshop. Business analysts joined the project managers and dashboard designers. Then came customer service representatives, brand managers, and sales engineers. In 2010 a smattering of line-of-business vice presidents joined us, and by 2012, I'd have a dozen or so bona fide executives sitting in.

These executives weren't above taking comprehensive notes in class, booking one-on-one guru sessions, and asking honest questions about their own competencies. Many were wondering how to establish cultures of "fact-based decision making." Others were under pressure to deliver corporate

strategies, sensibly recognizing the role that technology would be playing in strategic enablement and the new world of digital.

These business leaders didn't really care about technology standards or underlying architectures. They were there to understand how IT could drive value at their companies—and, by extension, contribute to their own success.

Unlike the IT-centric audiences in my earlier workshops, these leaders were concerned with how to incorporate technology into their overall road-maps. They wanted to understand funding models and organizational design alternatives. They wanted to know how to launch high-profile projects. They were laser focused on the rules of engagement between the business and IT. (Mainly because they didn't have them.)

The questions I heard from executives struggling with shifting expectations and changing market pressures reflected those of their IT colleagues. At the same time they viewed their challenges through a different lens:

- How do I know if IT is on the right track?

- How do I enlist the CIO's help in fulfilling corporate objectives?

- Wouldn't it be easier for each business unit to own its own technologies?

- What do I do when IT says they're too busy?

- IT is telling me I have to provide funding. How much of their development should come out of my budget?

- I'm feeling like the technical staff prioritizes existing technologies over innovative new products. How do I pin them down?

- My CEO is telling me that this project is mission critical. How much personal involvement should I expect to have?

- What should I outsource?

- What should I surrender?

Just as IT was feeling ignored, the business was feeling overwhelmed. Each group felt beholden to the other for their successes, and rightly so.

But the animosity ran deep. In my guru sessions, line-of-business employees would confide that they'd lost confidence in IT. "They don't get anything done," a bank's VP of retail products said. "We put in a request, and it falls into a black hole. They don't say no, but they don't deliver. I've decided just to handle stuff within my department. I just retained a consulting firm."

Indeed, beleaguered businesspeople complained of protracted working sessions, opaque development schedules, cryptic functional specifications, and jargon-heavy excuse making. Time-to-delivery conversations dissolved into a phenomenon colloquially known as "scope creep." Reward systems— or the lack of them—encouraged a culture of "No."

And so began the phenomenon of shadow IT, a thread that's woven into the tapestry of these chapters, and one that leaders on both sides are struggling to unravel.

Who Should Read This Book

This book is for IT executives and the executives who work with them. It's for CIOs who—in their one step forward, two steps back view of progress— are doing their best to reconcile traditional success metrics with growing pressures to innovate. It's for line-of-business managers who are trying to keep revenues up and customer attrition down, who are impatient with the glacial pace of change. It's for CEOs battling the uncertain future of the digital age.

It's a book about new models, revised rules of engagement, and rewritten charters on both sides of the business-IT divide. It might rock some paradigms. It might redefine ways that both IT and business organizations can work together to achieve overarching corporate objectives, with each impelling the other to succeed. It might even spark some revisions in your career plan.

From the business side, you should read this book if you fall into one of these groups:

- New CEOs who are looking for pioneering models for enterprise IT, or who might be struggling with how to position their CIOs or other senior IT staff

- Executive managers, including chief executive officers, chief operating officers, chief strategy officers, or any other company leaders who understand the role technology plays in driving efficiencies or fulfilling strategic goals

- Marketing executives, including CMOs, vice presidents, directors, product managers, and other marketing staff who might be considering—or reconsidering—IT's role in driving campaigns, optimizing analytics, or provisioning customer data

- Managers of strategic initiatives that mandate existing or new technologies

- Sales managers and field salespeople, for whom automation means less manual effort and more face time with customers

- Finance staff or CFOs who require technology to balance the books, and moreover to report on company performance to executives and shareholders

- Privacy professionals, including chief privacy officers, who have a mandate to individualize constituents on behalf of their companies in order to protect both, and must use technology to do so

- Customer support managers and representatives who rely on technology to determine "who's who" and to ensure that their interactions with customers are valuable and relevant

- Line-of-business managers who are finding themselves blessed (or saddled) with IT budgets for the first time, who must understand how to use that money effectively and what the risks are

- Executive sponsors of key business programs, most of which are enabled by IT efforts

From an IT perspective, this book isn't just for CIOs. It's for anyone struggling with IT's reputation, trying to resuscitate moribund relationships with business colleagues, or sensing trends that might impact their own career trajectories:

- IT executives who need to define—or redefine—the role of IT

- CIOs and CTOs looking to improve their reputations and distinguish their value

- IT project managers who are witnessing the erosion of IT responsibilities and who are finding themselves immersed in political battles against external service providers, cloud vendors, or systems integrators

- IT architects who need to support the alignment and integration of external systems

- IT practitioners who are realizing that the jobs they were hired to do are being threatened, both from the inside and the outside

- The "new chiefs"—chief analytics officers, chief data officers, chief digital officers, and chief risk officers—whose work needs to complement that of the CIO while simultaneously supporting critical business goals

Other professionals—many of whom may straddle the fence between the business and IT—will also benefit from reading this book, including IT and industry consultants, strategists, systems integrators, software and hardware vendors, and executive recruiters, all of whom are waking up to the facts that traditional IT institutions are outdated, any quest for a stable career path is pointless, and the five-year plan is an anachronism.

How to Read This Book

This book can be read in a linear fashion, chapter by chapter. I recommend that everyone read Chapters 1 through 3 to understand the problems driving wholesale change in the IT organization as well as the pressures on the business side that are often fanning the flames. Then readers with specific interest areas might choose to go directly to the chapters that are more relevant to them. In either case, the material in each chapter can stand on its own with minimal context from the other chapters. Table I.1 contains a description of each chapter and its primary focus.

TABLE I.1: How to Read This Book

Chapter	Description	What You Will Learn
Part 1: IT Challenges, Real and Perceived		
1. What's Wrong with IT?	This chapter paints a picture of the new market forces that are creating opportunities for companies to leverage IT differently. We'll share some real-life examples of why change is so hard. Chapter 1 calls out typical cultural norms that present barriers to IT modernization, as well as challenges that seem insurmountable to many IT leaders.	Whether you're in IT or on the business side, you'll recognize some of your own team's tendencies and behaviors in this chapter. (After all, the first step is naming them!)
2. The IT Leader's Identity Crisis	Chapter 2 colors in the challenges IT leaders face in managing expectations for transformation, modernization, and innovation. It offers a set of atypical questions for IT leaders to consider, including, "Who do I want to be?" Six IT archetype profiles are offered here to help leaders determine their current state as well as their desired state.	Taking the gloves off and answering some honest questions can put you on the path of not only understanding your choices but also selecting the one that best fits into your company's culture. The archetypes offered in this chapter can provide an effective vocabulary for rallying business-side leaders to support this change.
3. Self-Assessment One: The Scope of the Problem	Whether your company is regional or global, a medium-size business or in the Fortune 50, crafting a new brand for IT involves understanding the current state.	This first of three self-assessments will help you pinpoint the trouble spots that will be addressed in subsequent chapters of this book.
Part 2: Your IT Transformation Toolkit		
4. Strategy on a Page	Someone once said that the journey begins with a single step. Strategic planning needn't be a difficult and protracted activity. IT strategy should be business aligned, focused, easy to share, and above all, simple. Chapter 4 presents several tools to help you create and communicate a newly relevant IT plan. Real-life examples of Strategy on a Page illustrate sample structures you might consider adopting.	By reviewing successful frameworks from other companies, you'll have the basis for an IT strategy that gets people's attention. And if the IT plan is designed around business strategy, they can't say no.

(continues)

TABLE I.1: **How to Read This Book** *(continued)*

Chapter	Description	What You Will Learn
Part 2: Your IT Transformation Toolkit *(continued)*		
5. Operations: Rethinking Your IT Portfolio	The growing tension between the "keeping the lights on" and incubating new ideas keeps CEOs and CIOs up at night. Most CIOs are adept at creating operating plans, negotiating budgets, and allocating resources. Where they're less skilled is in reconciling operational and strategic initiatives in a common framework.	Prioritizing key IT initiatives is—or should be—a formal process no less important than choosing those initiatives in the first place. This chapter shows both IT and business leaders a structured process for prioritizing key projects, creating a plan, and enlisting constituents, thereby turning stakeholders into partners.
6. Organizational Models and IT Service Lines	No, there is no single template for an IT organization. In fact, there are numerous possibilities. Part of transforming IT usually means restructuring it. In the new age of business alignment, this chapter introduces the concept of IT as a series of service lines, circumscribing ownership, and inviting several organizational frameworks to support them. This chapter lays out the indispensable components of the new IT organization, and it proposes fresh models to inform ownership, reporting structures, and ongoing collaboration.	Leaders on both sides can use these new structures to redefine ownership and accountabilities, bringing their peers (back) to the table and involving them in recrafting IT's value proposition.

Chapter	Description	What You Will Learn
7. Innovation, Going Digital, and Other Uphill Battles	Every IT leader is juggling steady-state technologies with growing demands of the digital economy. Boards of directors are increasing the heat on executives to innovate, often to aid in competitive differentiation. Creating innovation labs and supporting the demands of digitization are often equated to changing the tires while the car is moving. Neither IT nor business leaders can ignore this challenge. It will only get worse (or better, depending on your perspective). In this chapter, you'll find the tools to transcend the act of thinking about "what's next" to formalizing a culture of innovation and the structures around it.	You'll learn that discovery, incubation, and "fail-fast" practices can generate a dialogue that supports innovation and more agile delivery. You'll learn whether new trends like launching an "innovation lab" or using big data in support of a digital strategy are right for your company. You'll also see an example of how to launch a digital initiative. By adopting some of the practices in this chapter, you'll not only bring your company into the world of new IT but you'll also be enhancing your brand.
8. Self-Assessment Two: Your Transformation Readiness	Now that you've read the tools and case studies about transformation in action, how ready for change are you? This second self-assessment includes questions about whether your company thrives in a collaborative model, whether delivery works best when it's top down or bottom up, and how open executives are to supporting a new IT model.	This assessment will quickly gauge your collaboration and transformation skills. It will also provide you with a ranking and accompanying next steps to consider before launching wholesale change.
Part 3: Leadership in the New IT		
9. Fighting the Talent Wars	Any leader will admit that a department is only as effective as its people. But how do IT leaders compete for top talent in the age of startups, consumer technologies in the workplace, data scientists, and competitors who were "born digital"? Why would talented job candidates choose your company? And why would they want to be led by someone like you?	Top IT leaders make common decisions around not only attracting new talent but also rewarding existing staff members in new, forward-thinking ways. You'll read about leaders on both sides who have found fresh ways to find, keep, and, yes, release employees to ensure that business requirements are consistently met and IT remains continuously relevant.

(continues)

TABLE I.1: **How to Read This Book** (continued)

Chapter	Description	What You Will Learn
Part 3: Leadership in the New IT (continued)		
10. Getting and Keeping a Seat at the Table	Managing change is one thing. Many IT leaders excel at nurturing small, incremental changes. But leading a transformation that can have a ripple effect from internal systems to the company's relationships with its customers, and with the market in general, is something altogether different.	This chapter will discuss ways that IT leaders and line-of-business executives alike can create a compelling case for change in their respective departments. It includes conversation starters that resonate with C-level executives, assuring them that the new IT drives business value and makes good sense.
11. Self-Assessment Three: Your Leadership Alignment	The frameworks, models, and case studies featured in this book collectively represent the tools in your new IT toolkit. But tools alone can't fix all problems. What leadership skills do you and your direct reports bring to the table to ensure that the changes you're ready to make have teeth?	Take this final self-assessment to determine your leadership score, adding that to the other self-assessment results to get a complete picture of your transformation readiness, and of your path forward.

Throughout the book, you'll discover conversations geared to your particular organization or role. You'll also notice a "Note to the CEO" at the end of every chapter. This section offers honest advice for senior leaders charged with establishing corporate direction and culture, as well as suggesting ways to ensure that the improvements stick.

Case Studies and Quotes

As in all lines of work, there are people who see change coming and rise to meet it, seizing the opportunity to test their own theories or leadership skills. And there are those who fight change to preserve the status quo—and often their own perceived power bases. In the latter case, I've omitted the names of many of my sources in order to protect them or their companies from scrutiny or because they've requested anonymity. While there is no shame in failing, these managers have good reasons for not being on the record about what went wrong.

But when it comes to delivering value, wherever possible, I've named names. The leaders quoted and featured in the book's "Executive Profiles" have done the hard work of transformation and are eager to share their stories. I worked with several of them in my role as cofounder and managing partner of Baseline Consulting, and—since we've spent time in the trenches together—I know they deserve the praise their risk taking has earned them. The leaders featured here illuminate the duality of perspectives between the business and IT on specific topics, and each is a paragon of clarity and collaboration. This book is likely not to be the last place you see or read about these forward thinkers, and rightfully so.

Rock and Roll

As an avid reader of business books, I appreciate the occasional reference to a classic literary work, sports hero, or dead European philosopher. I myself have been guilty of wedging the odd Kierkegaard quote or pithy Yogi Berra aphorism into my books and blogs. But if I see one more Sun Tzu command in a business book, I'll burn my own armada.

Since many executives in both the business and IT ranks are my contemporaries, I've opted to open most of the chapters with a classic rock lyric. When it comes to imparting the wisdom of the world, I'll put Tom Petty up against Jack Welch any day.

part 1

IT Challenges, Real and Perceived

What's Wrong with IT?

Sometimes I get discouraged
Sometimes I feel so down
Sometimes I get so worried
But I don't know what about.
 —Tom Petty & the Heartbreakers, "Century City" (1979)

I t's a frigid wintry morning in Boston, and I hydroplane my way across the hotel parking lot, cursing myself for wearing four-inch heels as I grope inside my backpack for my rental car keys. Despite the ordeal, I'm finding this an apt metaphor for the client I'm about to go visit, a CIO looking to navigate the slippery political terrain of his company, a multinational financial services firm.

When I arrive at Mike's office, his assistant ushers me in, and I'm struck by the spaciousness of his new digs. I'd worked with Mike at his prior company, a regional bank, and he'd obviously moved up in the world. It's been a year since I've seen him, and he gives me a big hug.

"Great to see you, darlin'," he says, and though never a bullshitter, he seems to really mean it.

Besides the increase in square footage and the expansive view, Mike's new office is different in another way. The walls are plastered with colored images of org charts, bar charts, and heat maps. I recognize a Forrester Wave and a few Gartner Magic Quadrants as well as some operating frameworks my consulting firm had built for his prior company. Sitting behind his massive desk surrounded by colorful matrices and charts, Mike seems almost childlike.

"Looks like you made a good move, Mike," I say, taking a seat at his conference table.

Mike is standing at his Nespresso machine, steaming milk for my coffee. He hands me a demitasse cup, takes a seat at the table, and then bellows, "Sara! Shut the door!"

The minute the latch closes, Mike looks at me, manages a tired smile, and puts his head in his hands. "This place is freakin' nuts," he says.

He then regales me with a litany of problems, uncharacteristically rejecting the sunny synonym "opportunities" he had used when we worked together at the bank.

"My predecessor was here for 14 years. Nice guy. They kicked him out just shy of his 15-year anniversary, but I suspect by then he was secretly happy to go. He tried to make changes, but ultimately he had no power. Everything here is a silo. And the legacy systems are all built on a house of cards. Half of my executive peers are pushing me to modernize. The other half are off doing their own thing. There's no way to keep everyone happy. As soon as I create an ally, I lose one."

I nod sympathetically. I'd heard different versions of this from other CIOs, and at this point, I'm thinking of what Tolstoy said about how happy families are all alike, but every unhappy family is unhappy in its own way. No two IT departments break in exactly the same place.

Mike starts in on some of his executive colleagues, and the overall lack of vision. He mentions a book called *Snakes in Suits*,[1] which links corporate behaviors to clinical attributes of psychopathology. I indulge him in his rant. He cracks a joke that if someone doesn't change the financial services industry soon, he'll be putting his retirement fund into an offshore account. He then launches into a tirade about IT industry analysts before I finally interrupt him.

"Mike," I say, "let me just ask you something."

"What?" he says, blinking.

"I get what's wrong. You and I have both seen it before. But what do you need?"

"Jill, isn't it obvious? I need an operating model!"

"Let me ask the question a different way. Who do you want to be?"

Mike puts down his espresso and looks at me as if I've just fallen off a charm bracelet.

The Problem with IT

It's a discussion in meeting rooms, boardrooms, hotel conference rooms, and post-conference cocktail parties: Why isn't IT working? Ask anyone in a corporate or government job and you'll get an earful. As I was writing this book, I'd occasionally throw the question out to friends, clients, and beleaguered airplane seatmates.

The responses come fast and furious. They don't speak our language. They're too focused on résumé building and tinkering, not on driving business value. We don't understand what they're saying when they talk to us. They play favorites with vendors. The CIO hides in his office. They're always "in the weeds."

A few years ago during a session with the marketing staff at a large consumer products company, I asked the group of marketing professionals to dictate a "take no prisoners letter" to IT. The letter would allow for an honest list of grievances. It could only be a single page long, so that the important points came through, and it should include suggestions as well as complaints. We wouldn't send the letter—this would encourage complete honesty—but we would use it as the lightning rod for the group's frustrations.

As the team talked, a litany of complaints emerged that subsequently took form in the following letter:

> Dear IT Team:
> Long time no see. And by that, we mean, Where the hell have you been? We know you're around. Seems you've been complaining to our execs about the lack of business engagement. That we never talk to you. And now you're mad that we've hired consultants to come in to help us build a roadmap.
> Well, guess what? We had no choice. While you're letting that big ERP vendor buy you lunch and having dashboard bake-offs and devising new coding standards—again—we have work to do. It may have slipped your mind, but . . . Newsflash! The company has just downsized. Despite this rough patch, our responsibilities haven't changed. Remember the CEO's companywide webcast in January? The one where he promised that in

the coming year the company would cut costs while increasing customer acquisition and driving innovation? Well, that's our job. And we're trying to get it done.

At this stage we're not sure whether to feel resentment or resignation. After all, we know what you guys have been spending, and, frankly, all that funding should support *our* needs, not yours. You've been loading data into a data warehouse for as long as we can remember. But no one's asked us if we needed any of that data. And if we hear the question, "What keeps you up at night?" one more time from one of your business analysts, we're going to throw the poor bugger down the elevator shaft. Odds are he'll bounce off one of those big servers in your data center.

We read someplace that IT is supposed to act as a supplier to the business. We deal with suppliers all the time. But none of them expect us to understand their internal processes—they just help us solve our problems. You guys keep insisting that we work within your framework. Whatever it is.

Here's what we'd like. We'd like to track the results of our marketing campaigns by the hour and make continuous adjustments. We'd like to monitor and respond to the buzz about the company through social media listening. We'd like the account reps to know about support and payment issues when they're writing customer bids. We'd like to understand what's involved in pushing product recommendations to customers in real time. We'd like our finance and sales numbers to reconcile.

So while you're mounting your crusade against our consultants and lamenting our shoddy technical skills, why don't you schedule a face-to-face meeting with us and ask us about this list? No, this isn't another requirements gathering session. Instead, it's *us offering you* an opportunity to participate. We're hopeful that maybe you can help us solve some of these problems? Or maybe it'll just be business as usual.

In characteristic anticipation of something new,
Your Marketing Users

This exercise was fun for this team, letting them blow off a little steam and renew their esprit de corps. I asked the team members if they felt like sharing the letter with anyone, or whether they'd like to keep it as an artifact of what we all hoped could be an evolving collaboration. Someone even suggested printing the letter and burning it, letting the smoke waft through the air vents and into the CIO's office.

Then the CMO suggested that perhaps IT deserved equal time. I offered my services as an honest broker to the IT organization. With the CMO's permission, I convened a handful of IT managers and directors, reading marketing's letter aloud and then leading the IT team through a similar letter writing exercise. Here's what they came up with:

Dear Marketing Team:

Thanks for your letter and for taking the time to write it. We're surprised you knew where to send it since we never see you over here.

In fact, we're working hard, and we're grateful for any type of feedback. Speaking of which, we invited you all to a lunch-and-learn session last Thursday where we presented a prototype of the customer event management (CEM) solution you've all been asking for. We're one step closer to predicting the churn of high-value customers, but we need your input. Most of you accepted the meeting invitation, but only four of you showed up. What happened?

Okay, we don't want to seem defensive, but if you don't feel listened to, well, neither do we. We understand that you're not wild about those architecture and infrastructure conversations, and we try to shield you from that stuff whenever we can. But sometimes we need your approval for investments in foundational technologies. If IT indeed supports the business, both sides need to know what's being supported.

But since you asked, we'll tell you where we've been. We've been trying to explain to you that we can't develop the custom software you've requested for a packaged price. It seems you all want "Google-simple" software on your desktops. Not to burst your bubble or anything, but here it is: there's really no such thing as technology in a box. Stuff needs to be integrated. So, to answer your question for the ninety-ninth time: no, you can't just "plug and play."

We've also been delivering the 24×7 support you've wanted—or haven't you looked at the service-level agreements (SLAs) we created? This stings a little since we're on call day and night. You don't know this because you're fast asleep while we're upgrading the operational systems that feed your campaign management tool. Sure, you want pretty dashboards on your desktops, but the company is running huge mainframe systems. We can't even get you guys to come look at the stuff we're building for you. At lunchtime. With sandwiches.

Our conundrum is this: the business funds IT, so we're beholden to you for money. Yet when we want to make sure your money is used well, we can't get you to share where you're going, let alone evaluate the solutions you've asked us to build.

Look, we're happy to rethink the way we work together, to collaborate better. We're even happy to fund a resource to shadow you while you do your jobs so we don't have to keep on asking you what's next. But we need you to meet us halfway. Shoot, we need you to meet us, period. How about lunch?

You know where to find us. We're (literally) always here,
Your Corporate IT Colleagues

It's an ongoing battle, and more often than not, IT gets the blame. Indeed, IT bashing has become de rigueur not only in boardrooms but in the popular press and online. Business magazines are rife with discussions of how CIOs can get a seat at the table, how often the CIOs report to CFOs and COOs (versus CEOs), and reasons why the collective reputation of IT leaders has nosedived.

Forbes asked, "Why Doesn't the Role of the CIO Ever Solidify?" echoing a *TechRadar* article that asked, "Is the Role of CIO Still Essential to Business?" Bill Inmon, known in analytics circles as the "father of data warehousing," ranted in a blog post:

So is it any wonder that the corporation does not trust its IT leadership when it comes to bringing in new technology? Hasn't IT leadership made every wrong decision in the book? If history is any indicator, why should any corporation trust its IT staff?[2]

Each of us has seen IT dysfunction in action, and it's never pretty. Scope creep invites projects that are late and over budget. Technically inclined staff are more comfortable playing in the technology sandbox than solving business problems. IT has a dearth of good communicators. Lack of leadership and direction by both corporate and IT management results in "bright shiny object syndrome."

For every problem, IT has its own halfhearted excuse. And when it comes to fixing those problems, the same tired shibboleths are trotted out as promising resolutions.

Kickoffs and Cold Cuts

My client Mike's desire for a framework—an operating model he could use as a template for redesigning his own broken department—was, in reality, a cry for help in the standard language of the CIO. Mike was simply, perhaps admirably, looking for a proven structure that he could leverage on behalf of his new firm. He had used frameworks in the past to communicate direction, and they had always worked. My team had designed an IT operating model for him at his old company, one that reflected its landscape of platforms and applications. He wanted a new one, a fresh one on which he could model his organization—and thus define his own role.

Indeed, IT leaders are comfortable with operating frameworks that mingle resource allocations, budgets, and projects. Absent such frameworks, IT executives are left to their own devices. They often blame others for their growing problems. I've heard variations of the situations listed in Table 1.1 firsthand from executives tired of repeated attempts at fixing IT problems, and they all fit within a few common themes.

TABLE 1.1: Common Excuses for IT Status Quo

Theme and/ or Excuse	Telltale Signs	Actual Quote from an IT Executive
Lack of leadership	• The CEO doesn't establish clear measures for IT executives. • Key decision makers ignore IT or fail to engage. • IT executives are not involved in business planning. • Charismatic or visibility-focused CEOs may not view technology as newsworthy.	"He keeps saying 'just keep doing what you're doing.' But I'm getting bad performance reviews, and I've been disinvited to the board meetings. I didn't do anything wrong. The question is, Am I doing anything *right*?"
Lack of strategy	• The CEO or board of directors doesn't clearly communicate corporate direction. • Key initiative owners don't involve IT in planning or budgeting. • There's a general failure to link technology to corporate goals.	"The only way I can figure out where the company is going is by reading our annual report."
The need for modernization	• Aging systems require inordinate time and resources to maintain. • Confusion about emerging technologies results in inertia. • Legacy systems have become part of the cultural norm.	"They keep talking about using IT for first-mover advantage. But I'm up to my eyeballs trying to replace our 30-year-old mainframe and our 20-year-old customer information file. There's no time for anything new."
Lack of budget or headcount	• IT budgets get incrementally smaller as lines of business launch their own projects. • New job openings linger due to low salaries or poor company reputation. • Repeated funding requests are rejected in favor of non-IT spending.	"The CEO and board keep telling me that IT is a differentiator. But I've had open job reqs for three director-level positions I can't fill because the pay's so low. I have to personally attend design meetings!"

Theme and/ or Excuse	Telltale Signs	Actual Quote from an IT Executive
Pressure to preserve the base	• Classic revenue sources are protected at the expense of new product ideas. • Fear exists that innovation will lead to cannibalization. • There is unwillingness to sunset outdated or obsolete products. • The increasing threat of disruptive competitors is being ignored.	"Sales for our bestselling products are down. We need to redirect resources to increasing those revenues. It's never the right time to explore new products or services—or to formalize innovation."
Style differences	• IT leaders cite personality differences with corporate leadership as a barrier to engagement. • IT's culture doesn't reflect that of the corporation at large. • Visionary CIOs have difficulty refocusing their staffs toward innovation.	"We can't stand her. She likes to hear herself talk in meetings, and she doesn't listen. She doesn't accept suggestions, and she is unavailable for one-on-one discussions. So I just keep quiet. My next company will get my good ideas."
Poor understanding of IT's value	• IT leadership reports to the CFO or COO, not to the CEO. • Backward-looking corporate boards perceive IT as a shared service. • There is pressure to outsource potentially differentiating technologies. • IT is marginalized as an operating expense. • A strict hire-from-within policy means a dearth of new thinking or fresh perspectives.	"I've been trying to sell the CFO on investing in analytics. Then he tells me to bring system upgrade cost estimates to the next executive staff meeting. I guess that's all I need to know about how we're measured!"

Reactions to these all-too-real phenomena tend to focus more on personalities than on processes or systems. In fact, the sentence "Maybe we need to bring someone in from the outside" has left the lips of CEOs and CIOs alike in an effort to rectify these and other problems. The outsider can be a technology consultant, a systems integrator, a strategy guru, or an executive coach. The point is that he, she, or they won't be on the inside, and thus they will bring an unbiased perspective to the issues. They will have the experience to recommend a plan of action, and they'll have the authority to be taken seriously.

The external firm comes in, holds a kickoff meeting (lunch will be from Panera or some other purveyor of sandwiches-and-slaw), in which everyone is asked for opinions. The extroverts participate, citing the need for more IT budget or the business side's poor attention span, while the introverts process and take notes. I call this the Kickoff and Cold Cuts Approach to IT planning.

The consultants listen and develop some initial ideas (often reflecting the viewpoint of the person who hired them), which they discuss at the bar after the session.

Then they draft up a PowerPoint presentation, delivering a "readout" to their sponsor. They tweak their bullet points based on their sponsor's feedback—which sometimes contradicts their original recommendations—and distribute the document to the meeting participants. This process is represented in the cycle diagram in Figure 1.1.

Figure 1.1 **The Ersatz IT Improvement Cycle**

The result usually falls short of the original goals. Rather than driving widespread process changes that might introduce significant efficiencies or encourage innovation, the exercise results in small refinements or incremental tweaks that ultimately don't cover the cost of the consultants. By failing to address the root cause, or worse, by not identifying who they want to be and what their organizations want to be, the executives are simply putting their fingers in a hole to stop the spillage, until another hole develops. Over time, the entire effort fizzles.

Many IT managers and executives have come up through the technical ranks, and they are therefore comfortable making incremental refinements to processes, just as they did to their code earlier in their careers. And most of them understand that an inability to drive wholesale change isn't their fault; it's the fault of the executives and boards they report to. A lack of vision for the future—indeed, the inability to see IT's potential to enrich the organization—is the fault of the company's top leaders.

The New Gatekeepers

IT is at a moment when its future is being redefined, and its cultural power is shifting to a new set of gatekeepers. I joke in my conference keynotes that "there's nothing more dangerous than a CEO who's just read an airline magazine." After all, we've all sat across a conference room table from an impatient executive who's asked about a current trend without understanding the complexity of its implementation. (Cloud, anyone?)

Who are these new gatekeepers? They fall into two classes, business units and customers, and their dominance in the IT conversation is growing.

The Business Unit Rises

Research has found that almost half of the CEOs described CIOs as being out of touch with the business and unable to understand how to apply IT in new ways. Over half also considered IT "a commodity service purchased as needed."[3]

Clearly most CEOs haven't positioned IT as a strategic differentiator, never mind inviting their CIOs to weigh in on the conversation. The result? Lines of business, particularly marketing and finance organizations, are obtaining their own IT budgets and setting their own technology courses.

There are certainly cultural and even economic reasons for this shift. But the overarching reason is that business executives are more comfortable with technology than ever before. Marketing vice presidents routinely procure and implement multi-million-dollar customer relationship management (CRM) solutions. Chief financial officers have their favorite applications for balancing their general ledgers. Product managers download inventory reconciliations onto their iPads. A doctor can view her patient's vital signs from her smartphone. Even our home appliances are talking back to us!

And vendors have capitalized on these tech-savvy business users. Visit any large company and you're likely to find a multitude of so-called packaged applications and niche technology solutions obtained without the help—and sometimes without the knowledge—of IT. Business units, measured on sales uplift, campaign response rates, or customer satisfaction, are neither accountable for nor concerned about the fact that they've implemented what are in effect new information silos. Integrated systems and data simply aren't their concern.

At first, this incites questions. "Why did the business go behind our backs?" IT asks. "Why didn't they engage us?" Resentment sets in. "They don't know the first thing about managing a relationship with a cloud provider!" This ultimately leads to inevitable political tensions, each side defending its turf while furtive efforts to showcase expertise results in circling the wagons.

These behaviors become entrenched, and eventually they become part of the corporate culture. At this point they're almost impossible to undo, so CEOs and COOs throw up their hands, in effect sanctioning business unit independence and encouraging other departments to build their own rogue systems. There are no penalties. Thus so-called shadow IT comes out of the closet.

Customer Focus Comes Home to Roost

As with internal business executives, external customers are also getting smarter about technology. A company's ability to leverage IT to improve its relationship with customers can affect nothing less than competitive advantage. The so-called consumerization of technology has meant that a shopper can now go online with a few taps of her smartphone to find the best price on the product she wants, and with a few more taps, buy it. Welcome to the digital enterprise.

Likewise, social media sites are connecting companies with consumers irrespective of brand presence or marketing budget. "I know how to compete with my known competitors," one retail CEO told me recently. "It's the small guys eroding my margins that I can't keep up with." Indeed, unencumbered by years of history, aging management teams, or established business processes, smaller companies with strong social media presence are nipping at the heels of established brands. We need look no further than Blockbuster, MySpace, and Kodak to view the carnage.

Indeed, consumers are moving toward technology and away from large advertising budgets and branding to decide where to buy products and attain services. The website Craigslist has replaced the Yellow Pages, and word-of-mouth is more viral (and to some more credible) when it happens online.

While this has been a boon to small startups and the venture capitalists who fund them, it can be unsettling to executives at established companies saddled with decades-old legacy systems and deep-rooted cultures. As Nicco Mele explains in his book *The End of Big*, the advantages of scale enjoyed by most big companies are collapsing:

> In the past, to have big and powerful clients as a lawyer, you needed to be at a big firm, because only a big firm had access to a wide range of resources: large research teams, expensive subscriptions to legal journals, and secretaries to help you manage large volumes of paper that provided you with a research advantage. Today, with the help of simple online services like Google Search and specialized cloud-based software for the legal profession, a big firm's allure has substantially diminished.[4]

As a result, says Mele, more and more small companies are cropping up and staying small. These companies are attracting the attention of your customers, and they could become your competitors.

For CIOs of more traditional companies, this means new pressures to modernize, exploiting their firms' scale and financial resources while at the same time thinking of new ways to become more nimble and innovative.

The problem is that CEOs aren't measuring these CIOs for modernization or innovation. Instead, they're rewarded for keeping the lights on.

Forging a New IT Identity

The new IT organization is hardly the result of a revolution. It's more like a picnic where everyone brings his or her own favorite dish to the table, often blissfully unaware of what's already being served. The result is often many salads and desserts and a dearth of main courses. Guests leave craving something more substantial.

After all, you can only eat so much potato salad. That's a metaphor for the usual tactic of replacing systems and platforms with something no one really has an issue with, but that likewise doesn't really satisfy anyone.

The lack of IT executives' influence is certainly part of the problem. CIOs, struggling with shifting reporting structures and fighting for a seat at the executive table, are undergoing nothing less than an identity crisis. As CEOs and CFOs continue to measure IT on the trendiness of their smart devices, email uptime, and office applications—constantly scrutinizing IT costs, system availability, and help desk response time—CIOs desperately try to reform their reputations.

A 2013 CIO survey found that 63 percent of the IT executives interviewed were meeting more frequently with influential stakeholders in order to increase their organizational profiles and shift their focus to more pressing strategic concerns. The same survey found that only 39 percent of CIOs reported to the CEO, with the rest reporting to CFOs, COOs, or other departments.[5]

The truth is that kickoffs and cold cuts only go so far. Leaders must take a deliberate and honest look at where they're going in order to induce change. Before you can really know where you're going, you need to know where you are and what's driving the need for change.

The first step is to pinpoint the current challenges IT faces in the age of the cloud, big data, decaying legacy systems, and digital everything. Figure out what the "ideal state" looks like. Then plan what IT assets will help bolster the brands of both the IT organization and the company at large. And, finally, start steering delivery. Figure 1.2 illustrates the steps for creating a new IT identity.

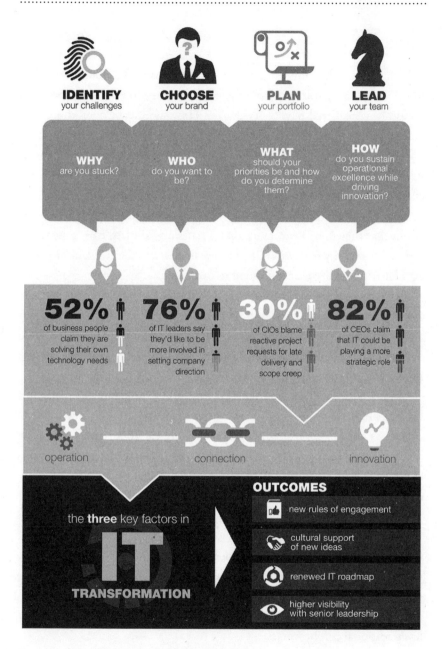

Figure 1.2 **What Factors into IT Transformation?**

Indeed, in order to successfully rebrand their organizations and redefine their own roles, IT leaders should consider three new decision levers that will drive change: operation, connection, and innovation.

Operation

Whether you're shedding commodity applications to the cloud or upgrading your legacy mainframes, as long as IT exists technology operation will always be considered part of its charter. How significant operational systems, enterprise applications, and user delivery technologies are in terms of IT's overall portfolio is the question (and one we'll explore a bit more in the next chapter). IT operations are foundational, allowing companies to execute critical business processes.

For better or worse, many IT leaders are so comfortable with IT operations that they don't venture beyond discussions of platforms, system uptimes, and security issues. While these are important, they underscore a risk avoidance mentality that is difficult to overcome.

"CIOs need to excel at running the day-to-day environment so there are no hiccups," says Rahoul Ghose, CIO of Lifetouch, the world's largest employee-owned photography company. "We need to be good at handling operational needs before we can turn our heads to the cool new stuff, like innovation via mobile apps."

Ghose stresses the need for CIOs to transcend operational focus and offer business solutions. "The pressure to keep systems humming is always there," he adds. "The reality is that when you hear about an IT executive who's fallen out of favor or lost his or her job, it's usually because of an operational failure. So, unfortunately, a lot of IT leaders stick within the safety of operational excellence when they should be doing more."

The question is, regardless of IT's existing competencies in procuring, administering, and managing technology platforms, what percentage of time do they command in the overall engagement and delivery cycle? And, more important, what priority should they claim moving forward? Technology operations are foundational. IT leaders must at once excel at operations, yet they must move beyond an operational focus and toward other less traditional competencies.

Connection

Connection takes many forms, and it can easily be applied to organizations, technology platforms, strategies, projects, or business processes. Many IT leaders conflate connection and integration, tying together diverse business processes via the applications and systems that automate them. With the advent of trends like big data, businesspeople are more apt to see connection through the lens of information, consolidating key data in an effort to reach a single view of the business. And executives see connection as an organizational move to align business units with each other, or with other "shared services" like IT and HR. Of course, connection is all of these things.

But many IT leaders mistake connection with centralization or colocation. Indeed, connection in its purest and most effective form is bringing together related capabilities to serve a larger purpose.

"Every company has the same basic set of technologies, give or take," says Dave Delafield, chief financial officer of Swedish Medical Group. "Everyone has an ERP system, and everyone has an enterprise data warehouse. The list goes on. But those are really the 10 percent problem. The other 90 percent is the complicated part: How do you take a big company and its people and try to drive a certain amount of alignment with technology, with limited capital and resources?"

Indeed, no successful IT organization has overcome its reputation of service provider and cost center without making sustained and meaningful connections, not only between systems but also with business constituencies.

Innovation

With all the buzz around innovation these days, you'd think that CEOs would put it front and center in their strategic planning. But they don't. Yet they expect IT leaders to order their staffs to start thinking up Big New Ideas, all the while retaining outdated compensation systems, thus cementing existing organizational dysfunctions and rewarding inertia.

As we'll see in Chapter 7, "Innovation, Going Digital, and Other Uphill Battles," executives can cultivate a culture of innovation through both emphasizing the strategic importance of new ideas and upending incumbent hierarchies and job functions in order to reward staff for out-of-the-box thinking. The emergence of big data analytics and digital marketing has given many in the C suite an excuse to, as many call it, "fail fast" with agile delivery processes, new technologies, and differentiated business capabilities.

As many executives look toward the future to redefine IT's role in their companies, they make the mistake of assuming that change must take place in an incremental and disassociated way. As the CIO of a Canadian bank told me:

> Once I replace my company's CIF [customer information file], I'll be in the position to start recommending how the bank can get closer to our customers. That's when my peers will start giving my team the respect we deserve.

It's the rare CIO who can stand before his IT infrastructure with its pulchritude of applications and platforms, wipe his hands, and declare, "Great! I'm done!" Most IT executives have numerous reasons for why they can't get out of the weeds. System modernization initiatives. Reduction of application bloat. Scrambling to support BYOD (bring your own device). Performance enhancements. But these efforts need to be placed in the proper context in the IT portfolio, so that IT leadership can drive a variety of heterogeneous initiatives across their systems and solutions—and make room to support business strategy and growth.

EXECUTIVE PROFILE

Ron Guerrier, Toyota Financial Services

When you pull up a chair in Ron Guerrier's office, the first thing you notice, just inside the doorway, is a bowl of tangerines. You offer a theory: visitors coming to pitch software or request funding for a new IT project have exactly the time it takes to peel and eat a tangerine. You then wonder how slowly you can chew.

But the vice president and chief information officer of Toyota Financial Services (TFS) demurs, citing instead his own personal experiment: when people have a choice, they'll choose the fruit over the candy stationed next to it. In effect, Guerrier is promoting the health of his managers and staff.

And not to put too fine a point on it, but Guerrier has been instrumental in the health of Toyota Financial Services. With $99 billion in managed assets, if Toyota Financial Services were a bank, it would be the nation's seventh largest. And Guerrier oversees the technology, solutions, infrastructure, processes, and staff that make it all work.

Taking the Wheel

Guerrier's IT organization has been celebrated in both the business and IT industry press. But what he inherited when he took over Business Technology Services (BTS) isn't what he's leading today.

"We needed a reset," he says of his early days as CIO. "We had a lot of outsiders coming in and telling us about ourselves. I actually wrote a white paper—I even remember the date: April 16, 2010—on the broken relationship between IT and the business. I described the problem and suggested how to fix it. If you don't tell your own story, someone else will tell it for you."

Guerrier set about reorganizing BTS, appointing division information officers (DIOs) as extensions of TFS business units. While they report to him, DIOs have dotted-line responsibility to the vice presidents of their respective business units. This ensures that each business group has their own dedicated IT delegate, in effect ensuring that each line of business has a seat at the IT table and vice versa.

"Putting the DIOs in place definitely improved our relationships with our business partners," says Guerrier. "Once we had more solid lines of communication in place, we could turn our attention to how we were actually communicating. Frankly, there were behaviors we needed to terminate as well as those we needed to encourage. For instance, we needed to stop leading every business conversation with a list of constraints. I tell everyone on my team that they are the 'voice of the CIO.' And that every conversation needs to be bidirectional."

(continues)

Those conversations aren't only bidirectional. They're also multidimensional. Communication mechanisms in BTS include town hall meetings, so-called huddles with smaller groups, and open office hours with Guerrier himself.

Driving Innovation

Guerrier realized that the communications and process refinements he was instituting would eventually allow him to turn his focus toward modernizing IT and introducing fresh technology solutions that could accelerate delivery and improve customer experiences with TFS. But first he had to tackle *muda*.

As a Japanese company, Toyota is steeped in kaizen, a business philosophy—literally translated as "change for the better" and popularized in the West by quality expert W. Edwards Deming—that enculturates continuous improvement and process efficiencies. Key to kaizen is the concept of *muda*, which loosely translates as "waste reduction." (So ingrained has *muda* become at Toyota that its *Wikipedia* definition even cites Toyota's production system.)

"When I was client delivery manager here back in 2007, we had a major kaizen initiative," says Guerrier. "I learned how superfluous work can get in the way of getting things done. So *muda* has become a major focus for us here. For instance, we just finished sunsetting Lotus Notes. That decision was about *muda*. These types of decisions give us more room to focus on new ideas."

New ideas include, for example, moving key applications to the cloud and to digital—Guerrier promoted Marlo Donate to chief digital officer in 2013 to lead the TFS digital direction—and social media technologies. And Guerrier recently introduced an innovation lab, iLab, as a proving ground for new technologies.

"If businesspeople aren't involved regularly with IT, they'll make assumptions about what we can and can't deliver. So they'll end up seeking solutions elsewhere. iLab gives the business a chance to come in and tinker with new technologies. They can engage directly with new tools—see them, touch them."

Guerrier has also invited software vendors into the iLab, allowing them to install their products and invite businesspeople to use them. "We're expanding to feature more functionality and more tool sets," he says. "In the past, when developing systems for the business, it was similar to picking up rocks from the beach. Businesspeople would describe what they wanted, and we'd run to the beach to pick it up. Now we use the iLab as a means of collaboration. Our partners are letting us borrow some of their newer technologies. In the iLab, they can test and prototype. Now it's like inviting our business users to the beach and letting them choose their own rocks!"

Speeding Toward the Future

When it comes to balancing an admittedly aging infrastructure with what he calls "cool new tools," Guerrier lives the challenge every day. "When you have an organization that's 32 years old, some people don't know the origin of the systems. They don't understand the logic of why things are the way they are. But that doesn't mean you have to stand still."

And that white paper Guerrier authored back in 2010? He credits the ideas he proposed for his promotion to CIO. Its title? "IT Delivery 3.0."

CHAPTER SUMMARY

Key Takeaways

- Technology executives across responsibilities struggle to define what IT should look like, often relying on boilerplate frameworks that might not reflect their unique cultures or skills.

- A "keeping the lights on" mentality among company executives means that CIOs have to overcome entrenched biases and behaviors in order to incite change.

- Business disaffection with IT can take many forms, but it is usually the result of lack of delivery or the perception of IT "science projects."

- Well-worn habits, such as retaining outside consultants or coaches, rarely result in systemic change. Rather, they drive refinements or organizational tweaks that might not be sustainable.

- Both internal (line of business) and external (customers and evolving social media technologies) forces are driving technology changes that affect more than just companies' technology plans. They can also change the way the market views your brand.

- The key question CIOs must ask is not, "What should I do with my organization?" but instead, "Who do I want to be in order to drive value?" and "What will my culture support?" We'll examine answers to these questions in subsequent chapters.

Note to the CEO

To transcend established practices and drive change, IT executives need your influence and reach. After all, you promoted that technology director to CIO. It's only fair that you're now willing to help develop your CIO's strategic savvy, highlight her as-yet-untapped coaching skills, and help her delegate more operational responsibilities.

Sometimes executive edict is the only way to leapfrog some of the well-worn excuses discussed in this chapter. As you continue reading, stay aware of ideas that might work at your company. Be prepared to not only advocate them but to also support your leadership team in changing roles and responsibilities, accelerating delivery processes, and rebranding IT. In the next chapter, we'll discuss where to start.

· · · · · · · · · · · ·

The IT Leader's Identity Crisis

Don't let the days go by
Could have been easier on you
I couldn't change, though I wanted to
Should have been easier by three
Our old friend Fear, and you and me

—Bush, "Glycerine" (1994)

Today's IT leaders are haunted by the idea of their own unmet potential. Chief information officers. Chief technology officers. Vice presidents of application development. Chief data officers. Centers of excellence directors. Chief architects. These and other IT managers are confronting the entrenched assumptions, legacy technology paradigms, and general cynicism that have branded enterprise IT.

The consensus among both IT and business professionals is that change is not only necessary but it is also inevitable. The problem is that many leaders are at a loss for what to do. Justifications for inertia may look like so much idle excuse making, but in reality the typical excuses are often barriers that are difficult to overcome. The usual ones include these:

- **"They don't give me the authority I need to do what needs to get done."** Expectations of the CIO range from fast deployment of commodity technologies to being the fulcrum for a range of diverse business requirements and their automation. Empire building, turf wars, plodding delivery speed, and cost overruns aren't exclusive to IT. But business unit leaders have their own problems, and if they don't understand how IT can help them with those problems, they simply won't engage.

- **"In order to build new things, I need to destroy old things."** I heard this one from the CIO of a Japanese auto manufacturer, who went on to explain that the task of sunsetting three legacy mainframes and replacing them with a combination of enterprise application and cloud solutions would take him the better part of three years. The trouble was that the business's perception wasn't that the 40-year-old mainframes were costly and slow. It was that *IT* was costly and slow. By the time key business processes had been automated anew, the CIO was gone.

- **"When they hired me, they didn't know what they were recruiting for."** IT leaders who say this are partly at fault for not asking the right questions. But the point is well taken. What companies say they're looking for—for instance, "a strategic thinker who can collaborate with strong leaders across functions, promote growth, and drive a digital strategy"—may turn out to mask the need for someone to manage network upgrades and craft a BYOD policy.

- **"The CEO told me I'd have influence beyond just technology."** Sometimes this is nothing more than the complaint of a CIO who hasn't earned the right to collaborate on more strategic conversations with his or her executive peers. But it's just as likely to be the failure of a CEO or other senior leader to understand the potential of technology to help the company enter new markets, pinpoint attractive acquisitions, or nab additional customer segments. It's a variation on the prior excuse, since often a technology leader is only as effective as the clarity of the mission.

- **"There's no mission here."** Some of the saddest IT leaders are those who, when it comes to a higher calling, have to define that higher calling themselves. Questions about where the company is headed, requests for strategic plans, and even online searches of the annual report leave beleaguered CIOs in largely operational roles, regardless of their many talents. Thus, even experienced IT leaders who may have excelled at their prior companies, or may have even filled other leadership roles, aren't allowed to contribute what they're capable of. Instead, they are relegated to operations management at the expense of helping to drive strategic direction.

These issues, and other reasons why IT leaders are questioning their positions, all speak to not getting power, and not being given power. (The two aren't necessarily distinct from one another.) But at the end of the day, they come down to two things: the ability of the company's executive leadership to include IT as a strategic lever and the tendency of the culture to allow this to happen.

Who Do You Want to Be?

In Chapter 1, I asked my client Mike, a CIO at a major northeastern financial services firm, who he wanted to be. He obviously hadn't heard that question before, and it threw him. He was expecting what he'd always gotten from his trusted advisors: a new framework he could socialize to revive interest in IT. A roadmap he could show the CEO to prove that he was on the right track. And a PowerPoint org chart that he could tinker with during conference calls. I had to break the news to him: there is no template.

As I explained to Mike, joining a new company is a lot like the first day of school. You come into the classroom and you take a seat. Then, over time, you figure out where you really want to sit. In other words, there's a seat you want to fill, and it's empty. It may be toward the front, closer to the teacher, or it may be at the back of the classroom where you can observe all the action. The point is that you're not stuck where you first sat.

Effective leaders get this. They understand that they have to earn the right to sit where they want. And where they start out is not necessarily where they'll end up. But categorizing IT leaders into personas or "types," à la Myers-Briggs, doesn't solve the entire problem. After all, you can anoint a CIO as an "innovator," but if the rest of his organization is maintaining legacy Cobol code, how innovative is he? It's true that the behavior preferences of the team can inform the model for the entire organization. But that's a more valuable conversation in the context of hiring complementary skill sets into your organization, and we'll talk about it in Chapter 7, "Innovation, Going Digital, and Other Uphill Battles."

There's also a recent move to define two different "speeds" for IT, one inwardly focused and operational, the other externally focused and innovative. Though convenient shorthand for determining an organization's proclivities and informing investment strategies, that perspective ends up being too simplistic and not doing justice to either category. And in the case of two-speed IT, the true challenges lie between fast and slow.

There's an issue that's more urgent than velocity, and it's that IT leaders must decide first how they define success. They need to be honest about their "as-is" environment and define their "to-be" state. Once they do that, the path forward becomes much clearer and the conversation about speed takes on a new relevance.

Defining an IT organization's ideal state isn't trivial. It involves understanding your internal brand so you can set about transforming it, determining the scope of IT's contributions, classifying both internal and external customers, and understanding looming opportunities. Knowing the answers to these questions will bring you that much closer to answering the question I asked Mike: "Who do you want to be?"

The point is to think holistically at the level of working systems rather than, as tempting as it is, at the level of individuals. Categorizing IT organization types also factors in individual behaviors. In this way, IT leaders can understand not only who they want to be but also what kind of organization they want to lead into the future.

The Six IT Archetypes

In working with companies across geographies and industries, I've observed six different organizational behavior sets in IT. I call them *IT archetypes*, and they connote not just theoretical models but actual focus areas, structures, and behaviors.

These archetypes can either be *actual*, signifying the current state of IT at your company, or *aspirational*, serving as a desired future state. Each is distinct in its own right. Depending on your company's culture, each of them has its own reputation, an internal brand. One company's operational manager is another company's bureaucrat. One company's IT broker is another company's cowboy. Management guru Peter Drucker was right when he said, "Culture eats strategy for breakfast."

Your company's culture very likely is what has informed its current IT archetype. Whether you use these different models to explain your current state or inform your vision, they can help reveal your company's appetite for change.

Type 1. Tactical

 CIOs whose organizations fit the Tactical archetype are commonly acknowledged for keeping the lights on. The good news about this is that most corporate business leaders will acknowledge that business couldn't happen without the infrastructure these IT groups sustain.

The bad news, of course, is that this type of IT isn't sexy. Worse, it's being increasingly commoditized.

Never mind the fact that the CIO of a major bank earned his stripes by deploying a core banking system that has kept the bank operational for the past two decades, or that the chief network officer of a cable company essentially runs the pipes that keeps the company in business. When IT leaders in this mode excel, they're extending the core foundational capabilities of their companies.

But executives are increasingly expecting more than what one CTO calls "maintaining the dial tone."

You know when your organization fits the Tactical archetype. Conversations with senior executives and peers consistently involve outages, uptimes, and upgrades. You are sought out for input not on business issues but on operations, automation, and cost. You'd like to drive a racecar, but they keep handing you a shepherd's staff and sending you back out into the pasture.

How do you know when you're ready to transcend Tactical? Here are some indicators:

- You get a budget for moving infrastructure or "steady-state" applications into the cloud.

- You are allowed to hire a senior-level manager to maintain these systems.

- A so-called IT modernization effort has been sanctioned across management lines, providing not only the funding but also the support necessary to overhaul outdated legacy systems and reallocate key functionality to more optimal owners both inside and outside the firm.

- The board of directors starts asking questions about the digital enterprise, big data, or other emerging business trends that mandate new technology and procurement processes.

Being tactical should not be dismissed as an anachronistic model responsible for the widespread disaffection with IT. Many large telecommunications companies and banks have thrived for decades in this mode.

For emerging IT leaders, running a department that fits the Tactical archetype can mean a way to earn one's way into the executive ranks. The Tactical archetype allows up-and-coming IT leaders to tackle complicated systems and prove they can apply new processes and skills to traditional IT environments. This can enhance the opportunity to examine other IT archetypes from a position of strength: there are platforms in place and an established systems infrastructure that's robust and proven. IT leaders can thus spread their wings, either within or outside their current companies.

Type 2. Order Taking

In their haste to be seen as business enabling, many IT departments master the art of release management. Business units approach them for new projects, which they unfailingly insert into a development pipeline. Despite protracted wait times and multiple iterations, business users eventually get what they asked for, and they are grudgingly satisfied. In these organizations, IT is even described as "business focused."

In the best scenarios, requests for IT resources are guided by an overarching mission that is represented by isolated business requests and fulfilled accordingly. The IT leader admonishes his teams to deliver against requirements, and they do.

At worst, the Order Taking approach marginalizes IT. The requestors not only tell IT what they need but often how to deliver it. It's as if IT were one big factory, churning out so much new code, turning the raw materials into finished goods, and awaiting the next fulfillment request. The requestors themselves may have only a partial understanding of how the envisioned functionality helps the business, and they may end up asking for a Band-Aid rather than a cure.

These days, far too many IT professionals confuse saying yes with being business focused. "If we say yes," the IT thinking goes, "they'll endorse us. They'll compliment us in front of executives, enhancing our reputation and cementing our value."

Not so fast. As Abraham Lincoln famously said, "You can't please all the people all of the time." And with the current resource constraints on IT organizations, saying yes to one request often means saying no to another.

The model of "We're here to help, what do you need?" is often accompanied by a backlash when budget cuts and headcount limits mean that saying yes is no longer the de facto response. Business constituents who once unfailingly lined up to take a number are now calling systems integrators to build their applications.

Some IT leaders don't even recognize that they're in Order Taking mode. Here are some of the indicators that they still are there:

- There is a preternatural emphasis on requirements documents and functional specs. While these are important, they are rendered holy in order taking environments where fulfilling exact specifications is synonymous with excellence.

- Developers jockey for projects involving new or emerging technologies, often inciting bitter political feuds.

- There is little understanding of the context of certain requests. "We need to reconcile customer email addresses" is a different problem than "Our new digital strategy needs to factor online purchase frequency into overall customer value." This lack of clarity can lead to the delivery of incomplete or one-off solutions.

The Order Taking archetype might be a means to an end. While programmers get busy fulfilling legitimate business needs, IT leaders can nurture gradual changes, perhaps collaborating more fully with business leaders on their end games, rather than functioning in isolation while imagining that doing so will help them get to where they want to be.

"Today's meeting will be endless, with a half-hour break for lunch."

Type 3. Aligning

In the mid-1990s, I consulted for an automobile company that was rife with politics between the business units and enterprise IT. Accordingly, the CIO instituted a new structure in which each business unit was assigned an IT representative called a "business relationship liaison" (BRL). These BRLs were colocated with their business constituents, ensuring that they were intimate with not only the business vocabulary but also with the evolving business initiatives that would require IT.

When this alignment model worked, the BRL had the full confidence of business colleagues. She was trusted to represent their needs back to IT, and she was often positioned as the face of the business to the rest of the company. She spoke their language, presented their plans, and advocated on their behalf for resources and budget. And the business unit was rewarded with regular new functionality and relevant technology solutions.

When the alignment mode wasn't effective, it usually came down to the BRL not having the organizational authority, or the appropriate business expertise, to represent the business unit's requirements. One BRL had transferred from representing sales to the financial services business unit, and he struggled with the jargon of a division that was less of a car company than it was a lending institution. He was consequently left out of important meetings, discovering after the fact that IT had been bypassed altogether for an important credit risk scoring project.

Every IT leader is trying to improve business alignment. Here are some indicators that your IT team has Aligning as its primary archetype:

- The team has formalized business-facing IT roles. Depending on the company's size and scope, this could mean anything from assigning individual business analysts to each department to dedicating line-of-business CIOs.

- The team uses business unit plans to inform a central IT-specific plan. This process is formal and performed on a regular basis.

- The team manages discrete requirements and development pipelines for each business unit, combining them into a central IT roadmap.

- The team enables information technology SWAT teams or dedicated IT organizations within lines of business, reporting to a central CIO or CTO.

- The team holds regular status updates or strategic planning meetings sanctioned—and often attended—by both business and IT leadership.

The best indicator that Aligning is your company's IT archetype is that the alignment isn't simply indicated by job functions but also by processes and behaviors that give it teeth—and staying power.

Type 4. Data Provisioning

 I'll admit to taking secret enjoyment listening to executives explain why they need to manage data as an asset. "Data is the new oil!" they declare (or the "new water" or "the new air"). "And the more data we have, the faster we can get out ahead of our market, and the smarter we can be about our customers."

I ask them if they believe their corporate data is an asset.

"Yes!" they insist, usually elaborating on how centralizing customer data in a data warehouse saved them millions of dollars, or even explaining a recent decision to fund a big data project, the goal of which was to pinpoint product component errors before they occurred or to predict customer attrition or the next likely purchase.

Then I ask them if they are willing to invest in data proportional to their other corporate assets. Many are flummoxed by the question, eventually admitting that they'd never thought about investing in data in its own right. Some argue that data is a by-product of the applications that generate it and thus should be funded by individual development efforts. Others appear crestfallen, as if their favorite dining spot just got downgraded by the health department.

The fact is that data is the raw material for a host of heretofore unforeseen products, services, and business processes. (If data is the "raw material," then information—where context is applied to data—represents the "finished goods.") Data is coming into and out of our companies at rates unimagined even a decade ago. The amount of data created every day by business alone is equivalent in volume to the digitization of everything anyone has ever said. Statistics like this abound as more and more information enters and exits our companies through a veritable revolving door of systems, subscriptions, and partnerships.

But ask decision makers in your company if they have all the data they need in order to do their jobs. Or what they could be doing if data were easier to locate, access, and understand. You'll hear sad stories about lost deals, abandoned acquisitions, product pricing and dimension errors, inaccurate revenue numbers and customer counts—sometimes discovered only after they've been reported to the street—stores or branches being built too close together, and mistreatment of high-value customers. These stories are legion, and they are very often accompanied by tales of irate company executives. I've heard all these mistakes and others. What they have in common is that they cost companies billions in escalating expenses and lost revenues every year.

Which is why some IT executives are starting to model their organizations around the ability to inventory, access, annotate, regulate, correct, integrate, validate, test, and deploy company data. The systems, applications, tools, and even the skills involved in this work become core to IT's value proposition, while other more operational capabilities are gradually outsourced.

Not only are executives starting to see the potential of harnessing the growing volumes and types of data for greater insight but they are also increasingly compelled by the possibility of monetizing their corporate data. Integrating, aggregating key data, and offering that data digitally to suppliers and partners for a fee can be a tremendous revenue source for forward-thinking companies.

For instance, general merchandise retailers are aggregating customer purchase histories, masking personal identifiers, combining the purchase data with demographic and social behavior data, and reselling the resulting reports to consumer goods firms who might be considering changing their packaging or paying for premium shelf space. Banks, insurers, and hospitality companies, along with retailers, routinely use advanced analytics to determine optimal product mixes to be directed to specific customers or customer segments. Casinos that give out player cards can monitor customers' gaming, shopping, dining, and entertainment activities, sending real-time offers to their smartphones to incent them to book additional stays at their hotel properties.

Characteristics of the Data Provisioning archetype are these:

- The company maintains a robust inventory of data from both internal and external sources.

- The company is comfortable with the security and privacy issues of key data sources being shed to the cloud or outside the firewall and has instituted the accompanying policies.

- The company establishes rigorous processes for ingesting data internally and deploying it externally.

- The company has invested in data-specific IT skill sets separate from the systems and applications that generate the data.

- The company has been able to quantify the value of business intelligence and analytics across organizations and products.

- The company invests in processes like data profiling, validation, cleansing, and master data management, along with the appropriate software, that are dedicated to the ongoing improvement and relevance of data.

- The company has earmarked big data or other strategic data trends as critical to its success.

- The company sustains an authoritative data governance board composed of leaders in both business and IT.

- The company supports experimentation—a.k.a. "data discovery"—to yield unanticipated and often breakthrough insights.

Few IT organizations belong in the Data Provisioning archetype, and moving in that direction is a calculated bet. But executives are increasingly realizing both the qualitative and quantitative value of their data and its role in supporting digital strategy and innovation, and they are willing to make significant investments to move in the direction of data.

Type 5. Brokering

 There are IT leaders who want to own everything. You've seen them: they'll fight tooth-and-nail for control and not cede an inch. Sometimes they're justified, bringing a hard-won and reality-based perspective to operational challenges that are more than often knottier than people realize.

But sometimes this behavior is based on a fear of the slippery slope. It's as if, by giving in this time, they'll begin losing ground. And there will be no stopping it.

Some CIOs are perceptive, seeing where their value lies and offering what remains to business partners and other ventures, thus transforming their IT organizations from being centralized and slow moving to being nimble and connected. The Brokering archetype relies less on a single organization, and more on a network. The network will likely encompass both insiders and outsiders. This requires being circumspect about the IT organization's competencies and bequeathing what's left.

"We want to become an integrator of systems that might not yet exist," says Michel Loranger, chief information officer of the Canadian insurance company SSQ Financial Group. "The future of our organization is to put people where they can really create value. So if there's a packaged application, we'll buy it. And management is newly receptive to the cloud. So we're seeing a shift from people working on development teams to people using partners and deploying what already works. Moving forward, we won't be seeing a lot of development from scratch."

IT groups in brokering mode apply not only a deep understanding of their own strengths and weaknesses but also their superior relationship building skills to cultivate collaborative partnerships with a potentially diverse group of players. They understand when it's time to outsource nonstrategic activities, and they have established a network of providers who can take them on. When a line of business has a requirement, the IT department will initiate repeatable processes to determine if the requirement is served best inside IT, elsewhere in the company, by a vendor or systems integrator, or out in the cloud. Suppliers, research scientists, programmers, designers, universities, customers, and even competitors may all be members of the network, and all of them may participate according to their charters.

In a brokering scenario, the business grows to depend on IT for building and maintaining this web of relationships. Sure, it may mean that more plates are spinning. But agile engagement and development processes are formalized, and deployment is faster than ever. IT handles procurement, so it can continue to evaluate not only the pricing of its partners but their performance as well. Everybody wins.

Characteristics of a Brokering archetype include these:

- A partnership network is developed across a range of competencies, and performance metrics are tracked for each.

- There is a willingness to divest in legacy systems.

- The company scales back in-house staff in favor of contract workers or more formal systems integration partnerships.

- There is a history with or familiarity with key vendors and suppliers who may be able to bring critical work efforts or systems on board quickly and effectively.

- A close working relationship exists with—or there is ownership of—the company's procurement function to ensure optimal pricing and service terms.

And a bonus: brokering is an attractive option for CEOs weary of calling for cost savings and speed of delivery improvements that have until now yielded scant benefits. According to Gartner, partnerships, alliances, and "value networks" of individuals and companies that can take on the work IT leaders no longer consider strategic are among the top five priorities of today's CEOs.[1]

Of course, the Brokering archetype means ceding control, if only temporarily, because when this model works well, control of how individual projects are deployed gives way to control over the optimal delivery channels. Those channels are subsequently rewarded with fees, prestige tiers within the network, and follow-on work.

Type 6. IT Everywhere

 Occasionally you'll hear an IT leader say something like: "I know I'm doing a good job when I render myself dispensable." Huh?

These executives may be reading the writing on the wall. Either shadow IT has become a reality in their organizations, or they've discerned that business units are competent to deploy their own technology solutions and what can't be developed can be pushed to the cloud.

Even executives who avoid the news can't be immune to the trend of IT consumerization. The Internet is delivering our vital signs to our smartphones, free play offers to our gaming consoles, and traffic statistics to our car windshields. Technology is everywhere.

IT Everywhere goes beyond the Brokering archetype, in which IT may still deliver key projects in-house while simultaneously cultivating a broad network of specialty technology providers by shifting the control of technology to those who use it.

Instead, IT Everywhere applies to inside the company and to the outside world. Finance buys its own general ledger software or outsources it to a cloud provider. Sales might choose to administer and maintain the product catalog and price list while outsourcing compensation and territory management. Customers manage and update their own profiles. IT is no longer a black box where all the magic happens (or doesn't). With IT Everywhere, IT becomes a thin layer of program oversight that monitors progress, reports on delivery, and projects future demand. It might not even be called IT anymore.

Interestingly, when some CIOs propose evolving toward IT Everywhere, many business leaders initially love the idea, but they then reject it. Sure, they've been complaining about IT, but that doesn't mean they're ready to take on technology themselves! It's a validation that the other IT archetypes still have some juice.

Nevertheless, a few IT leaders have begun putting the building blocks in place to support IT Everywhere. This means:

- IT development staff members are shifted into the lines of business. Some CIOs work with their business peers to establish "apprenticeships" in which IT staff colocate with business counterparts and watch them do their jobs. Thus they learn the vocabulary of the business (not to mention the personal relationships) and increase their readiness to join the business ranks when the time comes.

- A cloud deployment framework is formalized that applies metrics to outsourcing providers and enforces service-level agreements (SLAs).

- Independent entities are mobilized into a development network to build individual components of technology solutions that can contribute to a larger deliverable. This often requires new capabilities around performance measurement, collaboration, and oversight.

- A program management office (PMO) framework or some other governing body is introduced to monitor technology initiatives, track technology delivery from both internal and external organizations, and regularly update senior managers on progress.

- A willingness exists to sunset initiatives that aren't driving value and to otherwise "clean house." IT Everywhere won't work if it's bogged down maintaining brittle legacy systems or supporting multiyear projects.

Many see IT Everywhere as being the wave of the future. They believe it will place control of technology adoption and deployment in the hands of the businesspeople who are effectively the consumers of that technology, and they believe it will provide the oversight necessary to centrally track and holistically interpret value.

But this is easier said than done. It requires a multiyear roadmap, willingness of key staff to surrender hopes for a predictable organizational future knowing that new opportunities will arise, and solid relationships with external partners willing to assume more risk and accountability. Perhaps the hardest part is establishing a new set of behaviors that will, over time, bring IT leaders even closer to the business.

EXECUTIVE PROFILE

Sahal Laher, Brooks Brothers

"If I look at trends," says Sahal Laher, the CIO of 196-year-old retailing pioneer Brooks Brothers, "I have to say the biggest one is IT breaking down barriers. It's not about 'this is an IT project, this isn't an IT project.' They're all business projects. If you're busy protecting your IT silo, then you're just not strategic."

Laher was answering one of my questions on the future of IT. A retail veteran with management stints at Accenture, Deloitte, and Stride Rite under his belt, Laher places a premium on driving the value of technology. He'll tell you that this value is often despite IT, not because of it.

"People get that technology isn't a silver bullet," he says. "We need to redefine business processes, and we need to look at how we go to market before we shoehorn in a technology solution and pray that it solves all our problems."

So how is Laher tackling the technology challenges of a perpetually growing global retailer—and a household name?

"Well, I didn't walk in here and inherit an IT strategy. I needed to spend time with my peers on the executive team and with the business function heads. They helped me understand the critical business priorities and how we could partner together to make them happen—not only to enable technologies but also to fix business problems."

Recognizing that the scope of a global brand meant different solutions for different markets, Laher implemented an enterprise IT strategy that drills down to specific Brooks Brothers regions. Focusing on a mixture of cultural successes and best practices, Laher's team rolls out geographically focused solutions. "We always have to ask, 'What will this look like in Japan? How will it be different in Europe? And what about China?' A cookie-cutter approach won't work here. There are different ways to go to market, different regulatory issues. We have to be regionally aware."

Global Brand, Global IT

Laher puts an equal emphasis on the culture of his own team. "We spend a lot of time at work. So we need to be collaborative and innovative. That's part of why I joined the company in the first place."

Laher admits that prioritizing IT initiatives is a bit of a juggling act. He also acknowledges that many IT departments have a culture of saying no. Part of his prioritization process is triangulating three factors: scope, resources, and time.

"We need to balance our capabilities," he says. "If we consider these three factors, we can work with the business to come up with solutions together. For instance, if a project's scope is expanding, maybe we bring in some consultants to augment the team. If we make the business aware of the trade-offs, then IT can be transparent. We won't be a barrier."

Part of the transparency Laher values goes back to the vision of the company. He acknowledges that an established brand means that constituents both inside and outside the company may have set expectations. But he insists that's an opportunity to innovate and drive the business to the next level.

"There are two kinds of CIOs," he says. "There are those who are very content to keep the lights on. They're not doing a lot of transformation. I think I'd be bored with that kind of job. The other end of the spectrum are those CIOs who challenge the status quo and evolve their firms' capabilities. That's not for everyone, and it's not for every company. But it's right for us."

Listen and Act

Laher knows that not all companies have such a rock-solid vision, and not all CIOs play a strong role in IT driving corporate growth. In an earlier

(continues)

leadership position, he remembers, "Once a month, I'd give the CEO an update. But here, I can say that IT is on equal footing with other lines of business. I participate in meetings with other C-level executives where we can recalibrate our outlook for the coming quarter and refine our approaches. At minimum, I talk to the CEO on a biweekly basis, but there are multiple forums, so sometimes we end up talking daily."

Laher makes room in his budget for innovation because he considers it not just a strategic advantage but also a way to keep his workforce happy and engaged. We're always asking ourselves, 'What's the best practice for this?'" he says. "Our organization is full of good ideas. So we listen to them, and a large percentage of the time, we act."

Getting from Here to There

When reviewing the six IT archetypes, many IT leaders who consider themselves strategically aligned immediately look for a "strategy" archetype. Why no separate model for strategy? Because—depending on factors like your industry, incumbent infrastructure, vendor standards, and even the company's age and history—each of the archetypes described can be strategic in its own way. For instance, some insurance companies consider their claims databases strategic, even though they were built in the 1980s using mainframe technologies and network databases. Others rely on innovation to help realize fresh strategies, relegating everything else to outsourcers or the cloud.

After reviewing these archetypes, you're probably thinking that your IT department is a unique amalgam of all six. You might be right. But each IT department has a dominant set of behaviors that, for better or worse, defines it. People outside of IT rarely understand the complexity, nuance, and trade-offs that IT departments confront every day. When evaluating the six archetypes, it's helpful to ask, "What's our *primary* model?" This should help you focus on where you are—and where you want to be.

Drawing on these definitions, we can encapsulate each of the archetypes according to the IT department's expertise, behaviors, and core competencies. Table 2.1 illustrates an effective comparison of the six archetypes, including examples of initiatives that typify them.

TABLE 2.1: A Comparison of the IT Archetypes

	Tactical	Order Taking	Aligning	Data Provisioning	Brokering	IT Everywhere
Function	Maintains existing applications and legacy systems	Enables technology delivery to various lines of business	Supports business objectives of individual business units through technology	Creates processes and systems that streamline the access and deployment of cross-functional data inside and outside the company	Vets and sanctions optimal technology providers both within and outside the company	Sheds functional applications into business units; outsources commodity systems and shared infrastructure
Value measurement	System uptime and cost containment	Application delivery and conformance to requirements	Technology delivery in the context of often-heterogeneous business goals	Qualitative (better brand recognition) or quantitative (lower supplier costs) as a result of data usage	Best-in-class technology solutions; optimal investment allocation	Dispersed ownership and accountability for technology; low management overhead
Core competencies	• Cost reduction and management • Operational efficiencies • Financial risk management	• Formal processes for incoming requests and pipeline management • Tool sets for progress tracking, delivery scheduling, and release updates	• Synthesis of business plans into a holistic IT roadmap • Relationship management • Program management	• Robust processes for ingesting and deploying data • Ability to integrate heterogeneous data types • Authoritative data governance structure and team	• Research and market expertise • Contract and procurement processes • Skill set delineation • Negotiation skills	• Forward thinking and able to anticipate benefits and consequences • Contract and procurement processes • Negotiation skills

(continues)

TABLE 2.1: A Comparison of the IT Archetypes *(continued)*

	Tactical	Order Taking	Aligning	Data Provisioning	Brokering	IT Everywhere
Risks	Considered overhead by constituents, thus a target of cost cutting or staff cutbacks	Seen as a commodity; constituents permitted to use external or nonsanctioned resources in lieu of IT	Often only as effective as the least happy business unit; is especially true when IT is resource constrained and there is a backlog of requests	Focus on data and information at the expense of operations; protracted "discovery" projects sometimes leading to disaffection	Loose control over partner delivery outcomes	Business ownership of technology mandates departmental structures, skills, and executive support
Typical initiatives	Sunsetting or replacing outdated legacy systems; storage or network upgrades	Customizing packaged applications or provisioning reports	Vendor research to support marketing's new customer experience management initiative	Streaming sensor data on patient vital signs to doctors' mobile devices	Outsourcing proprietary billing systems while commissioning in-house data scientists to calculate credit risk	Recruiting for the finance department's new business unit CIO
CEO's view	Distant and heavily intermediated	Continues to approve funding, but is likely to marginalize IT as a service provider	Is kept informed of progress on key initiatives, usually on an as-needed basis	Engaged on opportunities and initiatives, regularly on strategic projects	Stays current on progress and engages teams in high-level planning meetings	Considers this model a differentiator; includes key players in high-level strategy and planning

Still wondering which archetype best fits your IT group? When in doubt, consider how your organization behaves when it's under stress. Do you revert to heads-down operations, doubling up resources to make sure things run smoothly? Do you look to outside partners for help? Do you cast off systems or teams that are underperforming?

In a *CIO Magazine* article, retired Fidelity Investments executive Bob Ronan asked, "Is Your IT Shop a Scrambler or a Leader?"[2] Irrespective of the IT archetype you might have now, if you're perceived as producing, you're in much better shape than if you're perceived as reacting.

Top Down or Bottom Up?

Chances are your company's priorities are dynamic, with changing strategic focus, recently launched projects, a demanding customer community, and funding that ebbs and flows. These forces and others can either render you inert, locked into a particular IT archetype whether you like it or not, or send you searching evermore urgently for a new model to adopt and prose-lytize. How do you know you might be ready to make the shift?

Often a company is ready for a wholesale change to IT, but it doesn't know it yet. In this situation IT leaders need to start promoting new ways of working. They'll do this in one of three ways:

- **Top down.** In a top-down culture, strategic initiatives and cross-functional projects typically inform the scope of individual development projects. These projects are often enterprise level in scope, require significant investment, and are very visible. Such projects can be the initial grounds for IT transformation efforts, in effect allowing IT leaders to test and retry key changes in the context of important business goals.

- **Bottom up.** Companies that work in a bottom-up way often launch grassroots projects or prototypes that need to prove value before being more widely adopted. IT leaders can introduce new job roles, team models, and investment structures into these projects in an effort to "land and expand" new behaviors.

- **Hybrid.** Some companies combine top-down and bottom-up cultures. IT executives must thus ensure that their organizations support sanctioned and visible work efforts while at the same time applying tactical improvements at the departmental level. Even large, enterprise-scale projects spawn subprojects that might end up as the proving ground for new technologies, ownership models, or even IT archetype changes.

One force that's very effective in evolving the IT organization is a perceived sense of urgency. Trends like digital marketing, cloud computing, omnichannel, and big data are forcing different and often difficult conversations about IT's identity, and thus inviting IT restructuring.

Don't Give a Damn 'bout My Reputation

No matter what its size, every organization has a reputation. Your team is no exception to this. (If you don't know what your team's reputation is, odds are your people are protecting you from the truth.) The reputation is rarely articulated, but mostly implicit. You've probably witnessed the gestures, the roll of the eyes or the wave of the hand, when a second-rate team with a less-than-stellar track record comes up in conversation. When a team underperforms or is deemed mediocre, words are unnecessary.

The self-assessment in the next chapter can help you determine your department's reputation. Complete it, and then refer back to the six archetypes in this chapter to determine the future-state archetype that could improve your reputation.

IT leaders who are newer to their companies—often hired to help the company adopt emerging technologies and establish new ways of working—have an easier time redefining the rules because they're not saddled with historical organizational structures or political loyalties. They can thus take a realistic look at what works. Here's one example of a CIO who did just that.

EXECUTIVE PROFILE

Tracy Austin, Mandalay Resort Group

"When I got to MRG as the first CIO, I realized that IT was perceived as an expensive cost center," says Tracy Austin, the first CIO of the Mandalay Resort Group (MRG), the Las Vegas-based entertainment company. "And the further from the business IT got, the truer this was."

Austin had arrived at Mandalay from Harrah's, which at the time was the acknowledged IT best practice in the gaming industry. Other casinos were all frantically trying to replicate Harrah's loyalty program, Total Rewards—for which Austin led the development and implementation. Total Rewards gathered invaluable customer information that Harrah's could use to analyze its marketing offers and products, thus driving improved customer service and outreach.

Austin credits Harrah's then-CEO Phil Satre for the change to data-based decisions. "Phil understood that Harrah's needed to move from gut feel to fact-based decision making, and he understood that Harrah's needed the right leadership in place to make that shift. He hired CEO Gary Loveman, who made a lot of that real. If Phil hadn't recognized the potential of information to transform the business, Harrah's would never have changed. He moved Harrah's forward, and that moved an entire industry."

When Austin arrived at Mandalay from Harrah's, corporate IT was either pitted against or unaware of the priorities of the properties (the hotels and casinos the company managed nationwide). Not only did Austin have to assume the helm of IT but she also had to define a new position in a company that had labeled IT a "cost center."

Time for a New IT Model

When Austin joined the Mandalay Resort Group, the company had 15 gaming and hotel properties. IT was struggling, there were few formal job roles, and there were even fewer development processes. And she was reporting directly to the president.

"There were no standards," Austin recalls. "And there was no governance. The property heads had their own IT groups, and they didn't really know what was going on in corporate IT. Everyone dreaded the hotel system upgrades—they would always fail. No one was communicating with the properties about what they needed. Things would just implode."

Austin realized it was time for a new IT model at Mandalay. She set out on a listening tour, talking to property heads and other executives about what they needed from IT—and what they didn't.

"The first thing I did as a new CIO was go and talk to my business peers," she says. "I did a little listening tour, and I heard what their needs and problems were. I got a mixed reaction. I heard everything from, 'Thank God, you're here!' to 'What's a CIO?'

"What I found was across lines of business, everyone wanted more information on business performance. Including executives. If you're

(continues)

in the gaming business, you're measuring everything from the exact placement of slot machines on the casino floor to the percentage of high-roller guest stays that are comped. You name it, it gets measured. Most IT executives would consider this a systems issue. But really, it's a data issue. We understood this at Harrah's before anyone else, and Total Rewards was the first program of its kind. We knew our customers better than anyone else. We had first-mover advantage. And we did it by collecting and digesting data earlier and better than anyone else.

"In addition, I found that IT results and capabilities needed to improve in a measurable way, and that meant standard IT processes, performance management, and looking at the true cost and value of a project were key—but in business terms, not IT speak."

Austin and her team defined their own success based on three targets: (1) management excellence—through which IT would acquire top talent; (2) return on investment (ROI), which would ensure that IT kept cost savings and revenue generation top-of-mind; and (3) being demand driven, which would force IT to remain flexible in an evolving industry. Austin brought on some qualified deputies, including executive directors who would isolate infrastructure and application development.

It's Not the Hand You're Dealt

Austin was, in effect, blending different IT archetypes while moving, ultimately, toward an IT Everywhere approach. "In the gaming and hospitality industry, innovation is about business processes and service delivery. Everyone's going more mobile, in-room technologies are here, and many early adopter IT organizations are swinging back toward bricks-and-mortar. I like the idea of dispersing IT to where it's needed—one organization can't own everything."

Austin encourages fellow CIOs to depart from their own industry playbooks. "I learned early to go shop my competition. But I also learned to look outside my own industry. When I was at Harrah's, I sat with retailers and grocers. I spent time with people in the travel industry. If I'd focused only on the casino industry, I couldn't have driven as much change."

Now a consultant and advisor to other IT leaders, Austin suggests that they understand business processes to influence change and surface business requirements before acquiring tools. "Very few IT executives do this," she says. "Instead, they go straight to the vendors, and those vendors' software packages drive the business process. One of the things I used to do at MRG was make people create business process maps, understanding the 'as-is' and the 'to-be.' This was part of every business initiative.

"Let's say we're going to put a mobile app out there. If you don't map the business process and desired outcome, how do you know that the new innovation is even going to make sense? How do you know that the customer will experience the benefits? You may have just introduced a new security risk and not achieved any of your business goals.

"And don't get me started on social media," she continues. "It's like in the old days of CRM—people just implement it and then wait for something to happen. Are you doing this because there's a business need for it or because some executive just got back from CES [the consumer electronics show] and can now turn his smartphone into a stun gun?"

Making Change

Austin believes that changes need to start with leaders' own behaviors. "Part of the change IT leaders need to make is to stop trying to educate everyone on the technology they're deploying," Austin says. "They need to adapt to the culture. Use business terms. Don't talk about implementing a data warehouse and why one data loading product is better than another. Talk about how marketing will have insight into targeting better offers to the customers and improving the response rate. Let's face it. A lot of CIOs were promoted based on their technical expertise. They don't engage the business because they don't think they're expected to, or they don't know how. They don't know that they're allowed—heck, they have a right!—to ask the business what it needs."

So how did Austin actually transform IT at MRG? How did she get support for changing the model?

(continues)

"I could have asked for support, and I would have waited a long time," she says. "The reality was that a centralized vision for the business wasn't coming given the regional approach. Yet, I was running a centralized service. No one was going to hand me a business plan that I could 'align' with IT. So I drafted a business plan based on what I heard. The regional heads had agreed to attend my steering committee meetings. They listened to me pitch my business plan and explain how IT fit. They suggested some changes, but they didn't push back. That was all the endorsement I was going to get. Ultimately, my instincts were right: by communicating how IT was going to support business goals, I not only changed people's minds, I made IT strategic."

Putting It All Together

I know what you're thinking. You're thinking: "Yeah, those IT archetypes are interesting. But the stuff on my plate involves ALL of them!"

No doubt it does. In subsequent chapters, we'll be discussing how to crystallize key initiatives to establish which target archetype is best for you. After all, this is about the evolution of your internal brand and, by extension, your professional legacy. Regardless of what you might be working on now, understanding where you could be can serve as a beacon to guide you forward.

We'll also be talking about prioritizing all that stuff on your plate. We'll give you a proven process to do it, and we'll also show you how to include some key collaborators in that process. This can establish a collaboration model that sticks.

CHAPTER SUMMARY

Key Takeaways

- There are often legitimate reasons for IT inertia, and many of them have been beyond the power of the CIO or CTO to address. Many reasons, like lack of authority or inability to confront cultural dysfunctions, appear as excuses by IT leaders who seem to be resistant to change.

- One of the biggest sins of the IT leader is not creating a target. After all, change is a means to an end. Show me a leader who cannot articulate where she wants to go, and I'll show you someone guilty of perpetuating the status quo.

- Understanding differing IT models can offer leaders not only a direction to plan for but also an understanding of some of the behavioral phenomena that currently inform their brands. The six IT archetypes can help identify predominant organizational behaviors that you can choose to embrace or overcome.

- One common denominator of IT change agents is that they define or redefine their own rules, often proceeding despite the lack of widespread support. The old adage "Ask for forgiveness, not permission" has proven to be very effective for these leaders.

Note to the CEO

It's your fault. Okay, sometimes it's not, but often it is. Why? Because you're not only leading the company but you're also implicitly or explicitly sanctioning a culture. The culture informs de facto norms at the company that are difficult to confront and even harder to undo. Perhaps no one takes on new projects or innovative efforts? That's because you've endorsed a culture of "No" in which people keep their heads down. Perhaps an ineffective team drags down the entire department? That's because you're managing by personality, not by objectives.

The examples go on and on. The fact is that transcending entrenched behaviors and expectations is hard for any manager, not just whoever's leading IT.

Your first responsibility is to encourage connection. Each of the IT archetypes depends on this. Leaders often assume that *connection* and *collaboration* are synonymous and that this is a personality issue, the natural ripple effect of getting people together. But it's really more about connecting departments to common business objectives. As managers bemoan lack of business-IT alignment and the fact that each side typically retreats to its respective corner, they hire introverts who simply want to write code or business analysts who insist they're "technical enough" to solve their own problems without IT's help.

In order to mitigate the IT organization to its rightful place as a value creator, leaders should prioritize connection through common business interests, encouraging collaboration through formal rules of engagement between IT and business units. The resulting behaviors should be rewarded.

As businesspeople continue to gripe that IT is slow to deliver, hard to work with, or "behind the times," look to the culture to see what's really not working. And sometimes you can look even closer than that—like, in the mirror.

• • • • • • • • • • • •

Self-Assessment One: The Scope of the Problem

ccording to *CIO Magazine*'s thirteenth annual "State of the CIO" report, only 25 percent of 722 CIOs surveyed felt that their organizations were seen as peers by their business colleagues. And 48 percent of the CIOs acknowledged that their teams were viewed as cost centers.[1]

Is the recurring phenomenon of IT not having a seat at the table due to a lack of leadership? Perhaps senior leadership can't see IT's potential. Or maybe the company is not in enough pain to need IT improvements. Or maybe it's just that old habits die hard. Whatever the reason, the self-assessment in this chapter will help you pinpoint some of the trouble spots that subsequent chapters in the book can help remedy.

Take the Assessment

In the assessment in Table 3.1, answer the questions at the left. For each question, you'll give yourself a score of 1 to 9 by measuring the degree to which the answer is positive or negative. The descriptions in the three columns will help guide you toward the best score.

Be as honest as you can, abandoning your personal biases and any defensiveness that might come up as you relate the questions to your own experiences. As my clients in healthcare always say, the better the diagnosis, the more effective the prescription.

TABLE 3.1: Self-Assessment One: The Scope of the Problem

Question	Scoring Spectrum			Your Score
	1 2 3	4 5 6	7 8 9	
IT reputation. Does the IT department have a positive reputation within your company?	IT is considered a cost center. IT people are considered difficult to work with. Not only is IT still firmly branded as a cost center but people also continue to question the expense.	Businesspeople admit that IT can drive operational efficiencies and economies of scale. Lines of business engage IT for infrastructure development and enterprise applications. IT leadership would like to implement chargeback, but they consider it politically risky.	IT is considered an active contributor to strategic initiatives and is involved early in business planning. IT is used to vet potential solutions against current technology capabilities, and IT owns establishing optimal delivery approaches. Innovation is part of IT's internal brand. Businesspeople regularly solicit input from IT on emerging technologies and their applications.	
Incumbent technologies. Are existing technology solutions highly regarded? Do employees consider the company's technology to be current with market trends?	In the past 3 years, IT budgets have decreased relative to overall spending. When people discuss the company's technology, they're typically referring to mainframes or core operational systems. Little attention is paid to competitors' IT strategies or industry benchmarks.	IT is seen as a component to various business solutions (e.g., the CRM tool enables customer loyalty programs). IT spending has been relatively consistent over the past 3 years. Businesspeople provide data and functional requirements to IT.	IT is regularly and proactively consulted by business managers for help exploring or acquiring innovative new solutions. IT spending has steadily increased, with significant budget increases for new solutions that support business strategy. IT is involved during high-level planning, and early in the project planning cycle, providing ample time for technology acquisition and development.	

Question	Scoring Spectrum			Your Score
	1 2 3	**4 5 6**	**7 8 9**	
IT governance. Are IT activities linked to larger business objectives? Does the company at large support this approach?	Right or wrong, IT is still seen as reactive or, at best, opportunistic. There is little proactive planning. Senior leadership is largely opaque about direction and does not provide guidance. Thus, IT governance only happens in pockets, if at all.	An annual IT roadmap is developed, but it is rarely seen or referenced outside of IT. The CIO interprets corporate priorities (via annual reports or CEO messaging) and factors them into IT priorities. There are a few key departments that IT works with closely.	IT governance is informed by overarching corporate strategy and cross-functional management input. IT applies a formal governance process for roadmap updates and refinements. Each business unit factors technology into its planning and enlists IT for help.	
Influence. Does IT have a say in major business decisions?	IT leadership is rarely involved in business plans or strategies. There are no rules of engagement for working with IT. IT staff feel misunderstood by their business colleagues.	IT involvement is opportunistic and often proportional to the size of the project. The business solicits input based on personal relationships, not process. There have been some positive collaboration examples on important projects.	The CIO and CTO participate in senior leadership meetings. Businesspeople have clarity around when to engage IT and what the boundaries are. IT clearly communicates its roadmap and competencies, making it easier for various departments to leverage tools and skills.	
IT leadership. Is the role of the CIO and/or CTO improving?	The CIO has been marginalized to "keeping the lights on." He or she reports to another C-level executive or director. The CIO will often get involved in IT projects to keep them on track or help reassess resources or spending.	The CIO has multiple vice president–level or director-level managers, with clear domains and measures. The CIO's responsibilities are expanding. New responsibilities (such as data governance or innovation labs) are actively supported.	The CIO is considered part of the senior leadership team. The company promotes the CIO as a member of the senior leadership team in external communications, in financial reporting, and on the company's website. The CIO is the go-to resource for questions or help on emerging technologies like mobile or big data.	

(continues)

TABLE 3.1: Self-Assessment One: The Scope of the Problem *(continued)*

Question	Scoring Spectrum			Your Score
	1 2 3	**4 5 6**	**7 8 9**	
Business executives. Have the CIO or IT managers been included in key business activities?	Business leaders in the company engage the CIO only when there is a problem or conflict. Shadow IT efforts crop up without the CIO's knowledge. The CIO has discovered more than one rogue technology initiative—after the fact.	The CEO has invited the CIO to be more involved in business planning. Business peers share their organizational plans and goals proactively with the CIO and IT managers. IT management is included in management training activities.	The CEO asks the CIO to own nontraditional initiatives, such as working groups or task forces. The CIO is invited to present IT plans or status at senior leadership and board meetings. Business peers solicit leadership feedback from the CIO or other IT managers.	
Staff tenure. Does IT retain good talent and acquire fresh staff when needed?	There have been 3 or more CIOs in the past 5 years. There have been multiple organizational changes in IT, resulting in significant employee turnover. Cost cutting or layoffs have hurt morale. The company is not considered an attractive employer for technology professionals.	New planning and prioritization processes have revealed the need for new skills. There is budget for new headcount in IT. IT measures performance against business goals. The company has instituted new functions or organizations and is hiring to staff them.	Digital initiatives have invited opportunities to hire and promote visible technology delivery roles. Technology-savvy resources are in demand within both IT and business organizations. This is a hiring metric. The company rewards new ideas and promotes people who consistently deliver. As a result of awards, positive press, or other external audits, the company has more demand for jobs than applicants.	

Question	Scoring Spectrum									Your Score
	1	2	3	4	5	6	7	8	9	
Customers. Is the company's technology prowess visible—either directly or indirectly—to customers?	Customers have cited the company's technology as a factor in poor service experiences, outdated website features, or lagging social media capabilities. IT is rarely asked to participate in customer-focused planning meetings. There is a widespread assumption that IT is too busy managing infrastructure.			Deployment of enterprise applications such as ERP or supply chain solutions can be traced to positive customer experiences. Technology staff are included in product innovation conversations. IT is involved in deploying data and analytics to enrich customer experience and drive revenue growth.			Company leaders acknowledge that technology is part of high-impact digital marketing and social media programs, and they have included IT in customer impact discussions. Customer compliments about the company's speed, nimbleness, pricing, or innovation are attributable to its technology. IT is acknowledged to have contributed to customer acquisition, retention, profitability, and/or revenue growth.			
									Total Score	

What Your Score Means

If you scored 3 or lower on a question, it suggests that some remediation might be in order, and fast. More than three questions scoring 3 or lower suggests that the IT organization is in a slump, and it may even be at risk if significant changes aren't imminent. Conversely, a score of 7 or above on a question suggests that IT could be a best practice in this category, and it could perhaps even drive competitive advantage.

- **A score of 8 to 24.** If a total score of 24 or lower worries you, it should. It hints of subpar IT investment and lack of attention to technology as a business enabler. As hard as it is to hear, IT probably has a reputation as an expensive and often unnecessary shared service.

- **A score of 25 to 48.** Successful efforts and connections are usually due to personal relationships and not from sustained processes or formal connections between systems and work groups. Successful collaborations between the business and IT are seen as happy accidents, more the exception than the rule.

- **A score of 49 to 72.** If you end up scoring 49 or higher, you should congratulate yourself for securing IT in the company zeitgeist, although as we'll see in subsequent chapters, there is likely more work to do.

The questions and their guidelines suggest that your IT function—be it centralized or decentralized, national or global, innovative or outdated—has a brand. The greater the level of organizational cynicism about IT, the more difficult it will be to overcome that cynicism through rebranding.

CIOs and CEOs alike often try the "people panacea"—creating new organizations or putting someone new in charge of an imperiled department or function—hoping that moving bodies around the organization will be effective. A 2013 Forrester study found that almost half of the leaders surveyed claimed that there was "a greater than 50 percent chance that they would redesign IT within 18 months, with a third responding that the probability of redesign was greater than 75 percent."[2]

But absent pervasive behavior changes, organizational changes by themselves simply pave the cow path. In Parts 2 and 3, we'll discuss how to introduce changes that stick and cultivate awareness of those changes so that they're not only supported (again, by people) but they are also effective in driving business results.

Save your total score! The book's final self-assessment at the end of Part 3 will combine the scores from the individual self-assessments and give you a total IT maturity score, along with some tactics to help drive further improvement.

NOTE TO THE CEO

With everything else they have on their plates, few CEOs wake up in the morning thinking, "Wow, I've gotta pay more attention to technology." If anything, most feel hamstrung by the demands of being an executive in an uber-connected world.

But if technology can move the revenue needle, why not? If you're a CEO and you know that IT could use some improvement, ask yourself three questions:

1. How can technology help the company grow?

2. How can it enhance our brand?

3. What do my IT leaders need from me in order to realize these two goals?

The CEO of a publically traded academic institution admitted to me over a cocktail once that he didn't take IT seriously because—well, frankly—his company wasn't in enough pain. The stock price was soaring, student enrollment was at an all-time high, and profitability was the best it had ever been.

I suggested that while both he and the company were riding high, it might be time to invest in building out a technology strategy that would stave off budding competitors. Start researching new ways to innovate. Beef up analytics capabilities. Engage the CIO and CMO in digital marketing discussions. Start monetizing data. That sort of thing. In my time working with the CEO and his team, I had observed that, flush with cash, the company was overinvesting in human effort.

As soon as I uttered the word "overinvesting," the CEO almost spit out the olive in his martini. "Wha?" he said, taking a minute to recover. "I'm thrilled we're doing well, but overinvestment is a four-letter word to me. I don't want to rely on people to do what technology can do." He promptly called a senior leadership meeting where they allocated a five-year technology budget. This was the year before the advent of massively open online courses (MOOCs), which turned into a disruptive threat for the company. Nevertheless, my CEO friend, unlike many of his higher education peers, is sleeping soundly.

. . . .

part 2

Your IT Transformation Toolkit

Strategy on a Page

I can see
It took so long just to realize
I'm much too strong not to compromise
Now I see what I am is holding me down . . .
I'll turn it around.

—Boston, "Don't Look Back" (1978)

I f you're on an airplane, odds are you're sitting amidst vice presidents, CEOs, marketing and communications executives, sales leaders, product marketers, directors, executive assistants, risk experts, and the odd management consultant—all of them en route to a strategy planning meeting. They've spent the preceding months huddled around conference room tables, standing at whiteboards, running through forecasts, conducting real options analyses, debating competitors' strengths, crunching consumer behavior data, and assembling PowerPoint presentations to share with their colleagues and senior leaders in the ambitious effort to prescribe what the company should do next.

Strategy, defined in its simplest form, is the set of actions a company takes to gain competitive advantage. Strategic planning typically includes a discussion of where the company wants to go, a critical study of the competitive landscape, an appraisal of emerging market trends, and the creation of a set of objectives against which the company must deliver in order to realize its goals.

An effective strategic plan helps executives pave the straightest path possible to growth. It should inform decisions about budgeting, resource allocation, hiring, talent management, data deployment, technology acquisition, and succession planning.

Although executives insist that strategic planning is still a key tool in their management toolboxes,[1] many strategies never see the light of day. Business managers often cite a lack of strategic transparency as one of the reasons for their slipshod planning processes or failure to execute.

It's no surprise then that when it comes to what IT leaders obsess about, corporate strategy isn't on the list of what keeps them up at night. In fact, many CIOs can't even articulate where their companies are headed, let alone describe key business objectives. It's not their fault.

"In my own travels I find it rare that a CIO connects the work IT does with value creation," says strategy and leadership expert Art Petty. The author of several books on leadership, Petty is sympathetic to the IT leaders' plight, laying the blame squarely at the feet of the CEO. "IT ends up being tactically compliant," he says. "It's a leadership issue more than anything."

Even experienced CEOs confuse short-term planning with long-term strategy. Many don't understand the true meaning of strategy—after all, how many of them have risen through the ranks based on strategy work? They conflate strategy with operations planning, innovation, and organizational change. Others decide to assign the task of strategic planning to external consultants, cherry-picking the least disruptive recommendations and allocating skeleton crews to deliver them. Still others, bruised by past experiences with ersatz strategic plans that were never implemented, declare strategy a four-letter word.

Confusion over the role of strategy often means that when CEOs relate strategy and IT, it's usually in the context of saving costs via shared services, improving business alignment, or outsourcing systems and skills. To these leaders, the term *strategic IT* often means upgrading everyone's smartphone and calling it a day. In their quest to standardize back office functions, CEOs unwittingly fan the flames of the raging business-versus-IT inferno that continues to scorch relationships on both sides.

Indeed, many CEOs are suspicious of strategy and often dismiss the word altogether. "Every executive worth his or her weight today is strategic," MapQuest founder Chris Heivly wrote in *Inc.*[2] "CEOs," Heivly wrote, "have been obsessed with the strategy of the company every hour of every day." Heivly advised readers to banish the word *strategic* altogether and instead

"THE CHAIRMAN WILL NOW DANCE HIS VISION FOR CRABCO IN THE TWENTY-FIRST CENTURY."

© Bill Long/The New Yorker Collection, www.CartoonStock.com.

work on "targeted areas of need." But, absent strategy, defining those "targeted areas"—are they strategies? programs? tasks?—can consume a lot more time and effort, particularly for companies in which demand for resources exceeds supply. Which means most companies.

No wonder IT leaders have trouble driving value! If a corporate strategy does exist, it might not be transparent, let alone clear enough to be the basis for deliberate and proactive planning. While they could be spending time rigorously exploring market opportunities and redefining their core business boundaries, executives are instead looking for ways to save money. Up until now, that's been acceptable. But the perpetual focus on the bottom line can sabotage top-line potential (not to mention opportunities to go digital or innovate).

Given that management consultants and strategy gurus have been speaking and writing on the topic of strategy for decades, why haven't more executives gotten strategy right? Art Petty confirms that executives, like many people, are victims of habit.

"So many times, strategic dialogue seems to be driven by last year's budgeting process," he says. "So everything that happens in a management team is a fight for budget and resources. We need to suspend those conversations and start asking about what's next for the company. Simply put, executives need to be willing to invest money now to enable their companies' futures. But that's hard to do if you haven't done it before."

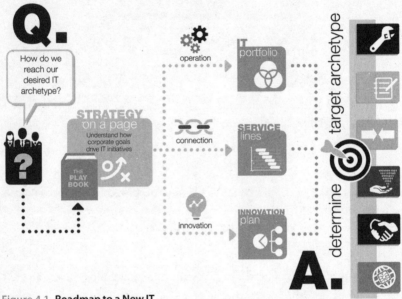

Figure 4.1 **Roadmap to a New IT**

The fact is, when it comes to clearly communicating their future directions, executives stay in their comfort zones, which typically encompass operational planning. Instead, what they really need is to resist what pioneering business guru and author of this book's Foreword, Geoffrey Moore, so aptly calls "the gravitational field of your prior year's operating plan."

But C-level executives aren't the only leaders uncomfortable with strategy. Fearing they're straying too far outside their own skills or organizational authority, many business leaders shy away from conversations about corporate strategy and how they can help drive it forward. Some fear they won't be allowed to participate fully in strategy creation, ultimately inviting more projects into an organization already starved for resources. Others fear that by being involved in strategic planning, they'll shirk their core responsibilities and end up failing at both.

But supporting strategy doesn't have to be a science project. In fact, a discrete exercise in strategic alignment can inform IT's long-term future, helping you target the right IT archetype.

This chapter discusses the first step in how IT leaders can push for strategic alignment, offering mechanisms for jump-starting strategic awareness while at the same time illustrating ways IT leaders can help not only execute corporate strategy but also communicate what change looks like. The whole, as they say, may be greater than the sum of its parts.

Figure 4.1 illustrates the process that will be broken down in Part 2 of this book.

Some of the tools that are described in the next three chapters can help you in the following ways:

- Communicate IT's vision more clearly

- Justify the projects that are on your plate

- Defend the projects that *should be* on your plate

- Make a case for projects to postpone, cancel, or outsource

- Explain in concise terms how IT adds value

- Enlist key stakeholders across both business and IT to define delivery priorities

- Partner with specific sponsors based on business goals

- Understand why your current IT plan might fall short

Note that the examples in this chapter have all been adapted, abbreviated, homogenized, or blended from real-life companies. As such, they're meant to be illustrative and not prescriptive.

Aligning IT Strategically

In my consulting practice, we used simple one-page strategy diagrams with our clients. Business executives love them because they communicate the company's intent and where it's headed in an intuitive and visual way. These diagrams can effectively link vision with the execution tactics required to realize the vision. IT people are increasingly using such constructs because, absent a deliberate and unified business plan that might serve as input, they offer something real and tangible to plan against.

Moreover, when it comes to developing strategy, to borrow a Zen aphorism, it may be the journey and not the destination that matters. When presented with an opportunity to help create a tangible and actionable point of reference, people who may heretofore have declined every meeting invitation from IT will nevertheless show up for a strategy session. They contribute. They connect. They feel ownership of the outcome. And this sets up a cycle of participation that—if the strategy is a sound one—incents future participation.

Of course, I'm not advocating formulating your company's value proposition in a single sit-down session, nor am I saying that IT leaders can get easy consensus in one meeting. Author Richard P. Rumelt distinguishes leadership and strategy this way:

> Leadership and strategy may be joined in the same person, but they are not the same thing. Leadership inspires and motivates self-sacrifice. . . . Strategy is the craft of figuring out which purposes are both worth pursuing and capable of being accomplished.[3]

Ideally, the structures we'll discuss here can be used to realize a deliberate strategic planning process that's been created based on sound techniques. As many executives have learned, strategy formulation is in fact a process—it has to be because companies evolve, organizational networks are complex, and markets change. Asking probing questions whose answers often suggest large-scale changes is the essence of strategy, and arguably those questions and answers are the reason so few companies deliver meaningful strategic plans. Absent this level of rigor, effective strategic alignment is tough to pull off. But common structures can fill the often unarticulated need of giving everyone a common frame of reference.

What follows are reliable structures that not only communicate the company's strategic priorities, but offer a way for IT to align to them. Regardless of whether you're on the business or technology side of the fence, they can help you cut through the habitual corporate storytelling, overcome old habits, and begin clarifying IT's focus areas. (You may even use them to better understand your IT archetype, as we discussed in Chapter 2.) At a minimum, these tools will encourage conversation and increase collaboration between disparate business interests. In the ideal case, your IT department can not only participate in this effort but also guide it.

Strategy Mapping

Strategy mapping was first popularized by Robert Kaplan and David Norton in their 2004 book *Strategy Maps*. Kaplan and Norton's groundbreaking Balanced Scorecard system redefined corporate performance parameters, adding intangible objectives to the typical goal of revenue generation, thus providing an integrated view of corporate value drivers. A decade later, the authors recognized that many of the companies that had initially adopted the Balanced Scorecard remained rooted in old behaviors, unable to capitalize on the (expensive and time-consuming) work of building their scorecards.

Citing Principle 5 of the Balanced Scorecard—"Make strategy a continual process"—the authors lamented this phenomenon:

> Because the new approaches had not been embedded in the ongoing management systems of the organization (Principle 5), the performance was often not sustained. We had not yet found a way to embed the ongoing management of strategy into the organization's way of doing business.[4]

According to Kaplan and Norton, strategy mapping offered a way to "express" the strategy—that is, a way to link corporate objectives with the tactical execution work necessary to realize them, thereby helping executives streamline delivery capabilities and prioritize investments. Once a strategy map was created, a company could not only better communicate it across constituencies but it could also help put the strategy into motion.

In my work with companies, I've used various adaptations of strategy mapping to show how overarching corporate objectives can drill down into tactics. The diagram in Figure 4.2, for instance, deconstructs a major automotive company's strategies (on the left) into some key analytics initiatives.

Figure 4.2 **Deconstructing Strategy at an Automobile Company**

This structure (which I've abbreviated and simplified) drills down from the company's vision of its future to the corresponding business strategies, helping the automotive company answer the following questions:

- Which strategies are ultimately linked to our corporate vision of being the premier seller of luxury vehicles in North America?

- What are the objectives of each strategy?

- What initiatives or projects must we put in place to help achieve each objective?

In essence, this structure provides a visual link to the two questions "What are our corporate priorities?" and "What work is required to realize them?"

In this particular case, the client noticed that each of the strategic directions would need to be enabled by business intelligence (BI) and reporting capabilities. The good news was that the company was already BI savvy, having invested in a variety of best-of-breed solutions that were streamlining decision making and enhancing outreach to dealers and drivers.

The bad news was that these analytics functions would require data that was not readily available to decision makers. In fact, we were confronting the brutal possibility that some of the strategic initiatives could not be achieved without significant investments in data management technologies, externally sourced information, and as-yet-unhired expertise.

But how to communicate that to IT and business leaders who were already arm wrestling over additional headcount and budget for their own pet projects?

We decided to deconstruct the strategy map in Figure 4.2 and go one step further with it, showing executives how each strategy relied on key data. For each strategy, we created a data scorecard—that is, a graphical illustration of the data that would be required to enable each of the initiatives in the customer retention strategy as shown in Figure 4.3.

CURRENT STATE

Legend: ✓ = created/supported · ⊡ = planned or in process · ✗ = no work performed · ⊘ = data doesn't exist

key data to support initiatives	definition	policy	data quality	system of record	current owner
CUSTOMER RETENTION — reward program					
customer contact info	⊡	⊡	✗	Salesforce	Rao
current purchases	✓	⊡	✗	Genesis	Variel
product usage details	✓	✗	⊡	Genesis	Variel
customer transactions	⊡	⊡	⊡	Genesis	Variel
return details	✓	⊡	✓	POS	Crane
campaigns & promotions	✓	⊡	✗	Campaign+	Hartt
win-back program					
purchase history	⊡	✗	✗	Genesis	Variel
customer transactions	✓	⊡	✗	Genesis	Variel
activity & usage history	⊡	✗	✗	Praxis	Welch
trouble tickets / service history	✓	⊡	⊡	PhoenixCSR	Karson
customer segment	✗	✗	⊘	Campaign+	Hartt
response history	✓	✗	✗	Campaign+	Hartt
customer value score	✗	✗	⊘	EDW	Patel
account rep history	✓	⊡	⊡	PhoenixCSR	Briggs
credit history	⊡	✗	✗	N/A	None
social network outreach					
online contact info	⊘	⊘	⊘	N/A	None
social profile detail	⊘	⊘	⊘	N/A	None
social channel history	⊘	⊘	⊘	N/A	Riley
social transaction history	⊘	⊘	⊘	N/A	None
community / blogging score	⊘	⊘	⊘	N/A	None
net promoter score	⊘	⊘	⊘	N/A (Campaign+)	Hartt

✓ created/supported   ⊡ planned or in process   ✗ no work performed   ⊘ data doesn't exist

NOTE: key data are representative examples only.

Figure 4.3 **Deconstructing a Key Strategy to Its Core Data**

As Figure 4.3 illustrates, we evaluated the required data based on the following:

- Whether the data already had a formal and documented definition

- Whether there were sanctioned policies in place for access, usage, and sharing of the data

- Whether data correction and quality processes had already been applied to the data

A checkmark meant that indeed these actions had taken place on the data; an arrow meant they were being considered or were in process; and an X signified that no work had yet been done. A circle with a slash through it signified that the data had not yet been provisioned in the company—that is, it didn't yet exist.

This example illustrates how a strategy as high level and lofty as customer retention can be distilled into the need for additional data in order to realize it in two colorful, easy-to-understand pages.

Explaining to a senior executive that a strategic initiative can be deconstructed into tactics in a simple way has the tangential effect of engaging executives in new conversations with IT. And explaining that in order to fulfill a strategic objective, corporate leaders must be willing to invest or innovate puts those leaders in the position of saying no. And when it comes to enabling approved corporate strategies, executives serious about strategy never say no.

IT Strategy on a Page

In his book *Escape Velocity*, author Geoffrey Moore counsels readers to articulate a compelling vision, set a strategy to realize that vision as a market leader, and resource that vision to successfully execute it. Moore's advice applies at a macro-level to companies as well as at a micro-level to IT organizations. As we saw in the previous discussion of strategy mapping, company strategies and IT strategies aren't mutually exclusive, and they can be deliberately linked in order to validate just how important IT is in enabling company goals.

It's one thing to link strategies, but it's another thing to communicate those linkages in a way that engages those outside of IT. I've used the Strategy on a Page approach with my clients to do just that. The goal of Strategy on a Page is to provide a visual framework to show what it will take to execute. Like strategy maps, Strategy on a Page illustrates a top-down relationship between high-level corporate goals with their associated execution tactics. Unlike strategy maps, though, Strategy on a Page communicates delivery components, concisely answering the question, "What will it take?"

Strategy on a Page can be customized. Its basic components are the following:

- **Vision.** The vision should be the aspirational statement for what IT should look like, defining its behaviors and priorities. Vision statements articulate the future that organizations want to create for themselves.

- **Performance measures.** For the purposes of Strategy on a Page, performance measures should apply to IT as a whole. (Later you can reduce them to measure specific initiatives, but that becomes too noisy for these purposes.) This answers how IT measures itself and applies to both the vision above, and the strategic imperatives below. In many cases, initiatives are assigned key performance indicators (KPIs) that define success.

- **Strategic imperatives.** These are mandates that support the company's strategic goals. For instance, a healthcare company we worked with had defined a strategy of "Pursue perfection in safety." Consequently, one of the IT organization's strategic imperatives was "Develop and deploy a networkwide Online Safety Scorecard."

- **Initiatives or projects.** These are the individual work efforts that will support the defined strategic imperatives—and thus deliver on the vision. You may think of them as projects, and many will have dependencies on one another.

Figure 4.4 shows the components of an IT Strategy on a Page.

When filled in, the Strategy on a Page can orient people around an IT conversation, a reliable reminder of what IT is working on and why. Many

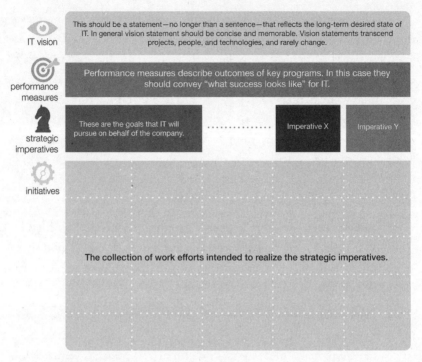

IT vision — This should be a statement—no longer than a sentence—that reflects the long-term desired state of IT. In general vision statement should be concise and memorable. Vision statements transcend projects, people, and technologies, and rarely change.

performance measures — Performance measures describe outcomes of key programs. In this case they should convey "what success looks like" for IT.

strategic imperatives — These are the goals that IT will pursue on behalf of the company. · · · · · · · · · · · · · · Imperative X   Imperative Y

initiatives — The collection of work efforts intended to realize the strategic imperatives.

Figure 4.4 **Strategy on a Page: Skeleton Structure**

leaders begin their management and staff presentations with the Strategy on a Page, in effect reminding their audiences of the inception of their work. This centers the discussion and provides an increasingly familiar touchpoint for subsequent planning and prioritization:

- "I was able to paint a vision for IT in my first 30 days or so," says Michael Smith, CIO at Mylan Pharmaceuticals. "We essentially created a one-page strategy 'house' structure. This resonated amazingly well with executives. I could tie all of our work back to my strategy house. We rolled it out more broadly in a video to the entire company. Often IT strategy stays within a small group at a company, but not here."

- Ron Guerrier, CIO of Toyota Financial Services, espouses the philosophy that everything his large IT team does maps back to a company initiative. He calls it the Business Technology Services (BTS) One- to Two-Year Strategic Goal Prioritization. "It's graphical, it shows how we're not only building but innovating, and it's available both internally as well as to our external suppliers. It gets everyone—literally!—on the same page. We update it every six months, and we enlist our business partners each time. So there's not only a reason but a value discussion around everything we're working on."

- "I have a one-page strategy slide that I use to talk to the board of directors and fellow executives," explains Michel Loranger, chief information officer of Canadian insurer SSQ Financial Group. "The details on the slide may change as the company evolves, but that one slide gets seen a lot across the company. It has to be really, really clear. And, more than anything, it has to continually communicate how we create value as a group."

The Strategy on a Page in Figure 4.5 is from a midmarket retailer, completing the skeleton structure (shown in Figure 4.4) to illustrate how the vision breaks down into more discrete IT projects.

To imagine that each strategic imperative is simply a matter of implementing technology is to further marginalize IT as a technology

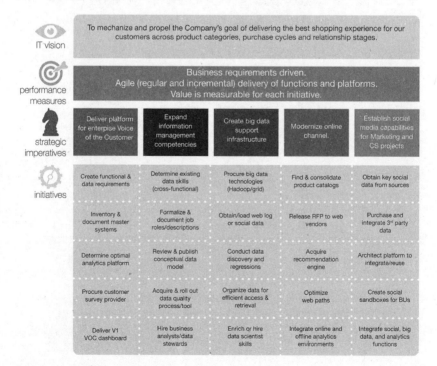

Figure 4.5   A Retailer's IT Strategy on a Page

procurement organization. Each strategic imperative will require a range of technical resources and business competencies. Once you've defined a high-level structure to color in IT's strategy, you can deconstruct it to support the three performance areas of IT: operation, connection, and innovation.

A bank I worked with has another version of Strategy on a Page, this one focusing more on letting the customer drive not only the business's vision of enriching customer experiences with the bank but also how IT will support this vision. As with the other Strategy on a Page examples, this one is top down, letting the company's vision, programs, and constituents inform IT activities. Figure 4.6 illustrates the relationships between the bank's business strategies and the resulting IT initiatives.

Notice how the IT activities shown in Figure 4.6 include projects that support both individual lines of business as well as enterprise initiatives

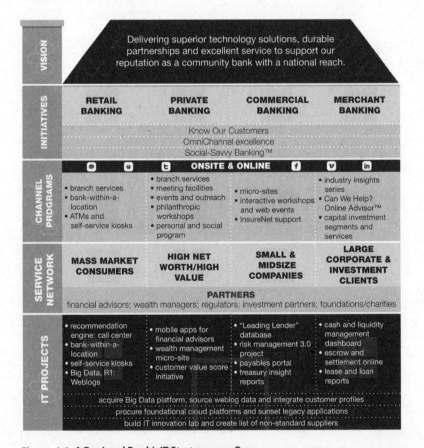

Figure 4.6 **A Regional Bank's IT Strategy on a Page**

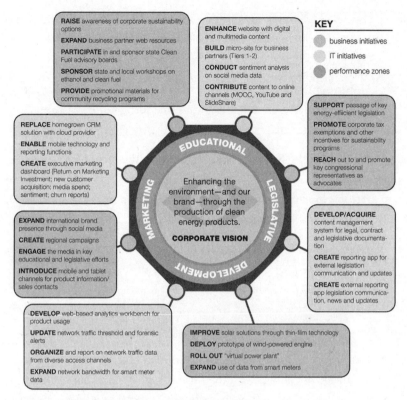

RAISE awareness of corporate sustainability options

EXPAND business partner web resources

PARTICIPATE in and sponsor state Clean Fuel advisory boards

SPONSOR state and local workshops on ethanol and clean fuel

PROVIDE promotional materials for community recycling programs

ENHANCE website with digital and multimedia content

BUILD micro-site for business partners (Tiers 1-2)

CONDUCT sentiment analysis on social media data

CONTRIBUTE content to online channels (MOOC, YouTube and SlideShare)

KEY

- business initiatives
- IT initiatives
- performance zones

SUPPORT passage of key energy-efficient legislation

PROMOTE corporate tax exemptions and other incentives for sustainability programs

REACH out to and promote key congressional representatives as advocates

REPLACE homegrown CRM solution with cloud provider

ENABLE mobile technology and reporting functions

CREATE executive marketing dashboard (Return on Marketing Investment; new customer acquisition; media spend; sentiment; churn reports)

EDUCATIONAL

MARKETING

Enhancing the environment—and our brand—through the production of clean energy products.

CORPORATE VISION

LEGISLATIVE

DEVELOPMENT

DEVELOP/ACQUIRE content management system for legal, contract and legislative documentation

CREATE reporting app for external legislation communication and updates

CREATE external reporting app legislation communication, news and updates

EXPAND international brand presence through social media

CREATE regional campaigns

ENGAGE the media in key educational and legislative efforts

INTRODUCE mobile and tablet channels for product information/ sales contacts

DEVELOP web-based analytics workbench for product usage

UPDATE network traffic threshold and forensic alerts

ORGANIZE and report on network traffic data from diverse access channels

EXPAND network bandwidth for smart meter data

IMPROVE solar solutions through thin-film technology

DEPLOY prototype of wind-powered engine

ROLL OUT "virtual power plant"

EXPAND use of data from smart meters

Figure 4.7 **An Energy Company's IT Strategy on a Page**

(at the bottom of the chart). A team will evaluate each initiative based on a comprehensive and culturally relevant set of metrics (as the next chapter explains).

An IT Strategy on a Page need not be a top-down rectangular structure. Another company, this time in the clean energy business, used the creation of its IT strategy as an opportunity to practice what the CIO called *mind mapping*.

"I typically hate getting everyone in a room," he admitted as we were planning the extended session with his executive team. "But I feel like everyone has a stake in this. After all, I'll be measuring them on their contributions to achieving these objectives. So they should have the chance to weigh in."

The resulting diagram, adapted and shown in Figure 4.7, was redrawn by a graphic artist and made into posters, which adorned the walls of the lowslung building that housed the company's IT group. Slowly the diagram was noticed by non-IT employees, and they acknowledged its inclusiveness and used it as a way to provide context in their conversations with IT.

In order for Strategy on a Page to be effective, it must be:

- **Unique.** Effective Strategy on a Page diagrams look different from other corporate documents, often including color, wording, and structures that are atypical and thus difficult to pigeonhole.

- **Recognizable.** Strategy on a Page should be recognized to reflect where the company is headed. It should feature sanctioned corporate vocabulary, leaving little doubt that it's an important artifact of executive-level thoughtfulness and vision.

- **Available.** Strategy should be transparent, and Strategy on a Page should be widely available via a variety of media. Perhaps it's featured on (and downloadable from) the home page of the company's internal website, tacked to the walls in hallways and conference rooms, and regularly mentioned in executive communications.

- **Distributed.** IT and business leaders alike should share the Strategy on a Page document with their direct reports, walking through the details and communicating the intent. It can function as a measurement "touchstone," representing the source for people's active projects and planning efforts.

Strategy on a Page can refresh people's ideas about IT and the value that it brings. Strategy on a Page can change minds about IT's relevance, showing how IT can contribute value, thus enhancing IT's internal brand.

EXECUTIVE PROFILE

H. James Dallas, Medtronic

In his book *Know-How*, management guru Ram Charan wrote, "When you are precise in your observations and take the time to connect multiple points of information, you begin to zero in on the real stuff." Charan's comment could be cross-stitched on a pillowcase in the office of

H. James Dallas. Dallas, the recently retired senior vice president of quality, operations, and IT at Medtronic, has used keen observations and connections as the basis for his successes across multiple IT leadership roles.

Prior to Medtronic, Dallas spent 22 years as an IT executive at Georgia Pacific (GP). "I went from producing quality products that improved people's homes to producing quality products that improved people's lives!" he says in a backhanded reference to the medical device company's mission. Indeed, mission is a theme for Dallas, whose leadership roles have all focused on enabling strategy.

Business-IT Alignment: It IS Brain Surgery!

It's not that Dallas has focused only on business strategy. He's delivered over 10 enterprise resource planning (ERP) implementations, participated in 15 acquisition integration efforts, and spearheaded 5 centers of excellence. He's seen his share of overbudget projects and enterprise software delivery snafus. And on the point of IT leaders needing to drive value, he's resolute.

"It wasn't that ERP didn't work," Dallas says, harkening back to a particularly challenging time in his career. "It's that the business units had their own instances of ERP and fragmented processes. We ended up consolidating 16 instances of JD Edwards into one."

Problem averted? Well, yes and no.

"The organizational, business process, and data changes were far harder than the technical ones," Dallas says. "Suddenly all the business unit (BU) CIOs were reporting to me. I needed to figure out when to be a diplomat, and when to be a dictator. These guys were closer to their business issues than I was. So I wasn't about to misrepresent my skills, and I wasn't going to just centralize everything.

"Sure, we needed to standardize some things in order to gain operating synergies and strengthen quality and security. But I had to give the BU CIOs the flexibility to decide how to go to market in their own divisions. The closer things got to the customer, the more flexibility I gave people, and the further away things got from the customer, the more we needed to establish common standards. By the time things

(continues)

got to distribution and manufacturing, we were really standardized—and really efficient. We took out $1.5 billion in costs."

A CIO at the enterprise level who is leading divisional CIOs is hardly a new phenomenon at a large company. But a CIO driving over a billion dollars in cost savings is. The way Dallas enabled this change, how he convinced people to participate, was masterful. "You can't lead from your office," he explains. "Medtronic's mission was to alleviate pain, restore health, and extend life. So I went and watched some surgeries. I saw heart surgeries, deep brain surgeries. . . . I actually saw a man's skull on the operating table!"

More important, Dallas says, is that he saw how Medtronic's products allowed people to lead fuller lives. He also spent time in the customer service department listening in on calls, and he went on the road with field salespeople. He took his leadership team to the warehouse, where they picked, packed, and shipped products.

"Sure you want to develop your relationships in the C suite," he says, "but it was just as important for me to develop relationships on the front line. Managers have issues dropped on them all the time. I wanted to see for myself what those issues and changes were. CIOs are often so focused on being behind the door that they sometimes forget that they need to leave their offices and get in the middle of the business. That's when the real conversations happen."

Strategy Matters

By cultivating solid relationships with his business peers, Dallas was able to collaborate with them to help them drive delivery and achieve their goals. He sat in on business review meetings, and he urged senior leaders to walk him through their business plans. He then used those plans to develop an IT roadmap and key themes, deciding to fund what was going to be common across business units, thereby letting individual managers allocate budget for their own unique solutions.

"Corporate IT budgets get the most scrutiny," Dallas explains. "When all the money is in one big pot, the CIO gets pulled in so many directions that success isn't as likely. But if you work collaboratively with various business leaders, you'll know when the business units should have IT projects on their books, and not on yours." Dallas smiles. "There's nothing wrong with shadow IT, as long as you're the one casting the shadow."

Surely things worked differently at a medical technology company than they did at a paper products manufacturer? What did Dallas bring from GP that he could leverage at Medtronic?

"Typically manufacturing companies have a top-down leadership style," Dallas explains, "but distributed companies have more of a distributed culture. At Medtronic, each GM was the king or queen of his or her business. So when I tried to sell an idea, if I linked it to our mission, it had a better chance of sticking. And if we could improve hospital, physician, or patient satisfaction, then it really had legs!"

Dallas made innovation a priority at both companies, creating innovation centers where small teams would test out new concepts and share them with the business. Interestingly, these were physical spaces where customers could also get a glimpse of innovation in action.

Dallas emphasizes the pressures on IT leaders to be both strategic and tactical. "You'll have your three- to five-year strategic plan, but you'll also have your annual operating plan. This will explain how you'll be funding things. I learned a lot at GP about having cost conversations. I learned that using technical jargon and a lot of PowerPoint slides got you nowhere. I led with strategic goals, and I talked about issues in business terms."

Dallas credits his time working with—and learning from—outstanding leaders at both GP and Medtronic. "The senior leaders I worked with showed me how people value security and significance more than anything else," he says. "The way you give that to them is by involving them, talking straight, and walking the talk."

Corporate Strategy Driving IT Strategy
Driving Corporate Strategy . . .

Whether in IT or on behalf of the corporation at large, disciplined strategic planning pays huge dividends. It validates how market forces contribute to industry success, how important competitive differentiation is, and how the resulting initiatives can inform new investments and resourcing rigor. Strategic planning justifies why we're in the business we're in—or why we've decided to depart from it. It colors in the word *value*.

Even leaders who are comfortable with strategy sometimes blur the lines. The relative definitions of *corporate strategy* and *IT strategy* are fairly crisp, but that doesn't mean there isn't overlap in ownership or execution responsibility. Figure 4.8 distinguishes some of the differences between corporate strategy and IT strategy. Notice that the successes are the same for both corporate strategy and IT strategy—the point being that IT can't be successful if it's not helping the business succeed.

Understanding how strategic your company is will give you better insight into the direction your IT organization should move toward—in

Figure 4.8 **Corporate Versus IT Strategy**

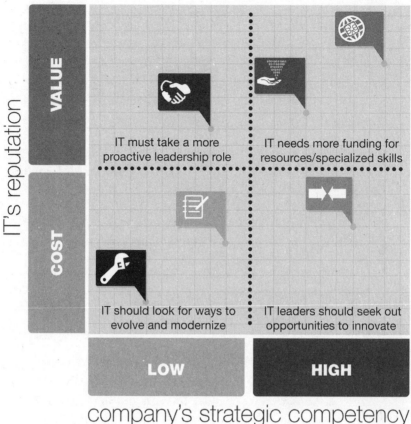

Figure 4.9 **Strategy and Your Desired-State Archetype**

other words, your desired-state IT archetype. (These archetypes were de-scribed in detail in Chapter 2.) Moving from one archetype to another usu-ally means evolution, not revolution. More often than not, the movement involves slow and incremental changes.

There is no "from" and "to" model that works better than others. The matrix in Figure 4.9 provides an idea of the IT archetype relative to your strategic competency. Hopefully it will give you a better idea of where it might be practical to end up.

So maybe you're lamenting the fact that your company's leaders aren't putting strategy into practice. Even not having a strategy is, in a way, a de facto strategy. Align with *that* strategy at your peril!

CHAPTER SUMMARY

Key Takeaways

- The word *strategy* is fraught with different interpretations. Most companies fall short of a regular and deliberate strategic planning process.

- Executives are often dismissive of strategy. This is usually based on bad past experiences with efforts erroneously labeled "strategy planning."

- Ultimately the lack of deliberate strategic thinking is a failure of leadership. The company, and its future, can suffer as a result.

- IT leaders are reluctant to get involved in strategy discussions because they're either uncomfortable with the topic or because the lack of transparency about company direction can force them into a guessing game they can't win.

- Strategy mapping and Strategy on a Page are two mechanisms that can help sort out complex company directions into IT execution tactics. Though they can differ in form and in content, they've proven to be useful tools in addressing what IT will be working on and why.

- The beauty of strategic alignment is that executives and boards of directors are often measured on and accountable for defining and realizing corporate strategy. If IT leaders populate their roadmaps with initiatives that support corporate strategy, they'll not only get full executive support but they'll also likely get funding.

Note to the CEO

According to a 2014 McKinsey study,[5] fewer business executives consider IT to be effective in helping to meet corporate goals than in prior years. Indeed, 37 percent of executives interviewed reported that IT helped their companies enter new markets in 2013, as opposed to 57 percent in 2012.

And 49 percent of those interviewed thought IT had assisted in the development of new products, down from 62 percent in 2012.

I asked Kevin Farley, divisional chief financial officer at Principal Financial Group, what advice he would give CEOs looking to drive business improvements through technology.

"The same advice I'd give an actuary," he said slyly. "Know your business. Know your strategy. Know where you fit into key strategic initiatives. And know how to extend into the distribution network—no matter what industry you're in—so that you understand the process from beginning to end. I've had different jobs in my career, but some of them took me further away from the end-to-end delivery process. As an executive, you never want to be too far away from provisioning products to customers."

Your company's activities mirror your mandates. Are you seeing business growth because you're strategic? Or because you've been lucky?

If it's luck, then congratulations. But the phenomenon of shadow IT discussed earlier will eventually become manifest. Line-of-business executives have neither the time nor inclination to go to the executive steering committee for "capex" budgets. If they can get their applications built using existing operating budgets, they'll do it every time.

IT is thus marginalized as a cost center, a reputation it increasingly battles. The CIO might be an innocent party—or the fault might very well lie with the leadership that doesn't cultivate and sustain structured strategic development processes. As strategy expert Art Petty observed, lack of corporate strategy is often a breakdown of senior management's ability to lead.

When I asked Petty his opinion of Strategy on a Page, he cited a Churchill quote: "Ask me to speak for two hours, I am ready. Ask me for one hour, and I need two weeks of preparation." His point is that Strategy on a Page is no shortcut. It requires a deliberate, regular, and executive-led process for distilling what's important for the company, and then documenting and committing to it.

The same applies to building an IT portfolio, as we'll see in the next chapter.

Operations: Rethinking Your IT Portfolio

All day long I think of things but nothing seems to satisfy,
Think I'll lose my mind if I don't find something to pacify . . .
—Black Sabbath, "Paranoid" (1970)

I spent over two decades as a managing partner at an IT consulting firm, so trust me when I tell you that I've heard my share of business gripes about IT. The gripers would usually begin with a series of subtle putdowns directed at IT leadership, then branch off into an indictment of skill sets or delivery velocity. They would conclude with a lament. "If we could only . . ." they would begin. For instance:

"If we could only get IT to understand what we're trying to do."

"If we could only get IT to deliver reports to our iPads!"

"If we could only get a single consolidated product list. (Yeah, on our iPads, where else?)"

It's not as if IT staff aren't busy. It's just that they're often busy doing the wrong things. Show me an IT department at a 40-year-old Fortune 500 company, and I'll show you herculean efforts to sustain costly, outdated, and unwieldy transactional systems at the expense of leveraging technology to drive business value. Cumbersome legacy system maintenance, hardware and software upgrades, and tire kicking in the name of research take up far too much of IT's time—time that could be spent building valuable business solutions.

Instead, they tackle what one chief operating officer offhandedly labeled "pitch and patch," spending most of their time lobbying for funding on behalf of projects that end up as refinements to already-brittle software code in an effort to sustain the status quo.

The Perils of Project Focus

As smart as they are, IT leaders often run their organizations reactively, managing pipelines of one-off projects to be delivered to a diverse and often unconnected constituency of business organizations. This is often the result of too many requests and too few resources, with constant assurances to the business that "you're next." IT leaders keep the plates spinning, reassuring as many managers as possible that progress is just around the corner. If businesspeople aren't actively engaged, then hopefully they're at least suspended in vague anticipation of something new right around the corner.

IT projects usually vary in breadth and scope. Figure 5.1 characterizes four types of projects that are the typical fodder for IT teams. The bottom

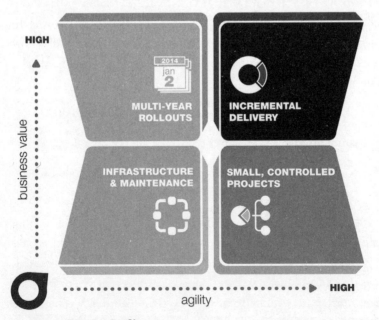

Figure 5.1 **IT Project Profiles**

left quadrant connotes building and maintenance work required for large systems. Even when outsourced, businesspeople view these initiatives skeptically, considering them "black holes" where money goes in, and nothing comes out. In the upper left quadrant are the multiyear rollouts, like large ERP or supply chain software deployments. While these solutions can streamline business processes, they often become bloated, late, and over budget.

Conversely, in the lower right corner, a range of smaller yet well-bounded work efforts usually fall under the rubric of departmental solutions and can be delivered quickly. Simpler to implement than their enterprisewide counterparts, they can end up adding incremental value. A specialty retailer recently added a new data visualization tool to its customer experience toolbox. The displays are so fresh and intuitive that even customer service reps who are normally engrossed in their spreadsheets have been requesting the tool.

Finally, even large projects, as represented in the upper right, can be broken up into what I like to call *human bites*. Such projects may ultimately be significant in scale, but they have been scoped into units of delivery.

Of course, there's another side to this story. IT departments are constrained by budget cuts and thwarted by often outdated paradigms of leaders who measure them on building and maintaining code. Reluctant to invite CIOs to the executive table, CEOs balk that IT is not the innovation incubator it could be. Case studies on companies that have failed to invest in IT innovations, and the resulting business impacts, abound.[1]

As CIOs pitch new IT projects, the mantra of "business enablement" is used synonymously with "operational systems development," in which commoditized systems of record are built, rebuilt, customized, and refined. Cost and effort estimates become elastic as teams undertake development and confront the inevitable data sourcing or code complexity challenges. Delivery plods along. Scope creeps.

The risk of overinvestment, miscalculated scopes, or inflated costs is proportional to an initiative's projected value, as shown in Figure 5.2. The result? Business disaffection with IT delivery has increased the phenomenon of lines of business obtaining their own technology budgets. At one large bank, the chief marketing officer (CMO) oversaw the acquisition, implementation, and delivery of a packaged CRM solution all before the

CRM vendor had even hit the radar of the bank's procurement department. The CMO boasted that she was automating business processes in the time it would have taken to get on IT's calendar.

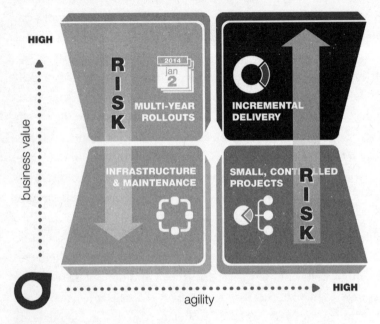

Figure 5.2 **Comparative Project Risk**

Shadow IT was born.

How do we change this? Should it even be changed? Have business units earned the right to assume traditional IT development work? These questions will confront executives within and outside of IT ever more urgently as corporate governance extends to IT expenditures and business unit executives look outside of IT for better ways to achieve results. You could argue—and many technologists have—that business leaders are never happy with IT. As guilty as IT is at coming up with new methodologies, processes, organization charts, and job titles, the business is often even worse—or better, as the case may be.

As we discussed in Chapter 4, when IT leaders are uncertain of priorities or direction, they often hunker down, tinkering with their budgets while trying to keep up with ever-shifting project demands. Have a problem? Let's launch a project. The dozens or even hundreds of concurrent IT projects, with their oozing scopes and ballooning costs, are a testimony to the project-as-panacea phenomenon.

But projects in a vacuum don't work. For one, they need justification in the context of something greater. And they need to be prioritized based on their business value. We'll talk about both of these in the remainder of this chapter.

EXECUTIVE PROFILE

Ryan Fenner, Union Bank

If you grabbed a microbrew at a Padres game and found yourself sitting next to Ryan Fenner, your first reaction would probably be to brush up on your batting averages. Fenner seems like a guy equally at home in a VIP box at Petco Park as he is in a conference room at Union Bank. And the well-worn baseball metaphors of teamwork, hits, and loaded bases apply equally well in both venues.

Fenner has certainly seen the game change at Union Bank. As a vice president, he's had a choice seat for some of the major cultural and technology decisions there. And in a job that requires ensuring tight teamwork between the business and IT, Fenner arguably understands what it takes to be an organization that wins.

Fenner started at Union Bank—then known as Union Bank of California—as a workflow automation specialist, moving on to key roles on the business intelligence and enterprise architecture teams. Across all his jobs at the bank, his focus on data put him right behind home plate.

The First Pitch

Most large companies tend to resist change until there's a problem. But in Union Bank's case, change came in the form of a consultant's Power-Point deck.

"It happens in a lot of banks," says Fenner. "We had an outside firm do an assessment, which was a catalyst for an initial set of serious changes. We knew we needed to fix some things. It was just a question of where to start."

(continues)

As anyone who's engaged a consulting firm can tell you, the recommendations of outsiders aren't new news. Many simply don't resonate. Others aren't tactical enough. Union Bank was the exception. The bank took the recommendations seriously, driving changes that were fundamental and cultural, resulting in the restructuring of IT around four key pillars:

- Infrastructure
- Data
- Integration
- Business

Fenner emphasizes that the business is actually the foundation for the other three pillars.

"Our businesspeople know IT, and they know what we can do," he says. "Sure, we've got shadow IT here—we're like most banks in that regard. So it's that much more important for us to align our architecture with business goals and continuously evangelize IT strategy."

One of the bank's core principles is this: "Reuse first, buy commodity, build to differentiate." The principle was initially applied narrowly to implementation decisions. "But over time it gave us room to start thinking about which systems and which activities were commodities," Fenner explains.

"For example, is Salesforce.com a commodity product? Can we differentiate it by configuring it differently? This has driven a lot of conversations about where and how we should invest. We could buy a so-called commodity product that could nevertheless become differentiating—actually strategic!"

Unlike many IT leaders, Fenner doesn't dismiss the IT-as-commodity conversation. "The fact that the business sees a team of people who can address the commodity skills is a huge bonus for everyone. After all, businesspeople don't want their organizations to manage servers. They have better things to do."

As the great outfielder Casey Stengel once said, "No baseball pitcher would be worth a darn without a catcher who could handle a hot fastball." So how does the business side run with some of these changes?

"I've been here for 10 years, and I've relied on my own relationships to evangelize my team's value," Fenner says. "But ultimately it's about embedding certain processes as the normal way of doing business."

Runs Batted In

And executive support doesn't hurt either. Union Bank's Bank Policy Manual lays out company-sanctioned practices in detail. One such practice is engaging with the enterprise architecture team, a requirement that had to gain C-level approval to make it into the manual.

"Architecture has become a fundamental component of quality here," says Fenner. "The team is really engaged across the project life cycle. We're involved in requirements gathering and planning—where we look at proposed solutions and how the business wants to implement them. Do they want to build or buy? We then make sure the business has input into technology decisions. And, of course, there's design. Projects need to engage the architecture team before they enter the design phase. And there's even a process for what we call 'project closure' to ensure that what was designed in the planning phase matches what was actually built."

How do you institutionalize new behaviors at a big bank?

Fenner laughs. "We talk about 'carrot, stick, and sledgehammer,'" he says. "The carrot is educating the business on the value of what we're doing. Businesspeople fundamentally want to do things better and cheaper, so they pretty much get that. The stick is regulatory pressures. Our data enables business processes like credit risk and regulatory reporting. Banks just can't ignore regulators and auditors."

And the sledgehammer? "Our current culture supports this," Fenner says. "Oftentimes, we have to break down barriers for teams to work together effectively. We have the freedom to take challenges to senior management for resolution when we need to. Leadership will listen and support us. The days of the lone cowboy are over. We need effective collaboration to succeed."

This suggests a certain level of executive support that Fenner confirms. From ensuring that IT was fully represented in the bank's operating

(continues)

policies through tiebreaking for knottier problems, the executive team at Union Bank has shown the IT team plenty of support.

"We have great leadership now," Fenner says. "The relationship between the business and IT is better than ever, and our leaders collaborate well. We're all willing to try new things and to share ideas with each other. The change in IT leadership [Union Bank's CIO has been in place for a little over two years] has certainly helped. Our executives are really behind us 100 percent."

Put another way, for one of the fastest-growing regional banks, driving business improvements through IT has been nothing short of a home run.

Building—Then Forgetting About— Your Operating Framework

Any IT organization is the sum of its complex, interrelated, and constantly moving parts. At the end of the day, the IT operating framework should serve as a means of connecting these parts and ensuring that they serve the IT strategy—and by extension, the business strategy—very well. These moving parts are represented in Figure 5.3.

This figure is represented more as a "constellation" than a hierarchy. This builds in the assumption that certain areas may need more or less governance. Two primary factors affect the amount of resources a single area receives:

1. **The projects in the IT portfolio.** For instance, if many of the projects for a given planning year require new systems or applications, the systems and innovation areas might receive more resources than other areas.

2. **The desired IT archetype.** You'll recall in Chapter 2 we presented six different IT archetypes: Tactical, Order Taking, Aligning, Data Provisioning, Brokering, and IT Everywhere. These archetypes can represent who you are now as well as who you want your organization to be. Say you want to move from Order Taking to Brokering. Then your operating framework might encourage resources be

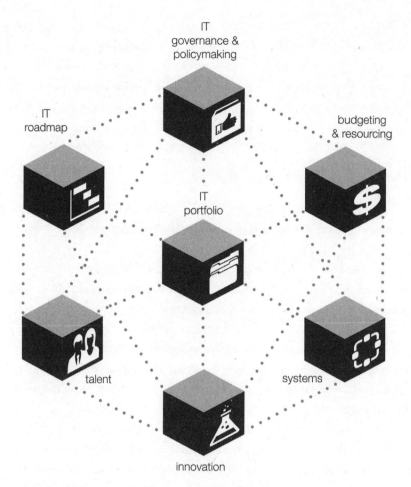

Figure 5.3 **Components of the IT Governance Framework**

aimed away from systems and talent and instead toward IT governance and policy making and innovation.

Let's briefly touch on the meaning and importance of each component in the IT operating framework.

IT Portfolio

Your IT portfolio is the collection of business capabilities and functions deployed by IT over time. It is ideally strategy driven, and its boundaries are informed by your IT archetype. We'll talk more about defining and prioritizing the IT portfolio later in the chapter. The IT portfolio helps communicate IT's collection of work efforts. It defines IT's job.

Why the IT portfolio in the middle? Because the portfolio ensures that—no matter what your IT organization's archetype—the focus is on delivery through a collection of technology-enabled business capabilities. We'll talk about how to build and prioritize an IT portfolio later in this chapter.

IT Governance and Policy Making

IT governance is the management of IT assets, be they systems, people, content, or other resources with value attached to them. Shouldn't this entire chapter be about IT governance then?

Governance is often misinterpreted as IT operations management. If not defined clearly and designed well, it can become an academic exercise, where reluctant members of a steering committee convene to debate priorities and make decisions based on assumptions of value. However, IT governance is maturing to include software tools that embed workflow and alert decision makers when they become bottlenecks to progress. When governance is done well, IT can often set the stage for other governance efforts in the company.

Much has been written about the importance of IT governance. But a lot of that discussion inflates IT governance as a set of processes and financial controls that can block out the sun, obscuring more tactical efforts that can drive more business value and shed more light on IT's contributions.

IT governance is really about the policy making and oversight of IT efforts. Its components are those we introduced in Chapter 1: operation, connection, and innovation. We'll talk more about IT governance in Chapter 10, "Getting and Keeping a Seat at the Table."

Budgeting and Resourcing

This component is what many executives often mistake for strategy in IT. In reality, the resources and budgeting enable business and IT leaders to deliver against their company strategies via their IT portfolios. They are a means to an end, not the end. IT budgets are rarely coupled with the company's strategic plan—longtime GE CEO Jack Welch didn't call budgeting "the bane of corporate America" for nothing. An outsized focus on resource allocation and budgeting distracts IT leaders from more pressing business needs.

Furthermore, routine budgeting and operations details can often be delegated to midlevel managers who could benefit from the experience. An effective IT leader manages downward, ensuring the proper mentoring and development of her team members. Such assignments can free a CIO to dedicate time to the rigor of cultivating support for and sustaining an aligned IT portfolio.

Systems

It all started with systems. Who knew that they'd be a mere component in the IT machine? Including systems as part of the IT operating framework is a given. However, in many ways this is the biggest commodity portion of the framework. Technology platforms are increasingly cheaper and easier to procure.

And, as we're seeing with IT organizations that have adopted the Brokering or IT Everywhere archetypes, they're also increasingly likely to exist outside of IT's four walls, making tracking and monitoring them all the more important.

Innovation

Including innovation in an IT operating plan ups the odds that it will be taken seriously by constituents who might be cynical about IT's ability to offer fresh ideas and nontraditional solutions. Innovation is more typically a residual IT conversation, not an acknowledged competency. I have seen leaders roll innovation into their operating models and end up with a cursory innovation budget—also known as "seed money"—as a result. A few small, incremental innovations can drive a cultural shift that positions IT as the curator, if not the owner of new technologies and delivery mechanisms. Chapter 7, "Innovation, Going Digital, and Other Uphill Battles," will talk about what it takes for a company to adopt an innovation culture.

Talent

Calling talent management out as part of the operating framework in its own right cements the point that IT skills are unique, differentiated, and important to nurture. With the rise of shadow IT, the management of technical employees falls to both business and IT leaders. These leaders should share a common philosophy of rewarding and keeping top talent and measuring it according to delivery. We'll talk about managing talent more in Chapter 9, "Fighting the Talent Wars."

IT Roadmap

The IT roadmap represents IT's delivery master plan. The roadmap might span multiple years, and it will usually include budgets, resources, and projects. The IT roadmap can be distilled down to reflect IT's delivery intentions. While many IT leaders would position the IT roadmap at the center of their operating frameworks, it's important that the roadmap be the result of deliberate IT portfolio planning, not the driver of it. The roadmap is enabled by the framework's other components—as they are all enabled by the roadmap.

Why Is IT Governance Such a Big Deal?

Governance is defined as the policy making and oversight of a corporate asset or capability. IT governance ensures that the approvals and the checks and balances are in place and formalized to ensure the successful delivery of the projects within the IT portfolio. Much has been written about IT governance—see Peter Weill and Jeanne Ross's book of the same name—and IT leaders have done an effective job of setting up governance structures. The problem isn't the lack of governance abilities as much as it is the failure to know what to govern.

All told, the operating framework is driven by your IT strategy, and that, as we discussed in Chapter 4, should be driven by your business strategy. Likewise, the operating framework supports the IT strategy that in turn enables the business strategy. As Figure 5.4 illustrates, the operating framework serves as a strategy engine.

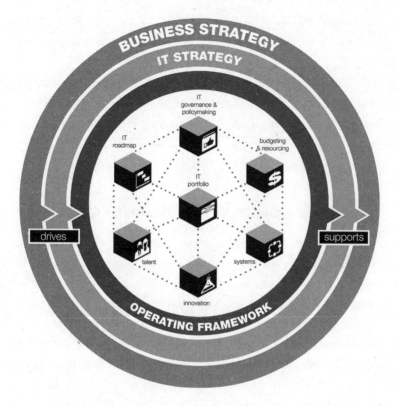

Figure 5.4 **The Operating Framework as a Strategic Engine**

As my story at the beginning of Chapter 1 relates, IT leaders love operating frameworks. Some use them to proselytize how complicated IT is—all the more reason to increase next year's operating budget! Some decide to structure their organizations according to the operating framework, putting senior managers in charge of each area. These leaders typically allocate the same levels of resources to each operational area year after year, emphasizing cost cutting and technology upgrades over and above the pursuit of execution on behalf of the business.

Using the operating model as the basis for IT's work begets an operational, not a strategic, culture. The strength of the operating model is not its complexity or that of its various components. Its purpose is to ensure that the mechanics of IT are functioning well. Organizing around service lines—the specialties the operating framework supports—ensures the optimal skill sets and technologies are always applied. The operating framework merely ensures that the right pieces are in place. IT leaders should design their operating frameworks, test their completeness, and then turn their heads to the work that needs to get done.

This is why leaders should adopt a portfolio approach to managing IT projects. Most of the literature on IT portfolio management seeks to rationalize IT investments, much the way consumers do in managing their personal investments, with the goal being return on capital. But with the rise of shadow IT, the fact is that every budget is an IT budget.

Problems with Classic IT Portfolio Management

I use the term "classic IT portfolio management" as if it's been institutionalized in most companies. It hasn't. Some companies maintain IT cultures largely composed of cowboys who pick and choose the fun projects—like shooting cans off fence posts. Others cherry-pick projects involving new or emerging technologies that will ripen their collective résumés, relegating junior resources to infrastructure projects and measuring their costs reactively. In the meantime, innovative and potentially differentiating efforts are dismissed either because of enculturated risk aversion or because "there's no open headcount."

For companies that have made the effort in IT portfolio management, though, most start by categorizing varying IT investments into buckets like "infrastructure" or "applications" and then treating each category in the same way, applying identical principles and a single budget pool across all categories. In the end, these companies end up overspending and delivering less than they could have.

Another problem is that IT staff create IT portfolios in isolation, failing to enlist business executives or stakeholders in the decision-making or prioritization process. The logic here is that IT people understand existing systems and applications much better than their business counterparts who would simply add "noise" to discussions of what the company already has, what it needs to replace, and what it needs to build anew.

Finally, many IT executives have treated IT portfolio management as a research project rather than a long-term series of practices that should prioritize work based on business goals, involve stakeholders, and become formalized as a sustained planning exercise. Thus, IT portfolio management starts with a bang, allocating investments using some amount of rigor, only to end with a whimper once IT acquiesces to pet projects and skunk works efforts that wring resources from the business.

"The challenge many CIOs still face is engaging their business partners in the roadmap discussion," confirms Sahal Laher, chief information officer of Brooks Brothers. "There are always trade-offs, so the ability to prioritize is key. For instance, if a project enables our 'Legendary Customer Service' program, it will probably be closer to the top of the list. IT leaders need to ensure that IT priorities align with business priorities and that they institute the necessary rigor."

The true value of managing IT efforts as a portfolio of projects is that it provides a means of prioritization, driving investment decisions in a more concrete and timely way. In fact, I would argue that IT project prioritization is just as important as IT spend, as it affects long-term ownership, outsourcing, development cycles, and resourcing decisions. In the next chapter, we'll see how IT should be restructured to support this prioritization.

Finally, in their quest to resolve evolving ownership and accountability questions, IT organizations assign ownership of the IT portfolio to a single individual who becomes a figurehead—and often a target—for IT investment decisions. A single IT portfolio owner is rarely effective. At worst, the owner succumbs to political agendas and alliances, advocating investments in projects or platforms that are seen as emerging or "sexy." (I call this "bright shiny object syndrome," and there's plenty of it on both the IT and business sides of the house.)

At best, the owner is overwhelmed by the complexity and disparity of technologies in the organization. "I'm still wrapping my brain around everything we've got here," one new CIO explained recently. "And what I'm realizing is that no one has pulled any weeds in a really long time. I'm going to have to get rid of a lot before I recommend building anything new."

Defining the New IT Portfolio

IT portfolio management allows IT organizations to influence company performance and revenues by determining the company's intrinsic IT competencies based on corporate strategic priorities. Strategy is where IT and business executives should ultimately come together and collaborate on more mission-critical development efforts. We saw some examples of aligning corporate strategy with IT strategy in the prior chapter.

IT portfolio management is changing. It's becoming more business driven, more holistic, and even more nuanced. Rather than prioritizing IT activities based on budget and resource availability, the new IT portfolio prioritizes projects based on a range of factors that are driven as much by corporate culture and past successes as by projections of cost savings or increased revenues. This in turn can drive more intentional technology investment decisions that serve a range of business needs.

"After our strategic plan had been accepted, I realized that we needed a single, unified portfolio to support it," explains Michel Loranger, CIO of SSQ Financial Group. "The portfolio represented the most critical needs of the business, not just within business units but across them. And this couldn't just be based on their ability to fund projects. It needed to be based on business value. So we began to identify a corporatewide IT portfolio."

Loranger has engaged the CEO in governance processes, and he is partnering with the CFO to evaluate business cases for projects in the IT portfolio.

"The challenge is that it's been classically difficult to compare projects. So next for us—and this is really the hard part—we'll have a way to vet projects according to specific metrics and prioritize them in a repeatable way."

A true IT portfolio results in a collection of applications, platforms, and capabilities that represent delivery. Deconstructing the IT portfolio into a series of projects ensures that the focus is on delivery, not on cost estimations and high-level plans.

The real-life story below illustrates how we developed a portfolio at a company called CheckFree.[2]

The Portfolio Story at CheckFree

When you pay your bills on your bank's website, odds are you're using software that was developed at CheckFree. The company blended the best of financial services savvy with a groundbreaking technology engine. But as in many tech companies, the smart people there initially worked in silos. CheckFree managers saw the potential to streamline business processes and create a more systemic way to deploy analytics projects. They asked for my consulting firm's help in creating a centralized program for business intelligence.

Like many companies, CheckFree based its technology investment decisions on a range of mostly operational factors, occasionally capitulating to strong personalities with urgent business requirements. We quickly saw the need to link individual technology activities to a broader set of corporate measures and cultural considerations. The resulting portfolio would establish an IT strategy that could support a range of business processes, organizations, and strategic needs, and it would also maximize resource utilization and technology reuse.

(The initial portfolio was geared to CheckFree's extensive business intelligence and analytics projects, yet it wasn't exclusive to these projects. In fact, CheckFree subsequently adapted the process for other enterprise technology efforts.)

As consultants typically do, we interviewed a few dozen senior executives. We asked questions about both corporate and line-of-business priorities, studied how they were measured, and walked through core business processes. Then we turned our heads to IT, examining operational systems and development methods and tools. We then attempted to encapsulate both existing and new development opportunities into a series of projects that would be prioritized based on a series of metrics.

We then convened senior executives and high-level directors at the company's verdant headquarters campus. In a wood-paneled meeting room, beamed from an overhead projector, the following challenge was displayed:

Think of a successful business initiative here that involved IT.
What characteristics or qualities made it successful?

We asked each executive to contribute his or her thoughts about the statement hovering on the screen in front of them.

"Customer satisfaction," said the VP of sales. "It really comes back to our customers being our first priority."

"Return on investment," countered the CFO. "Nothing really succeeds around here if we can't show some sort of ROI."

We facilitated a group discussion about what made for successful delivery at CheckFree, keeping a running record of the answers filtering out.

After about an hour, we'd arrived at a list of answers to the question. Figure 5.5 shows the list of resulting success metrics.

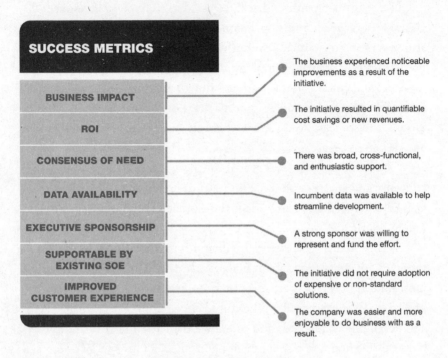

Figure 5.5 **Success Factors for CheckFree Business Initiatives**

Why this exercise? Because the resulting list illuminated not just what individuals considered important about a given project but what the *corporate culture* supported. By objectively recalling successful efforts—both within and outside of IT—then backing into why they were considered successful, participants in these sessions were forced to represent larger corporate priorities, not just their own narrow interests.

Note that although this list is very representative, no two companies have the same exact list of success factors. I've worked with groups who have come up with 20 factors. Others have only 3 or 4 factors. The point is that the list is inclusive, objective, and reflective of the company's values. By building this list in a collaborative, in-person meeting, each participant is accountable for his or her answers. There is often a debate on whether a project was really successful and what "success" really means. That's precisely the discussion we wanted to have. It was long overdue.

Once we'd arrived at our list, we then asked everyone to assign a weighting to each item. The weightings were based on the descriptions shown in Figure 5.6. Assigning weightings like those in the figure can help a company gauge the relative importance of each of these success factors.

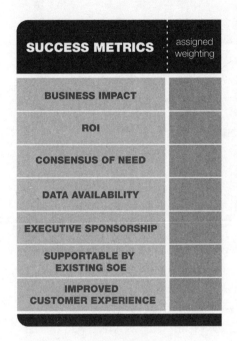 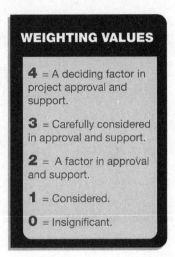

Figure 5.6 **Assigned Weightings**

The point is to assign a numeric weight to each success factor, resulting in a score for each one. There can be more than one of the same weighting—for instance, both ROI and improved customer experience received 4s, as shown in Figure 5.7.

At this point, the debate among participants can get lively. Leaders will defend their agendas, justifying why a particular project is critical to the company's competitive advantage, or arguing on behalf of a broad consensus to drive cultural change. But that's exactly the point of the exercise: leaders going on record about what's been successful—and by extension, what hasn't—illuminates how the company adopts or even embraces technology-enabled efforts.

Once the group at CheckFree agreed on the weightings, we adjourned the meeting and went out for cocktails, where the discussion continued,

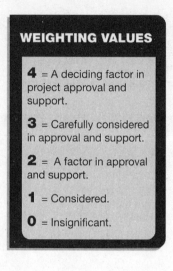

SUCCESS METRICS	assigned weighting
BUSINESS IMPACT	3
ROI	4
CONSENSUS OF NEED	2
DATA AVAILABILITY	1
EXECUTIVE SPONSORSHIP	3
SUPPORTABLE BY EXISTING SOE	1
IMPROVED CUSTOMER EXPERIENCE	4

WEIGHTING VALUES

4 = A deciding factor in project approval and support.

3 = Carefully considered in approval and support.

2 = A factor in approval and support.

1 = Considered.

0 = Insignificant.

Figure 5.7 **Weightings Assigned to Success Factors**

debates raged on, and agreement about where the company had delivered valuable new capabilities was reached.

We reconvened the group a few days later, after we'd recorded the varied projects we'd identified as part of our executive interviews. Some of the projects were already under way. Others were part of executives' wish lists. We listed each project across the top of a matrix and displayed it on the screen. Figure 5.8 shows three candidate projects across the top:

- **Web analytics.** Availing simple, visual reports on the company's web activity and drill down capabilities to highlight specific figures and viewer segments

- **Financial reporting workbench.** Integrating sales, cost, pricing, taxes, product, and asset data to generate a range of reports from top-line measurements all the way to sophisticated financial risk models

- **Customer value scoring.** Combining a range of customer attributes and behaviors to determine their lifetime value scores

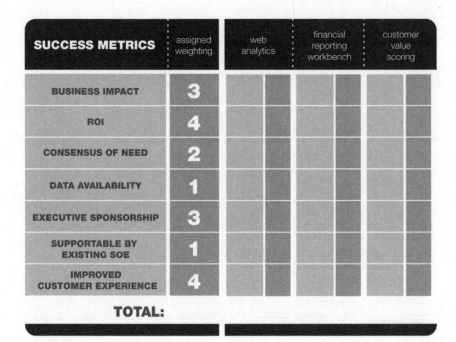

SUCCESS METRICS	assigned weighting		web analytics		financial reporting workbench		customer value scoring	
BUSINESS IMPACT	3							
ROI	4							
CONSENSUS OF NEED	2							
DATA AVAILABILITY	1							
EXECUTIVE SPONSORSHIP	3							
SUPPORTABLE BY EXISTING SOE	1							
IMPROVED CUSTOMER EXPERIENCE	4							
TOTAL:								

Figure 5.8 **Listing the Candidate Projects**

In reality, the matrix was several pages long in landscape mode, listing a diverse set of business applications from across organizations and that were at various levels of sophistication, complexity, and importance. We distributed one-page profiles for each of these projects to the group.

Then we asked the group to apply the same weighting criteria—the 0-to-4 scale they had used to weight the success metrics—to each of the projects listed across the top of the displayed worksheet. In other words, we asked them to answer the question "How would you score the projected business impact of the web analytics application?" So web analytics would receive a score for business impact. And another for ROI. And another for consensus of need, and so on.

The group argued and debated anew. These assessments were suddenly closer to home. Obviously, a CFO would argue that the business impact of the financial reporting workbench would be quite high, while the director of marketing saw customer value scoring as having greater business impact. The point was that business impact alone wasn't enough of a factor to determine the overall priority of either project.

SUCCESS METRICS	assigned weighting	web analytics	financial reporting workbench	customer value scoring
BUSINESS IMPACT	3	2	3	2
ROI	4	3	3	3
CONSENSUS OF NEED	2	3	3	3
DATA AVAILABILITY	1	2	2	1
EXECUTIVE SPONSORSHIP	3	3	2	2
SUPPORTABLE BY EXISTING SOE	1	2	1	1
IMPROVED CUSTOMER EXPERIENCE	4	2	2	3
TOTAL:				

Figure 5.9 **Scoring the Projects**

When the worksheet was completed, each application had a score based on each success metric, as shown in Figure 5.9.

Once each application had its own score for each success factor, we then did the simple math of multiplying each of the scores by the original assigned weighting, and we added up the totals so that each individual project had its own score. Figure 5.10 shows the results of the first three applications on the list.

The application that ranked the highest—in this case, customer value scoring with a score of 55—was put first in the priority queue, the second highest was put second, and so on, until we had a prioritized list of applications based on the identified success factors. The group then chose an executive sponsor for each application, and that person's responsibility was to work with IT to determine a development budget for that application. Once that exercise was done, the budgets would be analyzed and the list would be further prioritized to become the company's IT development roadmap for the coming year.

SUCCESS METRICS	assigned weighting	web analytics		financial reporting workbench		customer value scoring	
BUSINESS IMPACT	3	2	6	4	12	4	12
ROI	4	3	12	2	8	3	12
CONSENSUS OF NEED	2	3	4	3	6	3	6
DATA AVAILABILITY	1	2	2	2	2	3	3
EXECUTIVE SPONSORSHIP	3	3	9	2	6	3	9
SUPPORTABLE BY EXISTING SOE	1	2	2	2	2	1	1
IMPROVED CUSTOMER EXPERIENCE	4	2	8	1	4	3	12
TOTAL:			44		40		55

Figure 5.10 **Calculating the Priorities**

The Benefits of Portfolio Prioritization

This exercise isn't foolproof. It has often proven only as valuable as the authority of the managers participating. However, the advantages of this portfolio prioritization are many, including these:

- **The exercise reflects the company's culture.** Note that executives were pressed to consider which projects had taken hold at the company and to apply those attributes to newly considered initiatives—whether or not they had an individual stake in them. This prevents people from reciting their wish lists or parroting something they read in a magazine and instead encourages realistic thinking.

- **It prevents "squeaky wheel syndrome."** Often planning sessions are only as valid as the most persistent—or loudest—person in the room. By enforcing precision about success and the staying power of past projects, personalities are forced to cede to reality-based decisions.

- **It meets the company where it is.** A company whose leaders focus on operational excellence and efficiencies over strategic differentiation will fail if it suddenly shifts to a portfolio of projects intended to enhance competitive differentiation. The prioritization process accounts for current needs as well as future objectives, measuring both against a set of company-specific metrics.

- **It demonstrates rigor.** Although sometimes the meetings are protracted and the debates fierce, the portfolio prioritization exercise prevents the all-too-common scenario of applying tired budget allocation processes and selecting projects that most easily fit that process. I have walked through the exercise with CEOs who, when confronted with a numerical scoring model and a cross-functional team of decision makers, immediately bless the results. "I won't even argue your scores," a manufacturer's COO told me after five minutes. "This is the most deliberate planning I've seen since I got here. Go."

- **It mandates IT participation.** Business leaders often welcome portfolio prioritization meetings as the way to present their organizations' to-do items, discuss innovative ways to tackle emerging competitive issues, and explore options for moving toward digital engagement with customers. But absent the execution planning to accompany these discussions, they can die on the vine. IT managers deserve a seat at the table during project prioritization, and execution is unlikely without them.

- **It works even when strategy isn't transparent, or when there is no strategy at all.** Despite the popularity of strategic planning in executive circles, it doesn't always work. A 2013 study of executives by *Build* magazine found that, when asked to name their companies' top three priorities, executives were in sync at only 2 percent of the companies surveyed.[3] And many line-of-business executives complain that their executive leaders fail to communicate strategy when it does exist. Prioritizing a portfolio of applications may serve as a grassroots effort, corralling leaders for the purpose of blending aspirational proficiencies with cultural realities. Absent a strategy, such collaborative planning may be the best way to move the company forward.

Clearly the priorities might shift once the company determines the relative budget for each project. But that's the easy part for most companies whose budgeting, and the processes and skills used to determine them, are already well established.

EXECUTIVE PROFILE

Michael Smith, Mylan Pharmaceuticals

It began with an observation I'd never heard before from a CIO. "Culture eats strategy," the CIO said. And, one by one, the hands of fellow CIOs, systems integrators, and industry analysts began shooting up in the air. Everyone was eager for the speaker to elaborate.

That's the day I introduced myself to Michael Smith, CIO of Mylan Pharmaceuticals. A 22-year veteran of Nike, Smith understands the role culture plays in a large corporation. But more important, he understands how to use culture to steer an IT department that's on a growth trajectory.

"If you looked at Nike back in 1990, we weren't seen as a consumer products company. Back then, we were a billion-dollar footwear maker. Sure, there were a few T-shirts. But when I left in 2012, Nike was a $25 billion lifestyle company." The company's evolution was manifest—and so was IT's part in it.

Despite the differences between a brand behemoth and a growing pharmaceutical company—Mylan is a nearly $7 billion company with a workforce of over 20,000 worldwide—Smith is applying lessons from Nike. "As a company, Nike was constantly transforming," he says. "Sometimes I led the transformation efforts, and sometimes I supported them. Either way, I got to see transformational shifts happen from various perspectives. So it's a personal and professional challenge to support transformation at Mylan."

(continues)

Recruited to Drive Change

It's hard to imagine Smith, a stylish and soft-spoken man, pounding his fist on a mahogany boardroom table and justifying IT expenditure. And that's a good thing because he won't have to.

"There were a lot of things that attracted me to this role," he explains, "but mainly it's Mylan's mission: 'Do good, and do well.' The leaders here are bold and visionary, and they walk the walk. They see IT as fundamental to our mission."

Indeed, Mylan's CEO, Heather Bresch, recruited Smith, in part, because he didn't have a pharmaceutical background.

"I didn't arrive expecting to support the status quo," Smith confirms. "People expected change. But at the same time, that didn't really become real until we started delivering results."

Smith set about driving a set of changes that were at once helpful and supportive to businesspeople. He implemented a social business tool, Jive, that encouraged collaboration across organizations and teams. He also installed Workday, a cloud solution for HR and financial management. And he shifted the corporate standard from BlackBerry to iPhone, while at the same time supporting a bring-your-own-device model that lets employees use their preferred mobile devices. (Mylan is also migrating to Microsoft Office 365 from Lotus Notes.)

The common denominator for these disparate projects? "They're making people's lives easier," Smith explains. "IT needs to deliver results. People will support change if they see the value."

Govern Strategically, Deliver Tactically

And it's not just about updating technology with fresher solutions. Like many executive change agents, Smith keeps his finger on the strategic pulse of the company with a deliberate process for IT portfolio management. Deputy CIOs embedded within Mylan's various business units connect IT with business planning. This assures business leaders that their objectives are on IT's radar as it considers its own evolving roadmap.

"We're constantly sweeping our corporate strategic plan," Smith says. "We have 21 programs that will be in next year's portfolio. There may be 300 projects coming from my CIOs. We might look at those and find commonalities between them. We refine and group, resulting in a few strategic programs and a smaller number of supporting projects. This year, it's 21 programs and roughly 100 midtier projects. It ends up that we might not deliver the exact project you requested, but we will deliver the capability you requested through one of the strategic programs. And it is available for the world, not just your business unit."

This governance model—in which IT manages not only a portfolio of projects but a portfolio of investments—is a shift for Mylan. Before Smith, the company didn't have IT governance, an enterprise architecture, or other shared services to streamline delivery. "We're putting all these things in place in a unified way," he says, "and we're actually moving the needle."

But what about culture eating strategy? Has the tenet played out at Mylan?

"Aligning business strategy with technology strategy doesn't stop with the CIO," Smith says. "Every employee is a steward of strategy. And we capitalize on our cultural strengths: Mylan employees are committed, passionate, and relentless. To the extent that we can, we'll change the rules if they're not working. The good news is that our culture is ready to support these kinds of changes."

The other piece of good news is also clear: Smith wasn't only ready for Mylan—Mylan was ready for Smith.

Once your company has identified the components of its IT portfolio, a committee of IT decision makers and business stakeholders should collaborate to apply a structured taxonomy to IT initiatives-based quantifiable metrics. Categorizing IT projects in a sustained and structured way can inform development processes, resource decisions, new vendor conversations, and hiring strategies.

A Stakeholder Interaction Model

As many executives have learned the hard way, decisions on which technology efforts to undertake aren't confined to a few planning meetings by

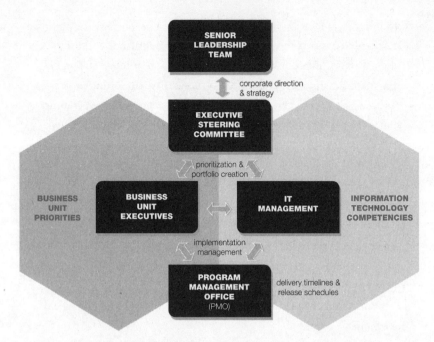

Figure 5.11 **Technology Portfolio Planning: A Stakeholder Interaction Model**

a fixed set of individuals. Often this type of planning approach—a few high-level managers accustomed to working together and sharing common philosophies—entrenches ineffective processes. At worst, it cements perspectives that don't move the company forward. As executive teams have proven time and again, lofty and formal planning meetings don't necessarily translate into effective delivery models.

Figure 5.11 illustrates an example of a stakeholder interaction system for technology project prioritization. By the way, the term *interaction system* is deliberate. It connotes fluid, bidirectional communications and multiple players for different types of decisions. It's not an organizational chart. Rather, it's a means of establishing decision levels based on authority and function. It encourages multiple players with different responsibilities and perspectives.

The interactions are beholden to the core decisions made by a strategic planning body, be it the senior leadership team or some formal strategic planning function. This ensures that strategy filters down to managers who are planning and ultimately delivering technology solutions. This might be driven by a PMO under IT or an operations function. Or it might filter back to individual line-of-business IT teams, depending on your organizational structure. (We'll discuss organizational options for the new IT in the next chapter.)

Studies have shown that when it comes to getting important work done, there's an increasing trend of interdependence among people and organizations,[4] and this is clearly true when it comes to technology project planning. This stakeholder interaction system is only one of many possible communications frameworks, and your mileage may vary. What's important is ensuring that key business units sit at the table with IT when it comes to prioritizing programs. As we discussed in Chapter 1, the effort executives put into connecting work functions can make a profound difference.

In a presentation to IT professionals, innovation expert Clayton Christensen talked about truly innovative organizations focusing on the job, not the product. "Innovators are organized around the job to be done," he said. "It's quite easy [for IT organizations] to add features, . . . but I think the industry would benefit greatly . . . to try to understand the job and then build the [products and services] from that insight."[5]

Think you're already doing an effective job of IT portfolio management? Ask yourself these questions:

1. Does our IT portfolio use a regular, repeatable, and sanctioned process to define and prioritize key projects?

2. Does it connect efforts across and between IT service lines (for example, platforms, analytics, and user devices)?

3. Is it linked to the company's strategy and/or to major business initiatives?

4. Can it be easily deconstructed into projects with clear success metrics?

5. Is it developed with the collaboration of diverse players representing different business functions, job levels, and skills?

If you answered yes to at least four of the questions above, you're not only clarifying the role of IT but you are also probably personally recognized as helping the company make difficult but ultimately transformative choices.

By adopting a portfolio approach to IT that involves the business in prioritization of work efforts, you don't just connect business and IT. You fuse them together. One of the benefits of a rigorous prioritization exercise is the rigor itself—using a process like the one described in this chapter factors in heterogeneous business, cultural, and political factors that reflect a broad range of considerations beyond traditional IT operations. Thus, everyone can support the company's overarching objectives through deliberate technology delivery.

CHAPTER SUMMARY

Key Takeaways

- The tendency to focus on isolated projects absent a connecting framework favors personality-based deployment decisions, and it risks marginalizing IT as passive and reactive.

- Risks of pursuing isolated and unrelated projects include overinvestment, duplication of effort, and the marginalization of critical infrastructure or shared capabilities.

- Operating frameworks should enable, not define, IT strategy. They are foundational.

- Traditionally, IT portfolio management has focused more on investments than it has on prioritizing technology delivery around business needs. By considering what's important to your company—either by looking to the strategic plan or monitoring where the company invests externally—IT leaders can rank projects, thereby creating more business value.

- Prioritization must involve a cross section of leaders from both inside and outside the IT organization, ensuring different (and sometimes competing) perspectives and agendas.

- There is no set means of establishing important prioritization metrics. They should come from a deliberate process of examining what's worked in the past and what's important for the future, with an emphasis on what the culture can accept and adopt.

- Senior leadership teams are more likely to approve technology development plans—and the associated funding requests—when teams can back them up with an incremental, business-driven, and formal process.

- Interdisciplinary participation further ensures that different organizations have a say in the direction of technology delivery. A stakeholder interaction system can be put in place to illustrate communication paths across the network of connected constituents.

- When done right, technology portfolio planning can ensure that innovation is part of a sanctioned process for planning and budgeting, rather than it being considered a luxury or afterthought.

Note to the CEO

Many CEOs remain disillusioned with IT and the technologies it delivers. But many of those same CEOs continue to support (either implicitly or explicitly) a bottom-up approach to IT planning. Successive incremental and reactive IT projects are much more likely to represent fixes than they are to support strategy or invite new ideas.

Often this represents a lack of context on the part of CIOs, who resort to drafting IT roadmaps based on best-guess assumptions of corporate objectives. Unimpressed by these roadmaps, CEOs may blame IT leaders for lack of vision or poor governance. They nevertheless fail to redirect their IT leaders toward solving the right problems. The root cause often lies in the lack of strategic transparency.

Whether your company uses a deliberate strategic planning process, hires a strategy consulting firm to help craft corporate objectives, or publishes a board-driven strategic plan, it's imperative that the CEO shed light on corporate priorities in a sustained way. CEOs need to begin shifting accountability for effective IT-enabled solutions away from IT and toward the business.

This means not only advocating but rewarding a multidisciplinary and collaborative approach to IT planning and funding, involving not only leaders from lines of business but also frontline workers who may be closer to customers, as well as vendors and partners who may be taking on increased accountability for hardware and software functions. Ultimately, even key customers can have input—but only after the process has been proven.

Understanding not only how technology can drive business value but also how it can support innovation and evolving customer needs is as much the CEO's job as it is the CIO's.

. . . .

Organizational Models and IT Service Lines

To what you wanted to see good
Has made you blind,
And what you wanted to be yours
Has made it mine.

—Soundgarden, "Fell on Black Days" (1994)

ay you work in a large company, and along with about 600 colleagues, you have a job in IT. Though you've been employed at said company for almost a decade, in that time you've had a dozen different jobs ranging from programmer to development manager to lead architect to network manager to director of quality assurance, just to name a few.

At first, you thought you were being exposed to different roles because they were grooming you for something bigger. Then you realized that it wasn't because you were that good. It was because they didn't really know how to use you. At around Job Number 7, it dawned on you that they didn't know what to do with you because they themselves didn't know what to do. So they kept moving people around, creating and dismantling organizations, launching work groups and task forces and—your personal favorite— tiger teams. You've been on all of those. Your boss, your ninth since you were hired, has just asked if you'd be interested in joining the Cloud Inquiry SWAT Team (already referred to by its unfortunate acronym, CYST). It's not a good sign.

An Argument for Specializing

I was first introduced to the concept of service lines after leading a consulting engagement with a healthcare company. Healthcare is a $3.5 trillion industry, representing 18 percent of the GDP,[1] and it's in the midst of massive transformation driven by federal legislators, emerging competitors, and perhaps most disruptive of all, patients demanding better care. If any industry is being forced to innovate, it's healthcare.

The term *service lines* connotes different specialties within a healthcare system. These specialties require their own skills, medical credentials, care plans, and delivery processes. Figure 6.1 illustrates a Midwestern hospital network's collection of service lines.

Figure 6.1   **A Hospital Network's Service Lines**

What's interesting about the service line structure isn't just which services reflect what that hospital network considers its core competencies, but noting which services *aren't* there. For instance, geriatrics is not a service line in this network. Nor is ophthalmology. Instead, for these and other specialties the hospital offers its patients referrals to partners in its network.

Figure 6.2 **Service Lines Supporting the Company's Mission**

Most healthcare companies define and build their service lines in accordance to overarching missions. For the hospital network represented here, larger missions support, and are supported by, its service lines, as illustrated in Figure 6.2.

The point here isn't to focus on healthcare, nor to portray the healthcare industry as leading edge. (Anyone who's ricocheted between care providers before getting a definitive diagnosis knows better.) However, service lines represent a useful construct for how internal and external forces are driving fundamental business model changes. Like IT organizations, healthcare providers are seeing forces of change circumscribe their areas of focus, their administrative mandates, and ultimately their success measurements. Not to put too fine a point on it, but both are also targets of disaffected constituencies.

Just as service lines have provided a framework for healthcare, they can also help IT organizations establish new delivery areas in order to categorize projects, allocate investments, measure outcomes, and support business strategy. The service line concept focuses discrete efforts and circumscribes a framework for delivery.

What's good for healthcare might also be good for IT.

IT Service Lines

The typical IT organization has evolved into a *shared service*—that is, a centralized department that offers a range of skills and technologies to a range of business units across the company. IT is seen as the purveyor of technology platforms and applications that can automate these business units' processes and supply the operational systems that run the company.

Savvy leaders understand that the value of IT isn't in the platforms and applications, or even in the economies of scale promised by the shared services model. Show me a successful IT leader, and I'll show you someone who can blend a variety of foundational, transformative, and innovative activities and demonstrate how they all support corporate objectives.

As they turn their attention to IT transformation and the new age of digital technologies, many IT executives start with the "who" conversation, focusing on organizational structures and roles as a means to drive change. The result recalls the metaphor of rearranging the deck chairs on the *Titanic*—only this time it's the passengers themselves who are being shuffled around. As the boat takes on water, they cling to their comfort zones, ignoring the calls to abandon ship.

In confronting the reality that fundamental IT models need to change, some IT leaders have turned to practice frameworks such as the Information Technology Infrastructure Library (ITIL) and its advocacy of provisioning IT services as the solution. ITIL is an effective structure, particularly for companies challenged with managing dozens or even hundreds of transactional systems or packaged applications that automate complex business processes. It establishes repeatable activities that companies can put into practice to ensure consistency.

However, the majority of IT organizations that have adopted ITIL operate in a highly controlled, shared services model. (This would likely conform to the Tactical and Order Taking archetypes described in Chapter 2.) ITIL becomes less helpful as companies explore noncentralized IT structures, rely more heavily on outside partners for development and outsourcing work, and embrace cloud computing.[2]

More important, ITIL's delivery stages can be overwhelming to senior business executives typically looking for the "what" and the "when," as opposed to the "how." ITIL's complexity is both its blessing and its curse.

In my work with CIOs and CTOs, I've found that executives in the midst of IT transformation embrace the idea of IT services, but they would like a simpler way to categorize IT into different delivery competencies— something they can use to connect with senior executives and business peers. Such a framework can also define "buckets" for investment and delivery. The healthcare service lines concept is a metaphor that can be applied successfully to IT, delineating various specialties that represent organizational competencies, as represented in Figure 6.3.

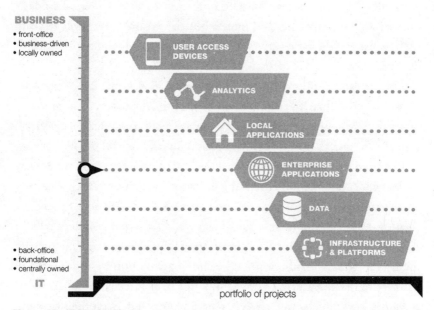

Figure 6.3 **IT Service Lines**

As the first CIO at Mandalay Resort Group, Tracy Austin—she was profiled in Chapter 2—had to drive change incrementally. "Before I got there IT was associated with systems and buzzwords," she explains. "That wasn't working. So we took a step back and mapped business service lines to IT service lines. This changed the vocabulary and brought us more in line with what the business actually needed. We could stop trying to explain terminology to everyone and start diagnosing and solving problems. IT was finally speaking the same language!"

The service lines structure also allows IT executives to determine ownership boundaries between lines of business and IT. This is perhaps the biggest challenge facing IT organizations today, and it is the single biggest issue in fighting the business-versus-IT dragon that rears its fierce head daily in corporate cubicles, executive offices, and boardrooms.

The service lines illustrated in Figure 6.3 are the most common in IT organizations. Let's take a brief look at each one.

User Access Devices

Five years ago, IT executives clung to the notion that their departments could legislate standards on which mobile devices people could bring to work. But as mobile devices have become more diverse—now encompassing not only smartphones and tablets but also wearable technologies and smart sensors—these executives have ceded to the reality of a multitude of devices.

Moreover, people's work habits are conforming to the use of their devices. The proverbial "smartphone in the morning/laptop in the afternoon/tablet at night" scenario means that people are more connected than ever. Of course, this "always-on" phenomenon has both positive and negative effects.

The point is that bring your own device (BYOD) isn't (and never was) a one-size-fits-all phenomenon. The driver of the delivery truck accessing a navigational app on his smartphone is using a different set of processes than the sales rep calling up a customer's purchase history on her tablet in the parking lot before her pitch meeting. In the former case, the logistics division might standardize on GPS technology to optimize routing for all its drivers. In the latter case, the company's sales force automation package must work equally well on sales reps' tablets as it does on their laptops.

For this reason, there's a trend toward letting business units manage their own data access through their own devices, establishing bespoke standards based on the context in which these devices are used. A mere two years ago, this was considered the nascence of shadow IT. Now it's considered common sense.

Analytics

It's rare to find analytics called out as an independent service. Large companies, including Walmart, Bank of America, and Verizon, have produced centers of excellence to centralize their business intelligence (BI) and analytics skills. But a growing number of companies have formalized BI as its own bona fide service line, with a dedicated executive, robust and specialized development tools, and a lens into corporate objectives that illuminates high-impact strategic opportunities that can be achieved through analytics.

Executives readily advocate the urgency of analytics, displaying Tom Davenport's celebrated *Competing on Analytics* on their bookshelves, wedged somewhere between *Good to Great* and *Who Moved My Cheese?* But when push comes to shove, these executives think nothing of pulling funding from analytics programs in favor of operational improvements delivered through new ERP or supply chain initiatives. When BI and analytics efforts are considered an offshoot of IT, they often end up competing for budget with the systems that arguably run the company. And they always lose.

Increasingly, though, BI and analytics programs are earning their keep, and they are thus more likely to have their own management, technology, and funding mechanisms. Companies like Caesars Entertainment and KeyBank have formalized the role of chief analytics officer. And you're as likely to see analytics organizations owned by one or more lines of business—see the executive profile of Dave Delafield, chief financial officer at Swedish Health, in Chapter 10—as you are to find them under IT's umbrella.

Local Applications

McDonald's has a standard menu at its franchises across North America. A hungry customer can get a Bacon McDouble as reliably in Youngstown as she can in Yuma. Nevertheless, every summer at select McDonald's restaurants in New England, a customer can walk up to the counter and order a lobster roll.

A large multinational bank I worked with has a centralized and powerful IT department that functions as a shared service. The bank's marketing department, frustrated with IT's slow pace and cumbersome policies, used its surplus budget to evaluate and procure its own CRM solution without either the knowledge or participation of IT.

When questioned about her decision to bypass IT, the chief marketing officer was defiant. "If I had involved IT, I'd be sitting in one of those 'Who owns the customer?' meetings right now," she said. "My CEO has new measures for me this year. My bonus is contingent on ROMI [return on marketing investment]. I'll be damned if I'm going to delay my team's effectiveness—and my own—waiting for technology people to deliver something they don't even understand." Indeed, Gartner has predicted that the technology budgets of CMOs will eclipse those of CIOs by 2017.[3]

The CMO knew this: the product managers, pricing experts, and brand managers in her organization understood the campaign management business process much better than the army of developers in the bank's IT ranks. The reality that business units are intimate with their own problems, combined with a newfound ability to find good technologies and the accompanying skill sets more quickly and cheaply than ever, means that they're increasingly bypassing IT altogether. If you ask the CMO, campaign management is a specialized business process beholden to targeted measures that are specific to marketing. In essence, campaign management is the CMO's lobster roll.

Some executives bemoan the trend of business ownership of IT, and they try to thwart it at every turn. Others embrace it as inevitable, allocating IT funding to business units who insist that they'll not only develop the application in question more quickly and cost effectively but that when the time comes, they'll also share the data generated by the new system with the organization at large.

Some leaders put controls in place in order to monitor and regulate runaway IT projects. Others assume that they'll be administering the infrastructure and platforms, ceding applications to others. As we saw in the CheckFree example in the previous chapter, your company's culture and the way it succeeds are paramount in determining what will work for you.

Enterprise Applications

Maybe it was a wry comment about how "ERP" stands for "everyone ruining processes." Or maybe it was a horror story of multiple botched implementations of a critical billing or supply chain system. Every executive working today has experienced the ripple effect of a complex enterprise system gone terribly wrong. It's just a matter of how wrong it went, and what the executive sponsor's role was in the failure.

As high-profile debacles at companies like Whirlpool, Hershey, and the state of California have shown, delivering enterprise applications such as ERP systems, human resources management, corporate websites, collaboration tools, payroll packages, content management systems, new email or office suites, and other widely deployed and generally used applications isn't easy. There's an argument for centralizing the procurement, funding, and delivery processes for these costly and time-consuming projects. Which is why IT organizations continue to own them, albeit with formal input from the business units likely to adopt them once they're complete.

However, as lines of business continue to attain their own IT budgets, some may have their eye on replacing in-house operational systems—many of which have entered the enterprise lexicon as "legacy systems"—with cloud-based or custom solutions that better suit their needs. Recently, IT leaders have been more receptive to this option, offering skills and support, but not ownership, in these business unit–specific undertakings. (See the Brokering and IT Everywhere archetypes described in Chapter 2.)

Data

A lot has been said (and written) about data's evolution from the by-product of corporate applications into a strategic asset in its own right. Consider the four criteria of a corporate asset:

1. **The asset has value.** For instance, a trucking company knows what it paid for its fleet of trucks.

2. **That value is quantifiable.** The trucking company knows the rate at which its trucks depreciate, and it can thus calculate the net present value of those trucks at any given point in time.

3. **The asset enables the company to achieve its strategic objectives.** In the case of the trucking company, the trucks deliver goods to customers in a timely and cost-effective way. Without the asset, the trucking company would fail in meeting its goals.

4. **The asset requires specialized skills to build and maintain.** The trucking company isn't hiring Honda mechanics to keep its trucks running but rather experienced specialists familiar with the truck's moving parts.

Now apply these criteria to your company's data. The fact is, more CEOs than ever before are considering data to be a critical business enabler. The good news here is that this translates into a willingness to invest in data—its skills, its enabling technologies, its quality, and its protection. The bad news is that executives are still unsure of the processes and tool sets necessary to manage corporate data in a sustained way. The rise of the chief data officer is less about the clarity of the role, and more about the need to make someone accountable for corporate information—irrespective of its systems of origin.

Data is a business asset, and it should thus be sourced, maintained, provisioned, and analyzed to support business objectives. But data is also a shared resource. Many IT leaders have identified data knowledge as one of their core differentiators. Indeed, as many CIOs hand over local applications to their respective lines of business, they simultaneously formalize shared data services as a flagship IT offering. (Refer back to the Data Provisioning archetype in Chapter 2.)

As data becomes a service line in its own right, leaders in both business units and IT are beginning to classify that data into three types:

1. **Consumer-generated data.** The reality of the big data trend is that most new data is created by consumers, via social networks, mobile devices, and sensor data (from, say, GPS or wearable devices). Fanning the flames of the digital trend, this data is of little value in its atomic state, and it needs to be integrated with more traditional data in company databases.

2. **Machine data.** Machines are generating data at a faster pace than ever. GE gathers data from its engines—"really, anything that spins," clarified a GE executive—in order to predict part failure before it happens. Patient vital signs, collected via an assortment of hospital and wearable monitors, can be streamed to a centralized repository to detect patterns that may affect public health (for instance, a spike in cases of swine flu in hospitals within the same geographic cluster). Abnormalities in a patient's vital signs may trigger an alert message to the patient's doctor—whether he is elsewhere in the hospital, lecturing at a university, or on the golf course.

3. **Transactional data.** Structured data generated by enterprise applications and internal operational systems and stored in traditional databases isn't going anywhere. Companies still get tremendous

value from analyzing customer purchase history, performing what-if analysis on product pricing, and mining billing records or ATM transaction data to detect fraud.

But the true power of this data is realized when it's combined, and data management and integration—not a company's ability to ingest unstructured data or its Hadoop programming prowess—are the differentiated competencies that will make the data service line positively essential to a company's strategic success. In fact—as the strategy map in Figure 4.3 illustrated—a company's ability to fulfill its strategic objectives is directly proportional to the degree to which its data is managed.

Infrastructure and Platforms

In their book *IT Savvy*, MIT professors Peter Weill and Jeanne Ross say this:

> Infrastructure investments are the foundation of the IT portfolio. The justification for these investments is sometimes cost reduction. Investments that standardize and consolidate technologies should reduce non-discretionary spending.[4]

Is it any wonder businesspeople don't consider IT sexy? Nevertheless, in today's digital era when social media interactions generate more records than telephone calls, someone needs to keep the lights on in IT. But even IT leaders steeped in the orthodoxy of centralized IT, with its incumbent legacy mainframes and multi-petabyte data warehouses, realize that in order to build something new, you might need to break something old.

A recent problem at a specialty retailer illustrates this conundrum. The CIO is under pressure from merchandisers to deliver a mobile app that allows the retailer to know when the customers are actually shopping in the store. This will allow the retailer to push real-time digital coupons to those customers based on where they're shopping. This practice, known as *geofencing*, will also help the retailer modernize its loyalty program by measuring how long shoppers linger in certain aisles. The goal is to incent these shoppers to purchase products in categories where they don't typically buy. Eventually, the retailer would also like to influence shoppers who aren't yet in the store by using wireless and GPS technologies to learn when a consumer is in the vicinity of a store, attracting them with promotional offers sent to their smartphones.

These same stores are running decades-old point-of-sale (POS) systems from multiple vendors. Store managers are crying for "modernization," while back office programmers responsible for manually reconciling heterogeneous sales data leave the company in frustration. The CIO is torn between delivering innovative digital marketing capabilities and catering to traditional expectations to maintain a legacy infrastructure that is deteriorating in lockstep with the confidence of his peers.

Infrastructure still matters. As tech-savvy employees eye jobs at coastal startups with their idea incubators, smoothie bars, and take-your-dog-to-work cultures, leaders across business and IT struggle with automating operations, while at the same time encouraging innovation with no new headcount on the horizon. The challenge for IT leaders is to support infrastructures while finding new avenues for increasing economies of scale and operational efficiencies.

Determining Service Line Ownership

IT service lines transcend the traditional notion of "departments," emphasizing communities of practice and specialty. They offer a means of categorizing work efforts and allocating resources, and they also offer a chance for IT executives to launch a deliberate conversation about what change will look like in IT. The service line concept is not an operating model. You'll still have to consider architecture standards, investment management, sourcing and procurement, technical support, and configuration management, among other core practices. However, I've found that most IT executives are more comfortable in these realms, already possessing the aptitude and supporting resources to manage them effectively.

Service lines can also help IT executives make the often agonizing decision of what to surrender to the business. Depending on a range of factors—clout of the business sponsor, cynicism about IT, organizational authority of the CIO, and other issues we'll discuss later in the book—IT leaders might choose to surrender control of certain technology categories to lines of business.

Interestingly, the CIO of the bank mentioned earlier ended up having an enlightened response to the CMO's technology procurement decision. He decided to give technology procurement authority to lines of business. He effectively drew a line in the sand to establish ownership boundaries, as represented in Figure 6.4, deciding that each business unit would own its local applications, analytics solutions, and mobile devices.

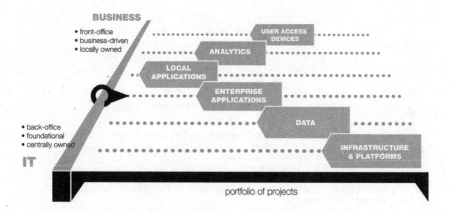

Figure 6.4 **Service Line Ownership Levels at a Bank**

For everything "above the line," the CIO would allocate a portion of his budget. Business units had the freedom to define, choose, and manage their own local applications, as well as their analytics capabilities and delivery devices. Business units could also opt out of this plan and continue to rely on central IT for all their work.

For the business units opting in, the CIO established a set of criteria for business-owned IT projects, which he distributed to all of the bank's business units (Figure 6.5). This represented a service level agreement of sorts, delineating the guidelines for business ownership, as well as an agreement for data sharing.

In the end, the bank's larger business units chose to opt in to this approach. Vice presidents from marketing, finance, risk and compliance, and customer service all chose to own their own technology projects, assuming responsibility for their financial oversight and delivery and agreeing to keep IT in the loop for program management, deployment calendaring, and budget oversight.

ABC company

LINE OF BUSINESS-OWNED TECHNOLOGY PROJECTS AGREEMENT

purpose

The following criteria will comprise the Service Level Agreement for all business units wishing to procure, customize or otherwise own technology software. All business units procuring software or data from an external party must abide by this agreement.

1. Product must be software or data. Any hardware procurement must come through IT.

2. Product's functionality must be used only "within the four walls" of the individual business unit (BU) and automate isolated, BU-specific business processes.

3. BU agrees to share any data generated by the new solution to a common extract file made available at an agreed-upon interval (hourly, daily, weekly, real-time streaming, etc.)

4. BU agrees to fund maintenance, upgrades, or bug fixes associated with this product.

5. BU agrees that any integration with incumbent systems will be done in conjunction with IT. Current cross-charging rates will apply.

6. BU agrees to employ all company contracts and non-disclosures with selected vendor.

7. BU agrees to deliver a status update at the IT Business Steering Committee meeting once per quarter.

1 | © 2015 ABC Company. Confidential.

Figure 6.5 **IT Ownership Handoff Letter**

EXECUTIVE PROFILE

Paul Obermeyer and Jim Cavellier, Comerica

Show up at Comerica's campus on the outskirts of Detroit, and you're likely to observe the usual large financial institution stereotypes. Sleek, official-looking building? Check. Fastidious security process? Check. Spacious atrium-style entry? Check. Suited professionals rushing through corridors to attend important meetings? Check, and check again.

But if you sit down with Paul Obermeyer and Jim Cavellier, you start to see this isn't the typical financial services conglomerate. Obermeyer, EVP and chief information officer, and Cavellier, his SVP of systems delivery management and architecture, are watching IT change in the financial services industry. And they're one step ahead.

Started as Detroit Savings Fund Institute in 1849, Comerica has steadily expanded its footprint over a century into multiple markets through both acquisitions and organic growth. The company's historical emphasis on optimizing the customer experience has driven both operational and strategic initiatives. Sure, many other banks would say the same. Obermeyer's team not only supports this direction, it also actively influences it.

"IT is going through a dramatic transformation," Obermeyer says, referring at once to the industry at large and to his organization at Comerica. He cites three drivers that are influencing that change:

- Persistent low interest rates

- Improved profitability

- A recognition that customers are getting savvier and requesting additional services and channels

"We're in the process of distinguishing the things that must get done that nevertheless might not differentiate us with those things that endear us to our customers," he says. "We need to enable a greater degree of self-service, and we need to give our customers direct access to us through their mobile devices so that we know them better."

That Obermeyer owns the service company for Comerica means that he oversees a playing field that's more expansive than just IT systems. Email, payroll services, core banking operations, procurement, corporate real estate, and other functions report to him, meaning his leadership is far-reaching, and the potential for process efficiencies is that much broader.   *(continues)*

"Systems delivery management is just one piece, the operational piece," confirms Cavellier. "The data center, help desk, application hosting, production operations around key business applications like web banking, check processing, and so forth—they're all really just one aspect of what we do in IT."

Evolving IT Functions

Obermeyer and his leadership team are focusing on new functions to streamline the operations piece, but moreover they are making sure to support the ongoing priority of customer experience management. Both Obermeyer and Cavellier emphasize that this is a series of initiatives and that they transcend mere systems.

Organizational functions are a major focus area for Obermeyer, and he repeatedly cites the value of close business relationships. "Our business relationship managers (BRMs) reach out to our internal customers across our lines of business," he explains. "We decided to embrace a broader view of this function. The BRMs help us understand the needs and perceptions of various organizations within Comerica. They communicate feedback both formally and informally, and this feedback conditions our delivery approaches."

"BRMs are teams," Cavellier adds. "They sit at the table with our internal customers, and there's a BRM team for each division. For instance, we have a business bank team led by a senior resource, with anywhere from 4 to 10 people on the team. And the BRM team for the retail bank has multiple people from multiple lines of business. This allows them to develop deeper business acumen and talk the talk." BRMs also collaborate with the company's Architecture Review Board, whose charter is to apply strategy and technology innovations.

Under Obermeyer's leadership, Comerica is also making room for IT innovation. The Comerica Innovation Center is an area that introduces new technologies that are aligned with the business strategies identified and shared by the BRM teams. This allows the bank to showcase technology vendors that best align with its business goals.

Systems Delivery Management, run by Cavellier, includes the operational functions of the data center, help desk, application hosting, and production operations around key business applications, like web banking and check processing. Infrastructure aside, Cavellier nevertheless maintains a strategic perspective. "As we shape our IT strategy, we're always keeping our internal clients and their business objectives at the forefront," he says.

... and Speaking of Strategy

With all the moving pieces involved in keeping a bank operational, how does Obermeyer avoid falling into simply maintaining commodity systems and skills? He's been careful to segment his departments' heterogeneous responsibilities into three segments:

1. Simplifying and standardizing at the core.

2. Developing an integration layer around that core. ("This enables us to move quickly and experiment.")

3. Creating unique service lines that differentiate the bank from its competitors.

"Calling something a 'commodity' doesn't demean it," he insists. "It just doesn't differentiate it. So I prefer to call these things 'nondifferentiated services.'"

Cavellier cites the book *The Big Switch* by Nicholas Carr. "Back in the day, factories began getting their power from power plants built near rivers, which revolutionized manufacturing. The notion of having to build capabilities within a company's four walls is over. For what we're calling 'nondifferentiated services,' we'll use someone who specializes in that work."

As an example, rather than funding and maintaining individual printers and printing services in every organization, Comerica uses managed print services. This absolves the IT organization from having to track and monitor printer types and locations across the company

(continues)

and its various offices. It not only saves money but it also allows the bank to introduce new features that previously required large capital investments.

"No one banks with Comerica because we're good at printing," says Cavellier wryly. "We understand what's not core to IT. We're going to be an enabler, and we're not building everything internally. And we have the internal credibility to pull that off."

Building Relationships Outside of IT

So is Obermeyer grappling with the same issues as other financial services CIOs, where lines of business are increasingly going it alone? Not really.

"We have very little shadow IT here," he says. "Sure, business-people can do analytics and other local functions, but they do it with the help of IT. You can't deploy reports or load anything onto servers without our support."

Obermeyer and Cavellier refer again to prioritizing business relationships. "The way you prevent shadow IT from getting out of control is that you keep good relationships with internal customers," says Cavellier. "They need to see IT as an enabler, not a roadblock."

They've combined internal client management processes, treating every new business request as a learning opportunity, with formal governance processes that manage the Comerica development pipeline. This includes procurement guidelines: any business-led IT investments that exceed $50,000 hit Obermeyer's desk.

"We're not a terribly complex company," says Obermeyer. "But we've been true to our mission for 35 years. We're a bank devoted to developing deep and enduring relationships with corporate wealth customers over time."

Clearly that customer focus applies both outside and within Comerica's four walls.

New Ways to Organize IT

Designing around service lines is an effective way to optimize IT around technology consumption—how people both inside and outside your company need to use technology and ingest data, irrespective of their job, their geography, or their organizational status. It instills a culture of IT as not just a shared service but rather a collection of delivery competencies that are constantly cultivated to meet the changing needs of the business.

Every IT organization is structured differently. Some rely on simplicity, limiting the number of units in IT to remain as elegant as possible. An example of this is the CIO of a clinical trial research company who breaks the IT organization into three groups: Old Stuff, New Stuff, and IT Operations. Though such models make operations easier, they nevertheless raise new questions about strategic alignment, prioritization of work efforts, technology acquisition, and career planning.

Most IT leaders, though, break their structures into more discrete functional areas. The manufacturing org chart in Figure 6.6 illustrates how service lines can be used to define or redefine practice specialties across IT domains.

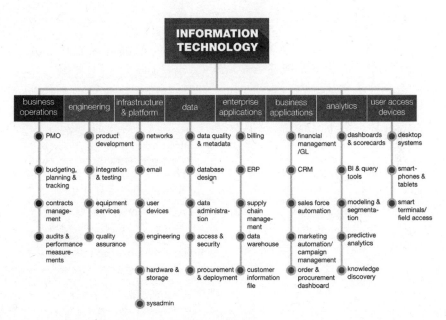

Figure 6.6   **An Organization Chart of IT Service Lines**

Of course, your IT team might not support all of these service lines. Depending on the size of your company and the scope of IT, you might need a separate operations function, as the manufacturer represented in Figure 6.6 did, to manage IT's portfolio.

Or you may have others that are particular to your industry: the manufacturer added an engineering service line to support the technology needs of its shop floor; one retailer I work with has an entire IT service line dedicated to supporting its multiple POS systems; and many banks elevate the urgency of risk and fraud detection and support it as one or more IT service lines.

Whether you work in IT or in a business unit, you've already confronted the reality that the CIO no longer owns all the technology. Once you've decided on service lines and ownership, you can be much more deliberate about how the IT organization should be set up, who should own what, and how the constituencies should connect. Table 6.1 uses the IT archetypes we introduced in Chapter 2 to color in ways to introduce change and drive collaboration.

TABLE 6.1: Collaboration Based on IT Archetypes

IT Archetype	Leaders' Concerns	Change Readiness	Collaboration and Organizational Change
Tactical	"Can we overcome the entrenched perception that we're simply installing and maintaining systems, or 'keeping the lights on'? And how will we keep high performers if the career path is limited?"	Low	Begin managing expectations among senior staff that IT employees are at risk and that there is a cost associated with losing critical skill sets. Publish staff attrition statistics. Meanwhile, develop an internal training program to enhance technical or leadership skills, and certify key staff members in those areas.
		High	Create awareness of technology alternatives to legacy systems and enterprise applications considered outdated or cumbersome. Research cost-savings potential of cloud solutions, and create a roadmap for gradual system replacement. Assign high-profile contributors to key business units as liaisons.

IT Archetype	Leaders' Concerns	Change Readiness	Collaboration and Organizational Change
Order Taking	"How do we educate business units that we can drive value beyond just building applications?"	Low	Retain an external consulting firm to deliver an IT maturity assessment. Note the opportunities for improvement, and share them with key leaders and stakeholders in order to remedy identified problems. Then couch these fixes in the context of an IT transformation or other lofty project, and measure and communicate the benefits.
		High	Enlist key decision makers in an IT portfolio planning process like the one featured in Chapter 5. Involve them in prioritization scoring to elevate the conversation beyond functionality and toward new business capabilities. Reconvene the group regularly to discuss new opportunities and sanction new projects. At the same time, begin adopting agile development techniques to enculturate more nimble delivery.
Aligning	"The same set of business units engages us time after time. How do we widen the circle and assure other business leaders that we can help them too?"	Low	Inventory key business applications that might benefit from being shared. For instance, marketing's CRM application might feature a product master list that could also help account reps track current pricing. Or perhaps there's an opportunity to consolidate ERP or billing systems to drive economies of scale, resulting in a higher ROI? Then update the affected business units on the resulting benefits, soliciting their support for further improvements that can be measured.
		High	The IT portfolio planning process described in Chapter 5 can help here too. With closer business alignment, you're likely to be able to enlist more senior business leaders. This group of leaders may eventually become your formal IT steering committee, with the portfolio being refreshed as needed in regular meetings.

(continues)

TABLE 6.1: Collaboration Based on IT Archetypes *(continued)*

IT Archetype	Leaders' Concerns	Change Readiness	Collaboration and Organizational Change
Data Provisioning	"We have all these big plans, but our data doesn't reflect that. And we have to balance our work accessing new data and cleaning up old data with our intentions to shed commodity systems."	Low	Accelerate the rate at which you move more operational applications to the cloud. Consider hiring contractors to perform operational system development and/or maintenance work.
		High	Enlist your HR department in recrafting job descriptions and performance measures. Make leadership aware of these efforts, establishing new rewards systems that ensure full-time IT staff are compensated for delivering new business capabilities and fresh thinking.
Brokering	"We'd like to widen the circle of suppliers and partners we do business with. And that means we might cease doing business with existing partners who no longer add value."	Low	Typically a low change readiness in the Brokering model suggests politics with legal, procurement, or HR, all of whom have a vested interest in the status quo. Convene key leaders in these areas, and present data on cost overruns, contract challenges, and other opportunities to realign business partners.
		High	Work with other internal leaders to create a sanctioned list of business partners. Use this as an opportunity to introduce new players—including smaller, specialized companies that might be motivated to offer more competitive pricing and terms—and eliminate partners who are no longer contributing value. Make sure there are "tiers" indicating preferred partners (for instance, those that offer enterprise licenses or volume discounts). Institute regular internal and external reviews to reevaluate partners, reassign tiers, and measure performance.

IT Archetype	Leaders' Concerns	Change Readiness	Collaboration and Organizational Change
IT Everywhere	"Business units accuse us of moving too fast. They can't provide the skills or processes necessary to inherit their applications. Some of them have changed their minds and don't want to."	Low	By definition, companies that adopt IT Everywhere have a high tolerance for change. If change is happening too fast, move headcount from IT into lines of business to ensure that incumbent skills are applied to technology solutions as they transition into lines of business or outsourcers.
		High	Create an IT governance committee composed of business unit leaders. Together, develop an incremental plan for the disposition of key systems and projects over time. Convene the committee regularly to update the plan and deliberate on new business requirements that mandate technology and innovation.

Letting your current IT archetype inform next steps for broader collaboration allows your company to take an "inside-out" approach to driving improvements. The opposite of this is the "outside-in" approach: someone digs up a competitor's IT org chart or another company's governance process and blindly applies it. This follows the well-worn, yet apt, maxim: "Meet your company where it is."

The danger—and I can't stress this enough—of redesigning the IT organization is that it is often a poor substitute for true, strategic change. Most managers are more comfortable having "who" conversations than "why" and "how" conversations. Connecting lines and boxes in new ways gives executives the false comfort that they're creating something, a structure on which they assign ownership and enforce newfound accountabilities. An organization chart creates the illusion that drastic change is afoot.

Reorganizations can indeed spark some short-term changes, and they can even instill improvements, but more often, they mask root-cause issues that are far more difficult to resolve. The truth is, the connection between performance and reward can only happen via strategy.

With the deliberate design of a new IT organization that maps to corporate goals, IT and business leaders can begin to distinguish themselves from their management colleagues, who increasingly have their own plans for technology delivery. They can begin positioning themselves as leaders in their own right, willing to drive transformational change and enlist their superiors and peers in decision making in an effort to garner support and drive wholesale improvements. The challenge, irrespective of your current IT archetype, is overcoming entrenched biases and assumptions about IT—and about those who lead it.

Funding IT Service Lines

Irrespective of the relationship of IT to the business, the days of reactive, project-level funding are over. Establishing IT service lines can help leaders in both business and IT determine how to categorize the company's technology investments. Clearly, as with healthcare service lines, each service line will have its own funding plan and ownership model. They provide IT with a way to categorize the types of investments within each service line. These investment types could include the following.

Infrastructure Investment

Investing in infrastructure means funding operational technologies and processes that run the business. The goal of foundational IT investments is to stay in business, reduce operating expenses, and automate core business processes. Foundational IT investments are critical to keep the company running, but they are not a source of either a superior brand or competitive advantage. An insurer's actuarial platform and a retailer's inventory management system are two examples of infrastructure technologies.

The infrastructure and platforms service line offers an apt example. Many financial services institutions are currently earmarking millions of dollars to replace decades-old core banking systems or customer information files (CIFs) that have become unwieldy and difficult to maintain. Large banks will typically spend between 50 and 60 percent of their IT budgets on infrastructure. Smaller or startup companies will spend less. Likewise, in the local applications service line, a sales and marketing department at a pharmaceutical company might need to standardize on tablet technologies for its field sales reps, thus allocating funding for new user access devices.

While inviting economies of scale and cost reduction, infrastructure investments don't get a lot of attention, and they won't transform a company's brand. In general, the older and more established the company, the greater the percentage of the overall IT budget that goes to infrastructure. This can perpetuate financial and cultural behaviors that may jeopardize innovation.

Strategic IT Investments

These investments drive competitive advantage for a company, helping it differentiate customer service, optimize pricing, or increase the velocity of significant decisions. Many IT leaders turn toward more front office solutions like CRM systems to help them track customer preferences, or they look to business intelligence software to help them measure sales performance and refocus marketing campaigns to help with these goals. Unlike infrastructure investments, strategic investments are intended to differentiate a company from its competitors. The faster a company's growth rate, the higher the growth rate of its strategic IT investments relative to its foundational ones.

The retailer struggling with shoring up a fragile POS network while aiming to deploy real-time offers to shoppers is a good example of this challenge. By investing in technology to push online coupons to shoppers while they are in the store, the retailer is increasing not only its revenue potential but also the value of the opt-in customer's shopping experience. The retailer's CIO understands that he needs to do both, and well. We'll discuss similar strategies of going digital in the next chapter.

Innovation IT Investments

Forward-thinking IT leaders are increasingly setting aside funding for innovation, meaning "outside-the-box" solutions that set a company further apart from its peers. Ideally, innovation investments break new ground, representing fresh thinking that comes from inside the company and is not simply representative of a larger industry trend. Of course, smaller or startup companies, unencumbered by decades-old legacy systems, often have the luxury of dedicating a higher percentage of their IT capital to innovation investments. But that's not to say that more established companies cannot allocate money toward innovation.

CVS, the large retail chain, launched its in-store Minute Clinics to provide basic healthcare services to its shoppers, introducing a disruptive market change. Competitive retailers spent millions trying to reattract customers who had defected to CVS, ultimately setting up their own versions of the Minute Clinic. Likewise, hospitals saw demand for flu shots and cholesterol screenings fall as patients procured these basic services while awaiting their pharmacy prescriptions and shopping for laundry detergent. Online check-in technologies and electronic patient records kept CVS a step ahead. We'll talk more about how digital capabilities can help companies leapfrog their competitors in the next chapter.

"There's a degree of rigor necessary in enlisting stakeholders for funding decisions," explains Lifetouch CIO Rahoul Ghose. An IT executive at Honeywell and Cargill prior to joining Lifetouch, Ghose has always taken a portfolio-driven approach—see Chapter 5—not only to IT planning but also to investment decisions.

"Typically, I like to take a base investment number and then break it down into categories such as compliance, efficiency, and growth. Within each category we would drill down into project criteria. We would rate projects against these criteria and come up with a composite value index to rank priorities.

"But at the end of the day the process wasn't so much a formula as it was an assist, a way to involve businesspeople in the decision-making process. Once we ranked the projects, the IT steering committee would sit down and consider our choices. That was where the final budgeting and prioritization decisions would be made."

Ghose admits that the process takes time to gel, depending on the organization's prevailing decision-making behaviors. "IT introduced the process and got it going. We brought structure to it. But at the end of the day, IT investment decisions were owned by the business. Every project in the portfolio had to have a business sponsor to represent the value proposition and defend the project."

Ghose sees the portfolio prioritization and investment approval processes as broad best practices that IT can bring to the table. "By introducing these processes, IT can help bring discipline to the organization," he says. "This process can easily extend to other investment decisions, like building a new plant or making a strategic acquisition—and it removes IT leaders from being labeled purely as 'technologists.'"

Technology investment decisions should be made both within and across service lines. In other words, there will be technologies that will exist intrinsically to a service line. For instance, smartphones and tablet devices fit neatly into the service line for user access devices. Other investment types will impact multiple service lines. For instance, analytics is its own service line, but its competencies will probably affect—and be affected by—enterprise systems, local applications, and even infrastructure.

The point is that these investments should be made and managed more deliberately on behalf of the services they support, and not just the projects or departments likely to leverage them. IT service lines can also directly play into more strategic activities like business alignment, risk management, IT governance, workforce management, organizational ownership, and communications planning.

Of course, we know that shadow IT is already out of the closet. This may mean that every department's budget includes funding for technology. Which makes the concept of service lines all the more critical.

CHAPTER SUMMARY

Key Takeaways

- IT executives, many of whom complain about reporting structures and lack of visibility, can easily get in the weeds when communicating technology delivery activities, compromising their reputations in the process.

- Industry frameworks, such as healthcare service lines, offer an effective and simple way of categorizing offerings for clarity and conversational level setting.

- Creating IT service lines invites "big picture" discussions while encouraging more specific conversations around technical capabilities, thus improving project scope and increasing the likelihood of timely delivery.

- What you do next in order to enlist stakeholders and restructure IT has everything to do with where you are now. Know your IT archetype and let it inform your action plan.

- Service lines can establish effective budget categories with teeth.

- Socializing the IT service line framework with business executives opens up budget and delivery ownership discussions, minimizing political friction and encouraging renewed partnership.

Note to the CEO

The days of keeping the lights on are over. The value of IT is to support business growth and evolution. As IT's boundaries morph, this opens up new opportunities to not only establish a fresh IT identity but also to support a new style of innovation.

Don't give into the temptation to reorganize as a quick fix. Ask your executive leaders about the work that needs to be done, whether that work should be done within or outside the company's four walls, and where ownership and accountability should lie. Let them define before they design—in other words, lay out the components of the new IT charter before determining who the players are and what they should own.

If business leaders complain about IT, encourage them to participate in this redefinition and be part of the solution. As for yourself, don't be afraid to ask, "Are we stretching enough? Can we do better?" Encourage your leadership in both IT and business units to ask the same.

Commodity IT is a thing of the past, and by clearing away stale ownership and power boundaries, a new type of IT organization—one that can streamline business delivery and drive fresh thinking—can emerge.

Innovation, Going Digital, and Other Uphill Battles

We are all in the gutter,
But some of us are looking at the stars.
　　　　　—Oscar Wilde (with a shout-out to The Pretenders)

I t's likely that the company you work for wasn't "born digital." Odds are your company didn't start in a dorm room or a garage, it never sponsored a hack-a-thon, and a masseuse won't be showing up in your doorway after your sashimi lunch. Sitting at your desk eating the sandwich you brought from home? Yeah, me too.

Even those executives who hold their cards close to the vest will freely admit that when it comes to innovation, their companies could be doing a much better job. They will also concede that new ideas rarely make their way from concept to reality. Ironically, it's these very same executives who cling to established company orthodoxies—"We're a retailer, not a software startup!"—as an excuse for sticking to the status quo.

Meanwhile, managers lack the power to fund truly innovative projects, and their employees gripe that no one really listens to their ideas. They quietly hope for change, keeping their LinkedIn profiles up-to-date just in case.

One of my clients called me out on this. "You've told me that my team's biggest challenge is our ability to focus," he said, barely restraining his index finger from pointing itself in my direction. "We're doing all we can to keep up with business demands. And now you're telling me to take on innovation?"

Yes, amid pressures to modernize IT, integrate applications, adopt big data, embrace enterprise mobility, get smart about social media, research location tracking technologies, consolidate consulting partners, monitor industry trends, govern information, increase system performance and uptime, get serious about security, investigate grid computing, and move to the cloud, launching an innovation plan is like lighting a match in a rainstorm.

So now you need to take on innovation? Well in a word, yes. And so does your CEO, whether she knows it or not.

Innovation's Different Faces

In the dark of night, many CEOs will agree with the statement, "If we don't innovate, we won't survive."

Many start by making innovation a part of the executive conversation. Bill McDermott, CEO of software giant SAP, recently urged his famously structured, resolutely German company known for its accounting and inventory management software to do "some crazy things," adding, "We have to be a little bit more like Google."

"Everything we've done around social and digital media has put us in the lead of almost every brick-and-mortar retailer," Howard Schultz recently told *Inc.*, sounding more like an engineer than the CEO of Starbucks. At Starbucks, every business function is fair game for innovation, which may blend in equal parts mobile payment apps, revamped store designs, and Fizzio handcrafted sodas. "The future of Starbucks is linked to our ability to create game-changing innovation," Schultz said.

Senior leaders are zeroing in on the digital space—not only to compete but also to be visible to the coveted demographic groups that spend time there. Many see innovation as synonymous with emerging technologies, focusing more on issues outside their companies' concerns than on those inside; more on the devices that let us interact and less on improving those interactions; and more on the tools and less on the answers. (This is also known as "paving the cow path.")

Digital devices and "bright shiny object syndrome" have blinded many corporate leaders to what might be more practical innovations for their companies. When faced with opportunities for fresh ways of creating value, most IT professionals spend more time considering new deployment channels than thoroughly researching solutions. We're underdiagnosing, overprescribing, and underdelivering, which is leading to increased cynicism among IT and business leaders. According to one study, only 2 percent of CIOs consider their companies' innovation potential to be fully realized.[1]

What qualities characterize an innovation-ready company?

- **Encouraging questions.** "Who do we want to be?" or even better, "Who *could* we be with new delivery or engagement mechanisms?" are questions that could lead to breakthroughs.

- **Maintaining an enthusiastic and up-to-date knowledge of emerging technologies.** At the same time companies need to take a sober approach to adopting them.

- **Shifting organizational competencies as the company's strategy evolves.** ERP was strategic a decade ago as companies reengineered their supply chains. Nowadays, it may be social media, 3D printing, wearable devices, or new machine learning capabilities that help a company achieve breakthroughs. True innovators understand that technology is a moving target.

- **Moving away from insularity.** Studies have shown that companies that innovate the most reach out beyond their four walls to partner with others, educating each other in the process.[2] Increasingly innovation is evolving as a network of like-minded individuals and organizations, fostering new ideas on behalf of their common domain. It's no wonder that just in the past several months I've met over a dozen executives whose titles are a variation of "Vice President of Innovation and Strategic Partnerships."

- **Considering research as no longer a means to an end, but the end itself.** This implies a willingness to support, fund, and cancel research into emerging technologies. Delivery is, and should remain, the goal.

"Something we do here that perhaps differentiates us from IT at other banks is that we allocate time for innovation," says Union Bank's Ryan Fenner. "We've actually incented people to innovate as part of their jobs, to come up with new ideas and strategies. And if they don't work—and inevitably some of them won't—people aren't penalized. So we give people the opportunity to do cool new things, with not a lot of downside. It's a great retention tactic."

But many executives continue to pay lip service to innovation, floating in the penumbra of good ideas, but never seeing them through. After all, who has the time? Meanwhile, many senior workers feel trapped by their company's emphasis on short-term goals and reactive fixes. One senior R&D director at a major high-tech firm recently changed jobs, taking half his team members with him. The reason? "At our former employer we were too encumbered by our install base," he explained.

The hallmark of progressive leaders is a willingness to try new things, to experiment and learn, and to design anew. Whether this means funding more software prototypes, hiring people with nontraditional skill sets, or exploring solutions in the so-called social, mobile, analytics, and cloud (SMAC) stack, leaders both inside and outside of IT need to support—and fund—trials and discovery exercises. This is true even if these efforts don't result in new technology adoption. They form labs or incubators that manifest these new behaviors. They fail fast, and they try again.

Effective technology innovation has three qualities:

- **It speaks to what is possible.** Innovative ideas need to be creative and occasionally even far-flung, but practical all the same. The question, "Can we build it or buy it?" needs to enter the equation at some point. Otherwise, an idea is really just a pipe dream.

- **It is future facing.** An innovation needs to drive an improvement or do something completely new. It needs to propel the company forward in some way.

- **It involves uncertainty.** There is no innovation without risk. Executives who introduce and support innovation must manage expectations that while all ideas will be considered, not all will see the light of day.

When executives discuss innovation, it's often wistfully and over an adult beverage. They characterize it as a binary proposition: we're either innovating or we're not. But these same executives often have wild-eyed ideas of sweeping new product offerings or drastically different business models. These innovations are devised in war rooms or incubators by millennial workers who, sandal clad and amped up on energy drinks, can spot trends that can cause, to use the well-worn word, disruption.

The reality is that most new ideas that deliver value in companies are less about innovation in its purest sense and more about *invention*—the execution of a practical new idea in the context of an opportunity. Where innovation is often vague, invention is practical. Where innovation is considered collaborative, invention is often borne from a single person's good idea. Where innovation must be rigorous, invention is organic. Where the concept of innovation has attracted a growing crowd of cynics, invention is routinely celebrated.

The savviest leaders recognize the difference between innovation and invention. In order to create a robust environment to encourage invention, they will nevertheless use the language of innovation to capture people's imaginations and invite dialogue.

Regardless of what you call it, where you start should depend on where the pain is, as well as what your culture should support. Figure 7.1 highlights the four candidate areas, assigning them to two main types: innovation, which signifies wholesale changes, or improvement, which is more incremental.

Innovation can be expensive, often upending existing business processes but conferring new advantages in the marketplace. The printing press, the Polaroid camera, network routers, artificial limbs, and Apple's iPhone are a few examples of innovation that drove drastic change and transformed life for those who used them. In the language of innovation, these would be known as "transformational."

Improvements, by contrast, are gradual and delivered over time. Although they aren't as splashy as innovations and probably don't get as much attention, improvements are easier to socialize and consume. CRM systems, data visualization software, and electronic medical records are all examples of improvements that were developed iteratively, but that radically changed company processes and job roles.

Improvements often begin as small, controlled projects, or pilots. "I am always going to continue the innovation stream and do pilots," AIG's chief data officer, Heather Wilson, explained to McKinsey.[3] "As the technology

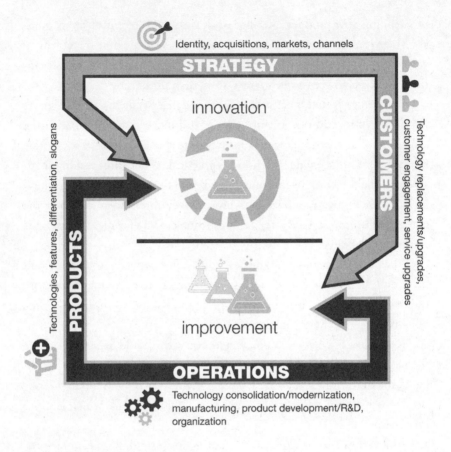

Figure 7.1 **Breaking Down Innovation**

continues to mature, I expect that we will continue to see new applications and capabilities emerge."

Innovations and improvements should have different support structures, decision-making processes, development timelines, and incentives. Improvements will show fewer immediate benefits, but at the same time, the people involved—innovation acolytes like the term *intrapreneur*—will be less beholden to bureaucratic constraints that might encumber progress.

When it comes to innovation, the experts' admonishment to "Think Big!" should be taken with a grain of salt. There is no single right way to innovate. The innovations that stick involve a series of smart choices that become second nature as bold new behaviors begin to take hold.

We're Ready to Innovate—Where Do We Start?

You can innovate within and across the four categories shown in Figure 7.1. The most effective way to determine where to focus is by asking these two questions:

1. **In which category do most of our strategic initiatives fall?** As we discussed in Chapter 4, initiatives that get the most support—and the most funding—are those that help a company execute its strategies. If you can link innovation to strategy, you're likely to get traction. Typically, branding and strategic innovations fall into the invention bucket.

2. **Where is our company investing externally?** When in doubt about strategic goals, look at where your company is spending its money. This is the best indicator of priorities. Has your company recently invested in a multi-million-dollar voice of the customer program? Then you might consider focusing some initial innovations around collecting customer feedback or new ways to deploy online surveys. Is there new investment money for streamlining the supply chain? Perhaps inventing a machine that accelerates and ensures full pallets on the loading dock would save you money. Is your company spending millions on acquisitions? Then perhaps overhauling the process for more nimble onboarding of staff and systems makes sense. Operational or customer-focused innovations typically involve more improvements.

Clearly, game-changing innovations can cut across strategy, operations, branding, and customers (refer again to Figure 7.1). Since these innovations challenge the status quo and shake up organizational silos, companies are often unwilling to embrace them. (Anecdotally, in my work helping executives with strategy, the older and more established the company, the more likely that the people in charge will be threatened by disruptive innovations.) Ultimately, it will come down to what the company's culture and its leaders can handle.

What cultural qualities can sabotage innovation? Here's a short list. Use it to gauge your company's appetite for innovation, and its readiness:

- **"Who else is doing it?" syndrome.** Sometimes a manager gets wind of an innovation being worked on outside of the company, and he uses the news as an excuse to start innovating. But if someone else is working on a new idea, then it's not likely to be truly innovative. Moreover, innovation works best when people are encouraged to solve company-specific problems, not co-opt ideas that might not be fully formed.

- **Confusing innovation with improvement.** There's a fine line between a new idea and making a good thing better. Improvements simply break an idea into manageable pieces. A textile company, for instance, figured out how to make its patented moisture-repelling fabric waterproof. That's improvement. One of its competitors figured out how to create a fabric that retained human pheromones, manufacturing a blanket that it marketed to new mothers to retain the scent for their newborns while they were away. That's innovation.

- **Impatience.** Often corporate leaders are so focused on the top line that innovation becomes a dangerous distraction from the real goal of revenue growth. If executives require pre facto proof that innovations will make the company money, then people will spend more time trying to figure out how to monetize their good ideas and less time actually executing on those ideas. Besides, if an idea is truly "breakthrough," you won't know enough to determine its potential ROI.

- **Fear of distraction.** Executives are afraid that innovation will take attention—not to mention funding and staff—away from the fire drills and short-term projects that represent their companies' typical means of getting things done. (These same executives use this distraction excuse to argue against the rigorous strategic planning we discussed in Chapter 4.)

- **Static measurements.** Many companies still don't measure people very effectively. When asked how they know whether they're successful in their jobs, IT and businesspeople alike will often shrug and mumble something about deliverables. The flip side of this is when employees are measured so specifically that new ideas are discouraged in favor of more immediate project delivery. Changing this phenomenon will likely require C-level involvement.

- **The Secret Society of Innovators.** Often leaders hand innovation over to a top-secret Skunk Works crew involving a few key contributors (usually those who are already well known in the organization), rather than making the innovation process transparent to the full population of employees. Perhaps most damaging is the implication that others who are not initially invited into this closed club are forever unwelcome. And thus an employee with a good idea will often keep it to herself, growing tired of the status quo and dreaming of the day when she can set out and make her good idea a reality, on her own.

"We're a small player in Canadian insurance," says Michel Loranger, chief information officer of SSQ Financial Group. "We're number five in group insurance. So if we want to compete with larger insurers, our strength is in our agility. We were the first to launch a mobile application: you can file a claim with your phone just by taking a picture. You can also fill out the claim online and get an answer within an hour. So we're not only proud of our ability to innovate but innovate quickly, and to keep innovating."

Innovation takes leaders who have a willingness to overcome historical folklore about their own organizations and who can tolerate the discomfort that inevitably accompanies change. Innovation should be encouraged up, down, and across the corporation, and everyone should be invited to the party.

Going Digital

Venture capitalist Marc Andreessen has said, "In the future, there will be two kinds of jobs: those where people tell computers what to do, and those where computers tell people what to do."

One of the biggest challenges for IT leaders is maintaining often complex technology infrastructures while simultaneously promoting new projects. They try managing for scale, shedding functionally specific applications into business units and whittling down vendor lists while they look for ways to contribute new value.

Far too many IT leaders never achieve the balance, ceding to tired expectations that they'll keep employees happy and systems humming. As with anyone who's struggled with shedding a few pounds, the self-talk focuses on what will happen once the pounds have been shed. "Once I lose the weight, I'll get back to the beach," we reassure ourselves.

In innovation-speak, this sounds like: "Once I [sunset the mainframe/outsource the billing system/get the new inventory system into production/hire a data scientist], we can start innovating." But new temptations get in the way, and we fall off the wagon. We may actually gain a few pounds, putting us even farther away from the beach.

Driving a digital strategy practically mandates change. The one key reliable incentive to get off the couch and onto the digital treadmill is the success of a competitor.

Consider the property and casualty insurer that watched as its policy renewals began to slide. The reason? A competitor had begun offering premium discounts to customers and prospects who agreed to fit remote transponder devices in their cars. These transponders tracked driving speeds and other driver behaviors, streaming the data into a central hub. Drivers who agreed to the program received lower premiums and other incentives to keep the transponders in their vehicles. Accident rates among participants plummeted, paying for the cost of the telematics technology in a matter of months and sparking a PR bonanza for the company. Fresh customer behavior and preference data to mine were a happy by-product of the program.

The insurer began its own retention program, which included allowing policyholders to file a claim from their smartphones, guaranteeing that, in certain cases, an adjustor would show up at the scene of an accident in 30 minutes or less.

Driving a digital strategy means being willing to topple established corporate structures. It also means introducing new business philosophies that might initially make constituents uncomfortable, but that promise significant improvements, and sometimes huge payoffs if done right.

Every business is a digital business. Or at least every business is *talking* about going digital. Many leaders across IT and business see digital as synonymous with innovation. While I would argue that digital is a subset of innovation, it is definitely at the forefront.

In the consumer space, video, radio, music, and television have all moved from analog to digital. Few companies nowadays operate on analog platforms. The digital doors have been thrown open, and everyone's rushing inside. That's precisely why IT leaders consider digital so promising— and at the same time, why they dread it.

Building Your Digital Vision

Your company is probably struggling with IT issues that are very different from those at Amazon.com, Facebook, or eBay—never mind Airbnb, Lyft, or TaskRabbit. You probably don't roam the hallways advocating for creative destruction. It's a pretty sure bet that your executives are only now turning their attention to the digital future.

So what does that look like? It first helps to identify the boundaries of digitization. A retailer's social-mobile-local (SoMoLo) strategy for tracking customer movement and offering store discounts in real time certainly has digital as its core. But so does the cable company's tiered service model, which incents customers, by guaranteeing them a faster service response, to post their service issues on Twitter or to transmit them via SMS messaging instead of using the 800 number. So does the healthcare provider's use of sensor data and wearable devices to remotely monitor the vital signs of at-risk patients, thus reducing admissions. And so does the insurer's telematics program.

Struggling to know where to start with digital? In general, a digital strategy will support one of the following three categories.

Category 1. Driving Revenues or Reducing Costs Through New Customer Experiences

Our right and left brains are converging. Companies can now not only track historical customer purchases but they can also use intuitive visualization tools to colorfully display demographics, product usage statistics, recreational and leisure preferences, and interactions with competitors. This augments outreach conversations and enhances the design and functionality of products that customers and prospects will want to buy.

The interface between humans and machines is drastically changing customer relationships. Digital is driving transformative customer engagement, retention, sales, advertising, product development, and media buying modalities. In the meantime, nontraditional data types like social media interactions, video, and sensor data increase the odds of reaching customers in a timely and relevant way.

Smart companies are turning toward digital marketing to analyze data about websites visited, searches conducted, content viewed, purchases made, and offline channels visited. (Surveys have confirmed that online digital offers encourage offline interactions.) Companies are pushing offers to consumers' smartphones when they're at home. They are then changing those offers, with the help of geofencing technologies, when those consumers are in the vicinity of a store. And they are offering additional perks when the consumers are actually shopping.

Retailer Burberry famously blurred the lines between the digital and in-store experiences, using a sleek combination of in-store video and radio frequency identification device (RFID) tags to display clothing on models and mixing and matching individual items as consumers were considering them. The company makes sure to gather contact information when the customer is in the store so that follow-up can be personal and relevant. The "always-addressable customer" is only possible in the digital world.

Category 2. Accelerating Business Processes with Digital Technologies

A recent Accenture study reported that most executives were using digital to boost internal efficiencies, not growth.[4] However, some of the efficiencies that digital enables can cause a ripple effect, pervading the company's four walls and ultimately touching its market.

What is the damage profile and the financial risk resulting from a hurricane in Florida, an earthquake in California, or a blackout in New York? Financial services firms have used complex analytics to determine risk for decades. But the property and casualty insurer mentioned earlier enriched its digital capabilities by combining a big data cloud offering with advanced analytics tools to accelerate its forecasts. This offered new capabilities for using satellite streams, soil samples, weather predictions, and other nontraditional data to increase the accuracy of risk profiles and to accelerate information availability, allowing the insurer to act in advance of catastrophic events and reduce losses. The resulting improvements to underwriting, pricing, and capital management processes have funded the digital investments many times over.

"Digital technology is turning our entire supply chain inside out," a movie studio executive told me. "The old days of selling a DVD for $15 are gone. Now they're $3. And they're going away." The movie studio has invested $60 million in a new digital strategy that will distribute movies over the Internet, designing a so-called digital supply chain that tracks the studio's film properties from content creation to storage and retrieval to packaging and distribution. "With digital, IT is no longer there to support the business," the executive said. "IT *is* the business."

No, this type of digital project isn't as sexy as sending time-limited discount codes to the smartphones of coveted prospects. But driving a digital strategy can be bigger than increasing revenue—it can also create value by streamlining cumbersome processes and reducing costs. Or, like the movie studio, it can keep your products circulating.

Category 3. Introducing New Business Models

Executives and corporate boards are excited about the prospect of using digital technologies to inform new operating divisions, products, and brands. Every shell of a video store sitting vacant in a strip mall is a reminder that digital enabled a radically new business model in the form of Netflix. Ditto independent bookstores and Amazon.com.

But digital technology will more likely extend your business than eradicate your competitors. GE uses a combination of big data and digital technologies to predict wear of its turbine engines and replace parts before—not after—they wear out. Car companies are experimenting with connected vehicles that can push information to customer service representatives about a vehicle's service needs and, in turn, pull information about weather or road conditions. Hospitals are exploring Google Glass as a means of performing remote physician consultations with patients who may be miles—or countries—away, thus introducing promising new service, cost, and care models.

Of course, there are challenges to delivering these business capabilities. Huge and diverse data sets, nonintegrated legacy systems, outdated analytics skills, cumbersome network speeds, and architectures that don't scale are all contributors to digital inertia. But the absence of data-savvy management and cultural fear of change are without question digital innovation's primary saboteurs.

Some executives, predicting an arduous journey from ideation to eventual digitization, become disaffected early. Others, hearing the phrase "total digitization," quickly become overwhelmed at the prospect of digital technologies pervading every nook and cranny of their companies. They're vexed, wondering where and how to begin. Suspicious that their incumbent infrastructures are insufficient, they overestimate the investment needs. "We need to be a digitally connected company," a CEO remarked recently, "which means I have to get the CIO to overhaul our IT infrastructure and ensure that each business unit is on board. That could be economically impossible." This type of assumption is not only wrong, but it also implies changes that are so dramatic and so immediate that digitization never materializes.

Creating Your Digital Roadmap

As McKinsey & Company heralded in a May 2014 article, "The age of experimentation with digital is over." Executives must move beyond research and create a deliberate digital roadmap for their companies. But when it comes to creating a digital strategy, one size definitely doesn't fit all, and business as usual may not apply.

How you roll out digital programs will be informed by the IT archetype that best fits your company today. Knowing your company's capabilities, limitations, and culture will help you create a realistic and executable plan. In addition, your industry, your company's cultural norms, and technological maturity will all determine how—and how fast—you can become a digital enterprise. For instance, communication companies have been tackling huge data volumes and visualizing their networks for a decade or more, and they are thus more comfortable than other industries with using big data and consumer devices to inform their digital planning. Likewise, high-tech companies, unencumbered by legacy infrastructures, are able to leverage open source technologies, programming prowess, and agile delivery processes to deploy digital solutions quickly.

Consider the strategy map shown in Figure 7.2. The objectives shown on the left side could each include a digital component. Encouraging customer retention through new digital capabilities (the third strategic objective) will involve several digital initiatives, each with its own list of enabling projects. These projects include releasing a mobile payment app for customers' mobile devices; introducing a points program, RewardPerkz on the Go, which will be administered online; a mobile product recommender; and a real-time customer segmentation capability that segments and resegments customers based on their interactions.

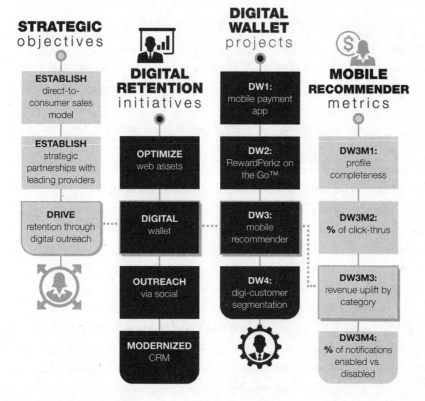

Figure 7.2 **A Digital Roadmap**

By letting business strategy drive digital initiatives, the company can avoid wholesale changes to its vocabulary and ensure that the business continues to own its own initiatives and measures. At the same time, IT organizations can position themselves as digitally savvy and distinctly valuable.

Innovative projects like mobile product recommenders might be set apart from traditional development in terms of ideation, context, and delivery. Depending on ownership, though, your digital initiatives may slide into your IT project portfolio, and they may be tracked according to similar (though not identical) measures. Over time, as innovation gets absorbed into the company's culture, digital strategy will become part of the larger business strategy.

EXECUTIVE PROFILE

Susan Neal, Men's Wearhouse

Calling yourself a "retail pioneer" to anyone who's worked in retail could be—depending on the listener—either braggadocio or career suicide. In this industry, thin margins dictate a company's ability to innovate (and everything else).

Susan Neal, executive vice president of marketing, ecommerce, and technology at Men's Wearhouse, personifies the retail executive of the future. Neal joined the apparel retailer in 2010 at the behest of the CEO and a board of directors that had begun envisioning the promise of a digital presence. She quickly set about fulfilling their vision.

Based in San Francisco—where she'd previously held a variety of leadership positions at Gymboree, having built its online business from scratch—Neal spent her first few months traveling between the Men's Wearhouse offices in the Bay Area and Houston. Her goal was to assess the company's systems, skills, and delivery capabilities.

"I saw what we were doing, and what we weren't doing," Neal remembers. "The CEO eventually gave me responsibility for IT, which at the time was concentrated in Houston. But we had businesspeople in San Francisco. I started thinking about how things needed to be organized and how to tie it all together to position us for innovation and success."

Ensuring the Right Fit

Neal hired a chief information officer, immediately relocating him to Houston. She also brought on a chief technology officer, basing him in San Francisco.

"The idea was that any technology that touched the customer would be run locally here in the Bay Area," she says. "Mobile apps, ecommerce, digital marketing, our marketing database—it was important to me that these functions be close to the business."

This defied the advice of some colleagues at other brand name retailers. "I had some pretty important CIOs telling me not to break up IT," she says. "They were adamant that colocation was critical. But, ultimately, I have to say that our customer-focused businesspeople are collaborating with the technology people who are also customer focused. My technology folks are sitting side-by-side with businesspeople. They're in each other's cubicles! You can hear them throwing around ideas. This kind of collaboration is invaluable."

There was also a website. But it was more about driving traffic into the stores than it was about helping customers make purchases. Technology was taken seriously, but it was used more as an enabler than a game changer. Neal drafted a strategic plan for a digital business and presented it to the board, advocating the need to not only catch up to the industry but also to surpass it.

The Customer Wears the Pants

Using information from the company's PerfectFit loyalty program, Neal and her team are testing real-time personalized product recommendations for customers and offering them incentives.

"As the email renders on your computer or your smartphone, the recommendations are pushed," Neal explains. "Because it's in real time, the messages can change depending on when you read the email. You can see the status of a shipment, an item that coordinates with a recent purchase, or get an update on your loyalty points."

Prom kids. Wedding groups. As these shoppers browse the selection at Men's Wearhouse, the company learns their preferred styles and brands.

Neal credits a robust customer database, managed internally by the CIO, for much of the program's success. "We're gathering and accessing

(continues)

relevant data for and about our customers," she says. "That doesn't mean all data, but the data that's meaningful for us. Sure, I could buy data that tells me that a customer drinks Diet Coke. But do I really care about that? We collect and use the data that matters and will move the company forward."

Modeling the Digital Future

Staying relevant with customers and keeping them engaged is the aspiration of every marketer. Neal's goal of innovating quickly extends from customer loyalty to customer service.

"My next big initiative is to be able to ship from the store. As we start to ask ourselves questions about inventory across stores, we need to be proactive in moving inventory such that it is as close as possible to the customer. Amazon.com is getting really good at forecasting demand, and that's where we want to be."

Among other innovation projects, Neal and her team are exploring in-store mobile applications and payment options. "As a company, we're pretty high touch," she says. "A wardrobe consultant greets you when you walk in the door, and we don't want to replace that. We truly have an omnichannel strategy, and we're constantly thinking about how digital, when used well, can optimize the customer experience."

Neal's advice for companies considering an innovation lab or chief digital officer? "Be willing to change your business culture before you hire a C-level person for this kind of work," she says. "Companies are bringing in the people, but then they're not willing to make the necessary changes. You need to build a strategy you can execute against. And you need the support of your CEO and board."

Ecommerce, IT, and marketing all falling under Neal's leadership may well be the key to the success of her digital strategy. But it could have been her downfall. When you talk to Neal, you realize that her decision to craft and present a strategy early on may have been the determining factor.

She is circumspect about her decision to refocus and change organizational structures before introducing innovation, but she knows in the end she got it right. "When I think about the vision of understanding customer information to provide a better experience across all touch-points, using innovative new technologies to deliver these capabilities quickly, bringing it all together makes perfect sense."

Digital Teams and Innovation Labs

The adoption of digital technologies like social platforms, mobile devices, analytics tool sets, and cloud computing—collectively known as SMAC—is, in reality, the easy part. The hard part is supporting the ideas that can leverage these and other emerging tools for sustained invention and improvement. Leaders on both business and IT sides love the idea of an innovation lab because it promises to kick-start the often alien process of creative thinking. But they can underestimate their readiness, as well as the adoption issues that so often accompany efforts to innovate.

What's in a Lab?

The mother of the innovation center of excellence was Bell Labs. Born out of AT&T and its subsidiary Western Electric, Bell Labs quickly achieved its own brand prestige. When AT&T realized that it had a small army of flat-smart, big-thinking engineers in its midst, it spun off Bell Labs and promoted the new entity as cutting edge. The Bell Labs campus in Holmdel, New Jersey—a structure nearly 2 million square feet in size—featured a giant statue of a transistor on the front lawn. In addition to the transistor, its researchers are credited with innovations in satellites, lasers, and several programming languages.

In his 2012 book *The Idea Factory: Bell Labs and the Great Age of American Innovation*, science writer Jon Gertner tells the story of Bill Shockley, one of Bell Labs' principal transistor technology developers. Shockley described a particularly difficult period of innovation as "the natural blundering process of finding one's way."

For corporate executives in the twenty-first century, the word "blundering" has been all but banished from the corporate lexicon. It shouldn't be. For executives to support innovation, they must implicitly support a culture of experimentation. Indeed, they might even need to tolerate some blunders.

Recognizing their own branding opportunities for innovation, executives in both business and IT are embracing the idea of the innovation lab. They see the lab approach as a way to formalize a structure for innovation, thus establishing cultural expectations and leveraging the lab as a type of Petri dish in which they can seed new ideas.

Companies that have introduced such labs have used them as a pretext for burnishing their reputations—"We are thinking outside the box, solving problems in new ways!"—as well as introducing a new channel for fresh products, business processes, and service lines:

- **Cisco.** Cisco's Emerging Technology group incubates ideas that turn into new business lines, including the company's Internet of Things Group, which has allocated $200 million for R&D.

- **UPMC.** Formerly, the University of Pittsburgh Medical Center, UPMC famously invests in high-tech startups, and it partners with vendors to jointly develop products. These new offerings improve patient quality of care. Moreover they represent promising revenue sources. The healthcare provider's Technology Development Center develops product prototypes and then considers which ones to market commercially.

- **Comcast.** Cable giant Comcast introduced Comcast Labs as its advanced technology arm. Its mission is to change how people are entertained and informed. The lab employs thousands of scientists, PhDs, programmers, and what Comcast calls "active inventors."

- **Lego.** Toymaker the Lego Group recovered from the significant financial woes of the last decade partly by coordinating distributed innovation efforts overseen by the company's Executive Innovation Governance Group. The group coordinates and monitors innovation across departments—even inviting customers to participate in its innovation network—and it measures the results. It also earmarks different kinds of innovation for different business units, including those that are "obviously LEGO, but never seen before."

- **Eastman Chemical.** The chemical, fiber, and plastics giant brought its lab directly to the Internet. The Eastman Innovation Lab (EIL) creates "stories of materials and design advancing each other." The EIL invites business partners—including companies as diverse as Patagonia, Rubbermaid, and Ford Motor Company—to collaborate with them on material formulations for automotive, medical, fashion, and consumer electronics products. Eastman then invites the partners to give testimonials on the social significance of the resulting products.

- **Johnson & Johnson.** Healthcare and consumer products pioneer Johnson & Johnson introduced three regional innovation centers in 2013, all focused on finding nascent technology and product ideas and helping them to bear fruit. These "prior to clinical proof of concept innovations" involve collaboration between J&J's regional innovation hubs and external partners. The company considers its centers to be incubators for new ideas in their own right, leveraging them as units of outreach to business partners, entrepreneurs, research laboratories, academic institutions, and venture capital firms.

- **Eli Lilly.** Pharmaceutical giant Eli Lilly has encouraged innovation by establishing its own venture capital fund, Lilly Ventures, and by partnering and collaborating with others in the biotech community. In this way, the company can control the outcomes, ownership, and impacts of its innovations.

- **Jet Propulsion Laboratory (JPL).** JPL has created a so-called technology petting zoo at its Pasadena campus, where employees are invited to tire kick gadgets, applications, and devices. The company partners with Amazon.com, Google, and academic institutions like Cal Tech to stay at the forefront of technology development.

- **Philips.** Electronics behemoth Philips maintains an innovation lab on the outskirts of Amsterdam, and its lab looks like the modern living room of a high-end city loft. Here it tests a range of emerging technology solutions, including LED lights that accept digital signals. The company also uses the lab to study consumers' responses to light.

- **Nordstrom.** High-end department store Nordstrom introduced Nordstrom Labs, whose mission is nothing short of plotting the future of retail. "What you do and how you contribute here is up to you," reads the description. The lab team works on short project bursts, interacting directly with customers in retail stores to test ideas. Nordstrom Lab values include "Bias toward action," "Build to think," "Flare, then focus," and "Show, don't tell."

- **Google.** Perhaps most famously, in 2010, Google launched its secretive research arm, Google X, where the company is breathing life into space elevators, driverless cars, and glasses that talk to the Internet.

As Bell Labs' Claude Shannon, the acknowledged father of information theory, once said, "I am very seldom interested in applications. I am more interested in the elegance of a problem. Is it a good problem?" The common denominator of these and other successful lab efforts is that they involve people up and down the organizational hierarchy. Many also invite outsiders to contribute to ideas and vet and test them. The promise of a lab is that it guarantees that innovation gets the attention and focus that has eluded the company thus far.

Launching a Lab: How to Know Where to Start

Starting up an innovation lab involves more than simply announcing the effort, anointing the staff, and relocating everyone offsite to a LEED-certified fortress of deep thinkers. An innovation lab should be as deliberately planned as any new business venture.

The focus areas showed earlier in Figure 7.1 offer an effective model of potential starting points for a lab, depending on your company's industry, interests, and pain points. Table 7.1 lists some sample innovation areas for a general merchandise retailer across these four focus areas.

TABLE 7.1: Focus Areas for Starting an Innovation Lab

Innovation Focus Areas	Goals	Success Measurements
Strategy	Increase customer volume and revenues by entering new geographic markets via renewed brand identity	Break even in first year of entry
	Explore a new business model of franchised stores	Create three "franchise of the future" stores and compare customer traffic and revenue volume
	Add leadership strength and broaden perspective by expanding the board with additional members representing larger companies (over $10 billion) and greater diversity	Three new board members vetted and seated by fiscal year end
Customers	Improve the customer experience through new engagement models and additional information usage within shopping and service channels	Customer satisfaction score increase of 19 percent or higher over prior year's survey results
	Determine and define new segments to drive innovative product offerings	Higher sales uplift on new segments versus control group
Operations	Accelerate order fulfillment through faster processes or new technologies	A 16 percent or higher fulfillment speed improvement within the first year
	Increase the number of inventory turns	Increase average store inventory turn from 4 to 5 per year
Products	Differentiate business capabilities through partnerships with innovative technology startups	Identify primary partner. Collaborate on a new product and create a joint go-to-market plan that results in sales growth across five consecutive quarters

Notice that the retailer in this case establishes particular areas of concentration within each focus area: these ensure that the lab staff doesn't dream up ideas for problems that don't exist. Yet the retailer isn't too prescriptive about the outcome. At the beginning, a balance between thinking and creating is key: the innovation lab must earn the right to exist beyond its first handful of projects.

(One common complaint from executive leaders is that the innovation lab concept started with a bang, but then it fizzled as ideas became less vigorous over time. Such labs were typically launched by a small set of enthusiasts who wanted a sandbox to play in. Such labs often folded after the innovations either ran their course or failed.)

As the innovation lab matures, people will become more comfortable with the processes for thinking and experimenting. Thus the need to establish proactive focus areas is likely to recede as the lab collaborates within its network and produces results.

Creating the Innovation Team

It's no coincidence that Bell Labs and Xerox PARC were owned and financed by larger corporate entities. The leaders of these companies recognized the halo effect that resulted from giving scientists and researchers the space, technical capacity, and funding to create anew. Perhaps most critically, they were given the freedom to think.

Management expert Roger L. Martin has studied the topic of how this century's teams of knowledge workers should be structured. In a 2013 *Harvard Business Review* article, he wrote:

> In particular, most companies make two big mistakes in managing knowledge workers. The first is they should structure this workforce as they do a manual workforce—with each employee doing the same tasks day in and day out. The second (which derives in part from the first) is to assume that knowledge is necessarily bundled with the workers and, unlike manual labor, can't readily be codified and transferred to others.[5]

In the spirit of creating a culture of innovation, the retailer described above has taken pains to avoid Martin's mistake, extending what it calls "managed experimentation" to its lab's staffing philosophy. Rather than employing a fixed innovation team, thus inviting a static innovation culture and slowing down ideas, the retailer encourages dynamic and continuous staffing of the lab.

The lab's innovation board accepts new ideas on a quarterly basis. Employees whose ideas are accepted, henceforth known as "innovators," are then invited to join the lab for the period of time in which their idea is explored. This allows the innovator to participate in delivery, play a role in selecting the team, and help drive the results. If the idea is successful—success is defined based on the idea, and it may involve profitability, cost savings, or customer retention—the innovator receives preferred status for submitting another idea. If the idea is rejected, the innovator returns to his regular job, but he is welcome to submit future ideas to the board. This has formed what the lab board calls "a loose affiliation of innovators" working both inside and outside the lab, which uses digital signage, interactive kiosks, and screen savers to admonish its members to "dream big and deliver!"

Contrast this with the mistake most companies make when forming an innovation team for the first time. Well-meaning managers appoint team members based on historical success and relationships rather than their forward-thinking ideas. They colocate the team in a building or on a floor and label it with a new name or even a logo. By isolating the innovation team in this way, managers are effectively creating an elitist group that over time invites the general *schadenfreude* of its peers and receives diminishing support. Perhaps the most perilous outcome of this is that new ideas never leave the four walls of the innovation lab!

Cultivating a Culture of Discovery

When you get a tour of the advanced analytics lab at a major U.S. insurance company, the first thing that you notice is the space. Although the lab is situated in the insurer's sprawling headquarters building, it bears little resemblance to the offices and cubicles that are replicated up and down the building's other floors. The lab itself is a series of pop-up meeting spaces, open testing rooms, and so-called proto-pods where data scientists, designers, and engineers can test out concepts.

The entire lab is enclosed by glass walls, isolating the purpose-built location within the larger headquarters. Surrounded by glass, the lab is in full view of passersby. It is well known within the company to be ground zero for new product and service ideas, as well as for having a "culture within a culture."

"By and large, the insurance industry is pretty conservative," the insurer's chief innovation officer told me as I toured the lab. "And so are we. But I'm cultivating a different mindset here." He invokes Jack Welch's measurement mantra and Steve Jobs's "Think different" slogans in the same conversation. "We need to measure our successes," he concedes, "but at the same time, those successes hinge on a culture of discovery."

A culture of discovery? In insurance? This lab, like many corporate innovation centers, bends the rules for those who are playing. The lab allows its team members to test out new ideas and—like many innovation labs—it embraces a mentality of "fail fast." (Facebook's motto is "Move fast and break things.")

"There's no penalty for failure here," the innovation leader reiterated. "Whatever we deliver that doesn't work, we learn from and we try again."

Testing, discovery, and experimentation are all rewarded in innovation labs where the trite metaphor of thinking outside the box is met with irony. (In this case people are thinking *inside* the box, albeit a well-appointed one.) The fail-and-try-again philosophy is not only embraced, it's practiced.

But this could be a wholesale philosophical change for many executives who are too busy fretting about the bottom line to pay much attention to cultivating any type of new culture, let alone one of discovery. Companies that have failed to drive change with innovation labs are those that isolate the people and consign the space, but fall short of establishing a new way of working.

Because cultural and work style issues are paramount in innovation labs, executive attention must be paid. Unlike many successful new corporate ventures, when it comes to innovation labs, a bottom-up, grassroots effort rarely sticks.

The insurer mentioned earlier considers its lab one of its top competitive differentiators—so much so that the company declined to be named on the record. How did they get funding to build the lab in the first place?

"Our executive leaders on the business side were starting to ask questions they knew we couldn't answer with our traditional approaches," says the chief innovation officer. "So we needed to incorporate new ways of doing things and use some different tools. We're looking at new member insights through social media data . . . targeted mobile apps . . . what we call our 'global wallet'. . . sensory telemetry—we're piloting a new telematics project right now using some fun visualizations. There's a ton of other stuff we're trying out."

And it's not just new technologies but also new data. Innovation labs are reaching out to more third-party data providers—the insurer is currently piloting data from the Federal Reserve—and ingesting nontraditional data types using big data technologies like Hadoop and Spark to accelerate the pace of delivery as never before.

Sure, it looks like a meeting of the geeks. "We're really good at computational biology. Behavioral economics. And, obviously, math," says the chief innovation officer. "But at the end of the day, the stuff we come up with needs to be usable. We don't have the luxury of just being a bunch of thinkers on steroids."

The public sector is also getting in on the act. Los Angeles Mayor Eric Garcetti recently appointed the city's first chief innovation officer allocating an innovation fund of $1.4 million. Initial programs include upgrading city websites, applying more robust analytics, and transforming city services—like broadening the city's MyLA311 problem-reporting system to become a central city information portal. Several other cities allow their citizens to pay parking meters and property taxes with their smartphones, and these cities are watching their revenues increase accordingly.

The public sector even has a newfound tolerance for the startup language of "fail fast." After witnessing a staff member's bold new idea go terribly awry, California Lieutenant Governor Gavin Newsom introduced the Failure Award "to whichever employee suggested the most fabulous failed idea."[6]

Federal, state, and local institutions are rewarding new ideas and process improvements that save taxpayer dollars and ensure citizen safety. The stakes have never been higher.

What Keeps Innovation and Digital Executives Up at Night

Most managers in charge of innovation centers are constantly rejigging their models, shifting their structures, and reprioritizing projects. Here are the issues that are top-of-mind for them.

The Innovation Funding Model

It's easier to convince a C-level executive of the company's need to innovate than it is to get her to put money behind innovation. Many executives will want assurances of ROI before allocating budget for innovation.

The insurance company's chief innovation officer explains their funding model: "The lab isn't tied to the old funding model where you create your business case and lay out what the end result will be. IT and the business are pooling money to support our discovery efforts. Our goal is to fail early if we have to fail in order to minimize the investment level. And then we move on to the next opportunity. We're training the rest of the business that you don't have to have all the questions defined up front anymore."

Executives at the insurance company have agreed to fund the creation of the physical lab. Business units will fund targeted projects. "Lines of business are coming to us and offering us money to explore new questions. Our leadership believes in this enough to pony up some money."

Other companies impose an "innovation tax" on lines of business whether or not they participate in innovation projects. The idea is that while innovation is optional—some might even call it a luxury—it is as foundational to the company's operations as electricity. Because everyone has access to it, and many use or will use it, it should be an embedded expense.

The introduction of new executive roles is often a pretext for first-time innovation funding. A newly announced chief innovation officer or chief digital officer will likely need a budget in order to meet his mandate. That 40 percent of all chief digital officers report directly to the CEO—only 22 percent report to the CIO and 16 percent to the CMO[7]—implies that procuring both budget and executive support for innovation is becoming less the exception and more the rule.

The hope is that digitization and innovation will pay for themselves over time. Ultimately, a company's ability to answer the question, "What percentage of our revenues has been generated from innovation or digital capabilities in the last two years?" is the most straightforward way to know for sure.

Democratizing Innovation

It's become a mantra in innovation circles: "Innovation is everyone's job." Innovation pioneer Gary Hamel expanded on this point in an interview with *McKinsey Quarterly*:

CEOs tell me, "Gary, we're really serious about innovation"—
and what CEO isn't these days? My response is to go down to
first-level employees and ask them a few questions. The first
question I ask is, "How have you been trained as a business innovator? What investment has the company made in teaching
you how to innovate?"[8]

In companies that have excelled at innovation, leaders encourage innovation. They ensure that up and down the corporate hierarchy, there are no
penalties for bringing new ideas forward and that recognition and financial
rewards are also possible. They also remove line-of-command and bureaucratic barriers that might discourage frontline employees from suggesting
new ideas or improvements.

As noted earlier, this democratization of innovation isn't limited to
employees. It may also extend outside the company, inviting partners and
suppliers to participate in the innovation process. These so-called open innovation networks have proved the idea that specialists collaborating temporarily on a common project can deliver a higher degree of business value
more quickly than static teams.

A major aircraft engine manufacturer was stymied about complaints of
a defect in its turbine engines. The manufacturer decided to apply what it
called "systems thinking" to its assembly process. Manufacturing engineers
videotaped the manufacturing of the part in question, allowing its aero-
space customers to view the assembly process online. Together, they were
able to pinpoint a problem with the compressor, working interactively on
material upgrades and visual inspection processes.

In the spirit of fail fast, forward-thinking executives are letting employees who try new things off the hook. Kevin McDearis, an IT executive at
the aforementioned CheckFree and now a CIO, has instituted what he calls
"amnesty days."

"There are no penalties on amnesty days," McDearis explains. "IT staff
are coming together to share problems and fix issues. We're not only stew-
arding the IT portfolio but also managing the accompanying risks. You
want to encourage calling out mistakes, and then fixing them."

McDearis's amnesty days hail a growing trend of professionals publicly accounting for their missteps or poor decisions together with their

colleagues. Popular Failcon events—"Embrace your mistakes. Build your success."—let investors and entrepreneurs share stories of where good ideas went bad. U.K. management consultancy NixonMcInnes holds what it calls the Church of Fail, complete with a tongue-in-cheek ceremony, giving employees an opportunity to admit errors, large and small. Formalizing these meetings celebrates accountability while simultaneously lampooning the ritual itself.

"Of course," says McDearis, "if the same people are always the ones admitting problems, then you might have issues with specific staff. But amnesty days have helped my teams fix what's broken and remediate as soon as we can."

It's now practically a given that no company should innovate in a vacuum. In addition to creating M&A strategies to enter new markets, companies are seriously looking at acquisitions as a means of innovating. They're also looking to their customers to help them.

Gamification and Crowdsourcing

Gamification is the process of making routine or tedious tasks interesting and alluring by making them a game. Initially introduced to incent people to complete corporate or HR training—it's proven to enhance learning, task completion, and user engagement—gamification has been adopted by corporations to increase customer conversations, social media participation, and website hit rates. Participants are often rewarded with points or prizes, motivating them to return to the game or recruit their friends.

Aetna used gamification techniques to encourage its members to increase healthy diet and exercise habits, Verizon used it to encourage more website hits, and Autodesk drove up software trials and subsequent conversion rates.[9] Retailer Threadless asks its customers to submit designs for T-shirts, wall art, and smartphone cases, among other merchandise. Threadless shoppers determine the winners, who receive a combination of cash and store credits. By engaging employees, customers, prospects, and the public through games, a company can achieve unexpected outcomes—and change the way they're seen in the marketplace.

Kaggle makes solving complex analytical or statistical problems a game by holding contests on behalf of companies seeking answers to real-life business problems. Companies like Allstate, Walmart, and movie review site Rotten Tomatoes have used Kaggle competitions to stimulate research and arrive at new business insights. The Kaggle community is over 150,000 strong, and its sponsoring companies typically offer cash rewards in the tens of thousands of dollars—often a small price to pay for discoveries that could provide a competitive edge.

Almost every company has a story about how customer feedback has driven product or service improvements. Using games and competitions is a low-risk way to not only solve problems but also engage a brand new audience in conversations with your company. It can result in innovative ideas from any direction. And it can instill goodwill in the bargain.

Branding the Innovation Lab

I once worked with a consumer goods company that was among the world's 20 most recognizable brands. In addition to the universally recognized corporate logo, each one of the company's major initiatives had its own logo design. Project teams competed for wall space at corporate headquarters, laminating posters that heralded their projects' brand identities and taglines.

I found this to be so much overkill and waste at a company that had spent millions aligning its strategy with its global brand. Shouldn't the importance and visibility of strategic projects be obvious? Why all the internal publicity and posturing?

Taking note of my wrinkled nose, a marketing executive took me aside to explain that—just as the company's brand was part of its DNA—establishing a subbrand for each project gave that project an identity. The company culture was so brand focused that individual workers felt loyalty to their project's brand. Being associated with a project with its own moniker encouraged esprit de corps and gave their work meaning.

Companies are increasingly assigning names and often slogans to their innovation labs. This directs attention their way and, more important, announces to the company at large that the innovation center is working differently.

Baking It In: A Seven-Point Innovation Checklist

A few years ago, Jessica Seinfeld, wife of comedian Jerry, wrote a cookbook called *Deceptively Delicious*, in which she shared tricks to convince children to eat their vegetables. One recipe advocated mixing broccoli in with a brownie mix: the small amount of vegetables would be a big nutritional boost, and kids would be none the wiser.

So it is with planning for innovation. By the time most IT roadmaps factor in platform upgrades, bug fixes, code enhancements, laptop replacements, email management, maintenance releases, and vendor contracts, there's little room for anything else. The portfolio planning process described in Chapter 6 can support not only existing business needs but also digital strategies, data exploration, or other promising innovations that often fall out of IT planning. The trick is to bake innovation into the existing budgeting process.

Some leadership teams earmark a portion of the overall development budget—say, 10 percent—and apply it to new technologies and focused innovation efforts. This approach delimits investments around nonstandard tool sets that could be rapidly deployed, while gradually fostering a culture of fresh ideas and experimentation without penalty.

IT leaders are transforming their organizations from "We build everything" to "Here's how to build it." This means gradually transitioning toward a competency focused on process creation and refinement. IT delivering proven and repeatable development methodologies straight to business departments streamlines deployment, ensures domain expertise, eases organizational tensions, and drives economies of scale.

Apple founder Steve Jobs famously said, "Creativity is about making connections." This implies not only adapting innovation, but understanding where you are today and the space that you're in.

Here are seven questions to ask yourself as you begin expanding awareness of innovation opportunities at your company:

1. Are we willing to make innovation a part of regular conversations and meetings? (This might mean including progress on specific innovation projects in status reports and leadership updates or creating an online innovation portal for company employees—in effect integrating innovation into the corporate vocabulary.)

2. Can we distinguish between invention and improvement, and can we establish the importance of each?

3. Are we willing to cultivate innovation talent, even if it means defying cultural norms?

4. Are we willing to modify reward structures to encourage new ideas and innovation delivery? Can we work with HR to modify compensation models?

5. Do we know who the detractors will be, and are we confident—with time and some successes—that we can convert them?

6. Can we decouple innovation from skunk works or stealth efforts, making it a general corporate goal and inviting everyone to contribute?

7. Are we willing to set aside seed money for innovation, abandoning established orthodoxies about time to delivery and ROI?

The answers to these questions will not only indicate your readiness for innovation but they'll also shed light on your commitment to making it real.

Such changes aren't easy. But amidst continued funding battles and organizational alignment struggles, they've been shown to drive widespread improvements. "When I hear people say 'the business and IT are fighting,' I just cringe," says Eugene Roman, chief technology officer of retail giant Canadian Tire. "Those people are done. In a world where everyone can be digital, everyone should be digital."

CHAPTER SUMMARY

Key Takeaways

- *Innovation* means different things to different companies. The buzzword can often obfuscate the meaning in the context of your company's specific opportunities. Cut through the buzzwords of *transformation* and *disruption*. Be willing to reward ideas.

- When it comes to supporting and implementing new ideas, understanding your company's strategy and culture is critical. Some companies can quickly support invention, while others must encourage incremental improvements. Both should be attached to focus areas, and both should be measured.

- Innovation mythology is widespread. By orders of magnitude, more managers are discussing it than are practicing it. Many leaders spend too much time searching for external examples from other companies they can imitate rather than earnestly searching inside their companies for opportunities.

- Your company's digital strategy will be informed by your industry, your culture, and your IT archetype. The old adage "Meet your company where it is" applies well to how you roll out digital capabilities.

- An innovation team or lab can jump-start invention and improvement as long as it's not viewed as a members only club or academic exercise. Make innovation efforts as transparent as possible.

- Innovation should be democratic, not exclusive. Involve, encourage, and reward everyone for new ideas.

Note to the CEO

When faced with the opportunity to formalize innovation at their companies, most CEOs err on the side of either being too tactical—emphasizing quick delivery and cost savings over fresh approaches—or too theoretical— believing that colocating smart people and asking them to think deeply can transform their businesses. The art, as they say, is in the balance. And so, perhaps, is your company's competitive differentiation.

"Fortunately, he gets it," says Susan Neal about Doug Ewert, president and CEO of Men's Wearhouse. "If your CEO is open-minded and really believes innovation is important, he or she will get other executives on board. They'll break down the organizational barriers for you, and they'll help you communicate your digital direction. But if you don't have that level of support," she cautions, "be prepared for a more difficult uphill battle."

Keep in mind that as your company becomes practiced, innovation and the people doing it will evolve. If launched correctly, innovation efforts blossom into often-proprietary processes that reflect the company's unique needs and assets. Companies can exploit this process to drive further innovation. It's your job to sustain a culture that supports this type of evolution and that welcomes ideas from all comers. If you're ready, start using the words *innovation, invention,* and *design* in your management meetings and town hall talks. Be ready for things to be different from what they are now, and be ready to handle the inevitable pushback. Be willing to start from a place of not knowing.

If you have to, begin with an ad hoc team and expand out from there. French philosopher Emile August-Chartier once said, "Nothing is more dangerous than having just one idea." But I would argue that in most companies, it's a good place to start.

• • • • • • • • • • • •

Self-Assessment Two: Your Transformation Readiness

our company was recently fined by a regulator for poor compliance reporting. One of your best customers just selected a competitor. Your most talented vice president abandoned ship for a startup. You just issued a product recall. Your boss has just told you that you might be spread too thin—code for splitting up your team.

There's a blessing in the curse: large-scale changes are typically made when something is seriously broken.

Smart executives get out in front of major problems and fix them early. They assess root causes, unafraid to call out the guilty to unravel knotty business processes and gnarled rules of engagement. Only then do they allocate new people and reorganize. They have the organizational authority to fix the problem and ensure that those fixes stick.

We'll talk more about leadership qualities in the next two chapters. But first let's look at your company's capabilities around the operation, connection, and innovation mandates we've discussed already and see how ready your company is to adopt some new practices in both business and IT.

Take the Assessment

In Table 8.1, answer the questions at the left. For each question, you'll give yourself a score of 1 to 9 by measuring the degree to which the answer is positive or negative. The descriptions in the three columns will help guide you toward the best score.

TABLE 8.1: Self-Assessment Two: Your Transformation Readiness

Question	Scoring Spectrum									Your Score
	1	2	3	4	5	6	7	8	9	
Strategy. Can company leaders connect strategy with the work being done across business units?	Our leadership doesn't discuss corporate direction. There is no strategy, or there is none that anyone is aware of. Someone mentioned strategy once, and that person is no longer with the firm.			Each department has its own plan, which in turn informs the projects we take on. One or more key line executives (like the chief marketing officer) think strategically and lay out a vision for the future. We have hired or promoted new executive positions lately (like chief analytics officer or chief digital officer) to see us into the future.			Strategy is an enterprisewide practice that executives participate in and support. Corporate strategy feeds business unit strategies. IT leaders are asked to participate in strategy formulation and ensure that IT projects conform to business goals.			
Operational planning. How formal is operational planning in IT?	IT is reactive. We wait to be told what to do, which often involves fighting fires. Budget money is doled out based on incremental spending and revenue growth, not on business needs. Headcount is paramount, and IT competes with the business for resources.			Project prioritization exists, but there is no formal governance team. IT is only as proactive as what we know about. Planning is based on personal relationships. IT leaders rely on the kindness of their peers on the business side, who often fund technology projects from their own budgets. The company does not put a premium on tech-savvy staff, but individual managers understand their importance.			There are structured processes for linking corporate strategy, business unit planning, and IT resources. IT is partially rewarded on its ability to meet corporate objectives and enable strategic programs (like "voice of the customer" or "supply chain renovation"). There is a common process for planning and budgeting across the organization.			

Question	Scoring Spectrum			Your Score
	1 2 3	4 5 6	7 8 9	
Collaboration. Do people work together easily? Are departments encouraged to share talent and ideas?	We're too organizationally siloed for collaboration to be meaningful. There's not enough transparency across organizations to know where collaboration might be possible. Knowledge is power here. There are more penalties than rewards for working with others.	Organizations collaborate on a situational basis, and only when they connect the dots. Personal relationships between staff members usually determine the makeup of work groups. Managers are more apt to encourage collaboration if other departments possess important skills.	Corporate goals determine which departments and skills should come together to achieve results. Cross-functional teams are rewarded uniquely for driving business value. Projects require documenting delivery methods for future teams to reference.	
Prioritization. Is there a clear process for prioritizing work efforts both within business units and across the company?	"He who screams the loudest" pretty much sums it up. Personal relationships and politics are big factors in what gets done first. Disagreements about the importance of business initiatives are common.	Business units have roadmaps that imply delivery priority. There is no macro-level prioritization process. It's usually subjective. Prioritization disagreements happen from time to time, but there is a clear escalation or tie-breaking process.	Governance informs delivery priorities, and there is a steering committee in place. The prioritization process is common across business units. IT's priorities reflect business priorities.	

(continues)

TABLE 8.1: Self-Assessment Two: Your Transformation Readiness (continued)

Question	Scoring Spectrum 1 2 3	4 5 6	7 8 9	Your Score
Organizational structure. Does the organizational structure reflect the company's strategy, priorities, and focus areas?	While there are departments, there is no formal org chart that links them together. Organizational charters don't exist. A department's success depends on the clarity of its goals. There is incessant talk of reorganization or corporate restructuring.	The organizational structure is clear to all employees. Department charters are published, and job roles are clear. Departments still largely work autonomously, with each aligning to strategy in its own way.	The organizational structure will change occasionally to accommodate evolving corporate goals (for instance, the addition of an analytics service line). Organizational success measures include macro-measurements (for example, companywide measurements) as well as specific measurements.	
Support for new ideas. Are employees at all levels encouraged to make suggestions for improvement?	People are comfort centered. They stick with the status quo. Employees are expected to go to their managers with improvement suggestions. Most never see the light of day. People take credit for other people's work here. Why would I go out on a limb?	The company has rolled out a process, website, or regular forum for submitting ideas. The CEO has begun talking about driving more entrepreneurial behaviors. Support for new ideas is pretty much limited to new technologies.	Structures are in place to support both strategic and tactical innovations. Leadership recognizes that technology is a key innovation enabler, and it has involved IT leadership in discussions of an innovation lab or internal venture fund.	

Question	Scoring Spectrum			Your Score
	1 2 3	4 5 6	7 8 9	
Partnering. Does your company reach out to partners to enrich its products and services or expand its reach?	We don't really partner. We've actually turned potential partners away because we feared loss of control. When it comes to developing something new, leadership has a not-invented-here mentality. We think we can build whatever we need internally.	We have a few partnerships. Most were the result of opportunism: they had customers or products we needed. We do have good partners, but they are typically former employees or have personal relationships with managers. We have partners, but no centralized ownership or negotiation.	The company forms partnerships based on a combination of our strategic direction and gaps in our own capabilities. We have a tiered partnership structure that connotes preferred partners. We rely on partners to help us enrich our product set and enter new markets.	
Openness to change. Does your company's culture support changes when they're necessary? Is change seen as a positive force for moving things forward?	People are penalized for sticking their necks out. There are no penalties for sabotaging new initiatives. It's safer to say no than yes.	There are leaders here who are lobbying for major changes. Some have been successful. Recently, the CEO (or other C-level executive) introduced a program that was atypically bold. We have centers of excellence or SWAT teams whose charters are to deliver new capabilities.	Both employees and leaders are results oriented, and they are rewarded for being part of new outcomes. Change is encouraged if it supports our company mission. A recent disruptive change met its objectives, and the people associated with that change were recognized.	
			Total Score	

What Your Score Means

A score of 3 or lower on a question means that your company has some shoring up to do before significant transformation can occur. Or that the culture simply won't support any type of major disruption. Or that the perception of pain isn't high enough to incent change. In this case—as counterintuitive as it seems—it might be better to wait for something to break. Ironically, lower scores are an indicator that change is urgent, but the changes necessary in these scenarios won't be the kind that will help reinvent IT. That work must be more foundational.

Unless you're the CEO, banging the drum for major change can backfire, causing you to be labeled as difficult. A rabble-rouser. Not a team player. For you, waiting for something big to happen is its own act of discipline. More than three questions scoring 3 or lower suggests that the company culture is so entrenched that many of the changes you've considered introducing simply won't stick.

Conversely, a score of 7 or above suggests that it's time to move to the next stage by driving process and organizational improvements, or by introducing wholesale structural change:

- **A score of 8 to 24.** A total score of 24 or lower is good news and bad news. On the one hand, your company falls into the category of having the most opportunity for change. However, you also have the most work to do. Truth is, in these environments the best way to drive change—and I say this with my best wishes—is for something bad to happen. Your company's leaders need to wake up and smell the competition. They're likely underestimating the severity of the company's problems. Or they're whistling in the dark. Smart leaders actually get ahead of these problems, using them as a pretext for significant change. Delta Airlines famously used the looming Y2K threat to overhaul its flight operations and tracking system. The Delta Nervous System cost the airline $1.5 billion, but it offered a consistent view of flight arrival and departure times resulting in customer satisfaction and operational efficiencies that took competitors years to match. The 9/11 tragedy, the financial crisis of 2008 and ensuing credit crunch, and Sarbanes-Oxley and other regulatory edicts have also invited broadscale changes. The resulting solutions ended up transcending their immediate impact. Find a pretext for change and capitalize on it.

- **A score of 25 to 48.** This suggests that there are pockets of opportunity for some heavy-duty transformation. You probably know what they are. A new chief data officer has been hired, and she is in the process of prioritizing data according to its ability to drive strategic programs. The CEO has just funded a voice of the customer initiative, and he has appointed himself the executive sponsor. The company has just bought a competitor and integrating systems, and data is Priority Number 1. Why not use one of those activities as the symbolic testing ground for some bold new behaviors?

- **A score of 49 to 72.** If you ended up scoring 49 or higher, your company welcomes change as long as it is deemed worthy of the necessary impacts. That doesn't mean that you're off the hook. Even companies whose leaders encourage change could do a better job rewarding change agents, formalizing innovation processes, and celebrating not only fresh ideas but also fast failures. Look for ways to help refine methods for introducing change, and make sure those changes are not limited to technology.

NOTE TO THE CEO

No pressure, but your company's innovation agenda is up to you. Technology leaders can do only so much to instill innovation as a priority. According to one study, 72 percent of CIOs agree that their companies spend too little time innovating, and CIOs continue to struggle with shifting priorities and operational focus.[1]

Maybe you're marginalizing your IT leaders to be super-technologists rather than business leaders. Maybe you're fanning the flames of interdepartmental strife that spark rogue IT. Maybe your version of fostering internal competition is just another way of explaining overinvestment.

Or maybe you've seen the light and you have changed your leadership lexicon to include conversations about innovation, social media, analytics, big data, mobility, the cloud, and digital technologies that can set your company apart. Maybe you're supporting IT in leading the charge.

Of course, introducing innovation will never be friction free. But you can still support good ideas, empower your executives, fund new technologies, and support fresh ways of hiring—and keeping—smart, delivery-focused employees. (There are some tips for the latter in the next chapter.) You can refresh success measures and rally behind new innovation initiatives. You can spend your time on activities that enable the company's future. You can build organizational trust and reshape priorities.

After all, if not you, who?

. . . .

part 3

Leadership in the New IT

Fighting the Talent Wars

If you think I'll sit around as the world goes by,
You're thinkin' like a fool 'cause it's a case of do or die.
Out there is a fortune waiting to be had
You think I'll let it go you're mad
You've got another thing comin'.

—Judas Priest, "You've Got Another Thing Comin'" (1982)

ere's what we know: there's a growing shortage of tech talent. Executives routinely report that finding and keeping skilled workers is their biggest challenge. The demand for programmers, data scientists, statisticians, database administrators, system architects, business analysts, and application experts has begun outstripping supply. In the meantime, companies are trying to shore up their talent pools by investing in science, technology, engineering, and mathematics (STEM) programs, breathing new life into staff development and training, instituting programs to attract a more diverse workforce, and cultivating employee-friendly workplaces.

But the flurry to foster a freewheeling, get-naked-and-party culture in order to lure younger technical staff only goes so far. Free sushi, Ultimate Frisbee, and nap pods won't keep tech-savvy millennials, whose average tenure at companies is a meager three years, from seeking greener pastures.

Furthermore, what works in Mountain View might not work in Moline. Companies are collections of heterogeneous physical and intangible assets. No two have the exact same core competencies, leadership characteristics, skills combinations, delivery capabilities, cultures, or strategic directions.

Deconstructing this even further, no two companies have the exact same priorities or project pipelines.

Thus, a single company will be best positioned to succeed if it can optimize its resources, including its human resources—not to out-cool its competitors or pump up its hiring statistics, but to fulfill its destiny. The companies I've worked with that most effectively attract and retain top talent, and the companies I've watched as that talent propels them forward, are those that match skills to projects.

Turn and Face the Strain

The problem is that despite the changing workforce demographics, most IT and business executives feel the pressure to work within their existing corporate cultures to hire and retain talent. The cultures of established companies are more than likely holdovers from decades of command-and-control management—they lack modern reward systems, there is poor performance transparency, and the leadership is unable to stay focused. "Other than that," one unhappy IT director told me ruefully, "it's a great place to work!"

Ironically many IT leaders are complicit in supporting the very corporate cultures that are sabotaging them. Think about your company for a minute. Could you affect change in the face of the following recruitment and retention trends?

- Studies have reported that 37 percent of technology professionals would take a 10 percent pay cut to work from home.

- The companies most successful at attracting and keeping skilled employees engage managers and senior leaders inside and outside the candidates' targeted departments in the interview cycle. HR's interviews are seen as merely one facet of the interviewing process.

- Google's famous "20 percent time" program encourages engineers to work on self-directed innovation projects, and it is being replicated at companies both inside and outside Silicon Valley.

- According to the U.S. Bureau of Labor Statistics, the size of the U.S. workforce is expected to decline. The so-called Silver Tsunami of aging baby boomers will make up a growing percentage of this workforce—by the year 2020, the median age of an American in the workforce will be 42.8 years.

- The gap between the necessary skills and the skills actually filled will continue to grow.

As a leader, would you institute a work-from-home policy? (According to Computerworld, talented tech staff are putting more stock in "softer" factors such as flexible work schedules and "job atmosphere."[1]) Do you have the organizational influence to enlist senior executives in vetting important job candidates? Do you have the clout to authorize innovation time? What about the ideal mix of workers from the millennial, Gen X, and baby boomer generations? In competing for these resources, what qualities set your company apart?

The problem most companies have is their lack of principles to guide them through talent management. Staffing is dependent on revenue forecasts and budgeting, not on the work pipeline. Overinvestment in effort is the order of the day, as senior leaders whisper to one another, "We have all these people. . . . What are they all *doing*?" Or worse, they begin to calculate profit per employee and are gobsmacked by the number.

Author and management professor Peter Cappelli wrote about this phenomenon in *Harvard Business Review*:

> Talent management is not an end in itself. It is not about developing employees or creating succession plans, nor is it about achieving specific turnover rates or any other tactical outcome. It exists to support the organization's overall objectives, which in business essentially amount to making money.[2]

Cappelli argues that talent management processes should resemble the manufacturing supply chain, allowing companies to anticipate shifts in demand and tune their talent needs accordingly. Executives need to shape corporate priorities effectively in order to drive accurate and effective human resources decisions, even if it means scaling back their business plans if the talent requirements are too lofty.

In my own experience, the companies that have consistently achieved strategic objectives are those with the highest staff retention rates, and for good reason: the connection between talent and performance is only as effective as corporate priorities are clear.

"We've invested heavily—if not always wisely—in talent."

© Patrick Hardin/The New Yorker Collection, www.CartoonStock.com.

Determining Priorities for Talent

Regardless of your targeted IT archetype, you need to begin hiring and managing staff differently. This change is largely the result of the inevitability of the cloud and the demands of digital, combined with more deliberate outsourcing decisions.

Typically, conversations around staff hiring and retention revolve around these central questions: "What do we want to own? What do we want to outsource? Where do we need some sort of hybrid model?"

Here we'll return to the three categories we introduced in Chapter 1: operation, connection, and innovation. Executives, business managers, and IT leaders should all be on the same page regarding the priorities placed on these three factors.

I used the questions in Table 9.1 in my consulting practice with many of my clients to gauge the business-IT divide. But the table also offers some effective questions to ask in order to determine consensus around skill priorities. I asked individual groups to answer the questions with a simple yes or no, noting variations in responses. (You can also use a scoring mechanism here to apply more rigor if you wish.)

TABLE 9.1: Determining Your Company's Commitment to Talent Management

	Operation	Connection	Innovation
Are the skills that support this category effective? Are they doing what they were designed to do?			
Do we consider our skills and capabilities to be modern?			
Do our skills and capabilities define IT's reputation?			
Do we evaluate new job candidates on their interests and proficiencies?			
Do executives emphasize organizational competencies in their internal and external communications?			
Are there reward systems in place that drive delivery and quality?			
Are employee specialists across departments involved in the definition and evolution of this category?			
Are there discrete training investments dedicated to this category?			
Is there time set aside for staff members to share and learn from one another?			
Have outside experts been retained to help the company improve?			

I would then share the answers in a group setting with everyone who took the test, asking them to explain their perceptions and highlighting areas where the company needed to pay more attention or invest more deliberately.

Items that received a unanimous "No" were prioritized for further exploration and possible investment.

Typically your company's IT archetype—refer back to Chapter 2 for a discussion of the six IT archetypes—will determine its staffing mix. For instance, in the Brokering model, there will be a heavier emphasis on collaboration competencies and networks, and less emphasis on platforms because the company's enterprise systems are likely to be outsourced or deployed in the cloud.

As you consider talent acquisition and retention, you can gauge what's important in the context of your IT archetype. This may mean managing talent around your desired, rather than your current, archetype. Figure 9.1 illustrates the importance of each change area relative to each IT archetype.

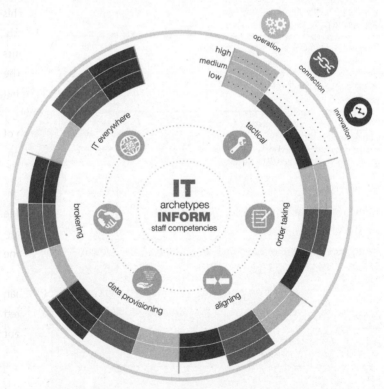

Figure 9.1 **Mapping Talent to Your IT Archetype**

Here we've defined the organizational competencies relative to each IT archetype. This conversation can help explain to executives why IT is where it is—and where it needs to be. But when it comes to deciding whom to hire and how to prioritize your staffing and retention decisions, we need to return to corporate strategy.

but also Mark's Work Wearhouse, FGL—Canada's largest sporting goods retailer—and Partsource, an auto parts retailer. In addition to its established brick-and-mortar presence, Canadian Tire has a robust and growing online channel. And its Thursday advertising circular is a beloved part of Canadian folklore, having arguably become the company's most successful marketing channel to date.

Roman considers himself a change agent at Canadian Tire. But with a brand that is a revered part of Canada's commercial history, admirable year-over-year revenue growth, and a stock price that analysts trumpet as "outperforming," what's to change?

Understatement isn't one of Roman's strengths. "This is all-out digital warfare," he says.

Roman sees the future of retail, indeed the future of IT, as digital, proclaiming that those companies—never mind how large or established—that meet the digital demand first are the ones that will win. He names several large vendors, all pervasive in the retail sector, pronouncing them "obsolete."

"Speaking of obsolete," he continues, "retailing is obsolete!" He pauses for a minute so we can experience the full irony of that statement leaving the lips of a top retailing executive. "It will all be replaced by e-tailing! And by 'e-tailing,' I mean *extreme retailing.* So if you're doing a paper flyer, it had better be the BEST paper flyer—but it must also be digitally correct. Over time, all paper, all mailings will disappear. So the question isn't, 'How good is your flyer?' It's 'How good is your *e-flyer?*'"

E-flyer?

"It's now all about *digital asset management* in IT," Roman explains, writing down the letters on his glass-topped conference table to underscore his point. (In case you wondered about that acronym, it's DAM-IT.)

Three Ps and a W

So how will this vision of extreme retailing at Canadian Tire be realized? Roman embraces a philosophy he calls "Three Ps and a W." What are the three Ps?

1. The first P poses the question, "What's possible?" Roman advocates thinking big and outside the box.

2. The second P asks, "What's probable?" Here you need to think realistically about what the company can absorb. But, Roman cautions, your company can always surprise you. ("The probability of Canadian Tire hiring an old general to run IT was really pretty slim. When Stephen Wetmore [the CEO of Canadian Tire] called me for this job, it was the furthest thing from my mind.")

3. The third P asks, "What's preferred?" Here Roman counsels that the culture needs to be amenable to the proposed change or improvement. Options must be weighed, and viability needs to be considered.

What's the W? The "wildcard," of course. Roman holds up his smartphone. "This," he says, "is the wildcard. I believe fundamentally that the future is 'automatically mobile.' Mobile is everywhere. Canadian Tire is an old culture that so fundamentally believes in the automobile. So we're calling it 'auto-mobile.'"

Roman is driving Canadian Tire into early adopter territory. He extolls the benefits of the cloud, content management, and social commerce. His IT staff includes far-flung development centers in Eastern Europe and India, with developers both ideating and implementing. New projects include an innovative "search-and-shop function," a new website featuring "full flyer integration," and a proprietary "extreme commerce" initiative that features "buy online, pick up in store" (BOPS) capabilities. "We were the first one to deploy and use this technology," Roman says.

Eugene Roman, Change Agent

For all his technophilia, Roman gets energized—yes, even more so— when I bring up the topic of instilling change in a culture as established as Canadian Tire.

(continues)

"Any type of change agency is *cultural* change," he insists. "I learned this at Nortel. They called us 'Global Warriors.' They assessed us for our individual competencies. Mine is situational awareness. They had these psychologists assessing us. They asked me for 300 ways to use a belt on a desert island. I came up with 320 ways. No one else got past 150."

Seriously?

But that's the point. Roman is serious. With the full backing of Canadian Tire's leadership team, he is pursuing not only new ways of working but also new ways of thinking. About smart systems. About how humans work with machines. About what he calls "netputing"—that is, interconnecting systems in real time.

"I gave everyone on my leadership team a compass," he says. "It's because we're going in a new direction. I tell my people, *Do. Not. Get. Lost.* People wore these compasses around their necks. Soon, they were being stopped in the hallways. Everyone wanted to know where the compasses came from.

"Soon after that, I gave all my direct reports whistles. You might get a call to play. Then I gave everyone a lock because security is important here. Some people got laser pointers to signify laser precision.

"The point is that the ability to change must be manifest and visible. Everyone initially laughed at these props. But everyone wanted them."

Business Strategy Driving IT Talent Management

In Chapter 4, we discussed distilling discrete initiatives from larger corporate strategy, and in Chapter 5 we discussed prioritizing those initiatives. The companies I've worked with that have hired and kept the most effective staff (and this applies to both line-of-business and technology roles) are those that link their skills back to strategy.

Once strategic initiatives are established and prioritized, they can be used to drive the demand and prioritization of which resources to hire and when to hire them, or whether to outsource the work.

The advantage of considering your IT portfolio for hiring decisions is that it's simultaneously strategic and tactical: strategic in the sense that it's informed by corporate priorities and can incorporate weightings to rigorously rank the importance of individual initiatives; but tactical in the sense that each initiative becomes a project, with its own success metrics, release schedule, delivery timeline, technologies, and, yes, talent.

Consider the strategy map in Figure 9.2. It takes the digital roadmap shown in Figure 7.2 one step further, illustrating how the company deconstructed its digital strategy from objectives to projects all the way down to discrete skill sets.

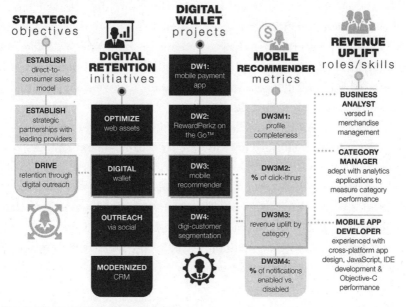

Figure 9.2 **Strategy-to-Skills Mapping**

Figure 9.2 shows how the strategies were deconstructed into initiatives, which were programs that encapsulated individual projects, each measured distinctly. The question, "What skills do we need to deliver this project in a way that fulfills the stated metrics?" ended up informing how the company would determine the skills for the project in question. This provided a structure that managers could use to be more thoughtful about whether internal people were qualified to fill the role or whether an external search should be launched.

The map in Figure 9.2 was built through an interactive exercise between managers and other members of the project team, who worked together to ensure that the right skills were applied to the job at hand. Creating such a collaboration not only had the "soft" benefit of letting people feel like they were part of the talent management process but it also ensured that all bases were covered when it came to newer or more innovative projects. Ultimately the map ensured that the strategic objective would be realized through execution.

"I had to consider the company's five-year strategy," says Peter Mueller of biotech giant Lonza. "This helped me establish my group's priorities. It also informed my hiring strategy: the first person I hired was a systems architect, someone who would be responsible for going after the data in our systems, which were both global and regional. Then I hired a data architect to help publish the data. Then it became more practical to deploy our reports. The point is that I had to understand the business needs before I could staff it in an intelligent way. Not to state the obvious, but it's really the only way to get real work done."

The truth—and many IT leaders find this a bitter pill to swallow—is that teams should be formed only after IT service lines (see Chapter 6) and individual skill sets have been identified.

For instance, managers often adopt vague-yet-catchy team names in the hopes of garnering some coveted buzz. One manager decided that the internal brand of the RapidFire Growth Team or the Strategic SWAT Scrum would grab people's attention. He didn't predict that after the initial exuberance of the splashy team name wore off, his colleagues would still be flummoxed about the team's charter.

By contrast, Figure 9.2 suggests that the business analyst and category manager might be in the category management business unit, while the mobile app developer belongs in the local applications service line. Once the work and success metrics are defined, you're free to earmark your mobile app experts the "Mobile Tactics Squad"—a.k.a. "MTASq," pronounced "M-Task." (True story.)

What about the unpredictable projects? The inevitable one-offs that may be unforeseen, yet considered critical by management or business partners? I've watched as managers realize that they must finally get serious about the IT modernization efforts, outsourcing, and new procurement processes. Regardless of your IT archetype, your company will need to scale up its workforce not only to deliver on strategic projects but also to mobilize round just-in-time business needs.

The structure shown in Figure 9.2 can be extended to the actual staffing process. For instance, Figure 9.3 shows the project manager's notes on how he is planning to source each role on the Revenue Uplift project release.

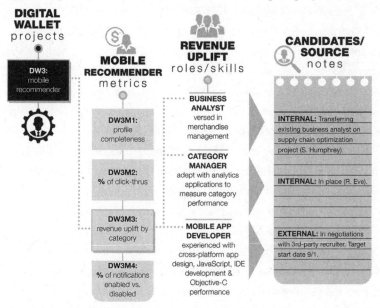

Figure 9.3   **Staff Assignment Status by Project**

Project management tools can track candidate interviews, qualifications, rankings, and hiring status at the strategy, initiative, project, or release level. The point is that even explicit staffing processes and decisions can be mapped to corporate strategies, allowing hiring managers to forecast and prioritize staffing according to the importance and time frames of various strategic initiatives.

Of course, the mapping approach above can backfire if your company moves too slowly or if strategy is a loose collection of high-profile, independent tasks rather than a closer coupling of efforts linked together via a common mission. Which is why companies are slow to move away from their traditional staffing and retention behaviors.

How IT Change Agents Manage Talent Now

Eugene Roman of Canadian Tire gets personally involved in hiring at all levels of his organization. He regularly hosts mentoring sessions at local universities, and he has been known to offer candidates jobs on the spot.

"I'm acquisitive," he says, "and I'm looking for Siberians." At first, I'm thinking he wants people accustomed to remote icy tundra, but after several references to the word, I realize that Roman is coining the term for the new denizens of cyberspace: *Cyberians.*

"My newest employee has a master's degree in health informatics," he says, then promptly whips out his iPad to show me a picture of a fresh-faced young woman who exudes the confidence of being both young and gadget savvy. "She tracked me down, and after I talked to her, I realized that she possessed a degree of situational awareness like no one else I've seen at her age. I talked to her for two hours; then I hired her."

Roman isn't letting the traditions of his almost century-old company deter him from new thinking. "Simply put, I'm looking for geniuses. I want to see the coup d'oeil. That twinkle in the eye."

How will he use this young woman's genius? What will he do with her?

"It's gonna be magic," he replies.

And this is the great lesson of hiring in the twenty-first century: if we always hire as we have been, we'll end up in the same place. But for each executive I spoke to with fresh pitches and new ways to meet and engage job candidates, I found many more concerned with keeping the good people they already had. After all, the lure of startups, with their cappuccino bars and same-day dry cleaning service, is hard to ignore.

Some visionary executives are realizing that keeping talented contributors means offering them the skills and work environments they would get working for a flashier startup, without having the relocation, cost-of-living, and family disruption impacts of moving to Silicon Valley.

"We're in the midst of developing a world-class training program," says Comerica's Paul Obermeyer. "This will happen with both new and existing staff. Part of this means moving away from legacy technologies based on 20-, 30-, or 40-year-old development platforms and focusing on newer technologies that make us a more attractive place to work, with solutions that are relevant to today's market.

"On the retention side, we're also working on workplace design, focusing on more temporary and collaborative spaces where you can boot up your PC from wherever you're sitting. A physical environment that's bright and fun helps make Comerica an employer of choice."

Many executives at larger companies are resolved to make their workplaces more attractive, often citing family-friendly work policies and emphasizing a quality-of-life focus to attract and keep top talent.

"Principal Financial Group is pretty diverse," explains Kevin Farley, one of the company's divisional chief financial officers. "It's not like the executives are all cut from the same cloth. There's a standard of living and a community-focused culture that's very inclusive. Sure, compensation plays a role. But I feel like Principal supports balance. And that's something that comes through in our recruiting and hiring."

In the effort—okay, the war—to attract and retain top talent, the qualities that companies relied on in the past are being replaced by a new crop of trends that are redefining or, in some cases, defining success.

Local to Global

A 2012 McKinsey study found that 30 percent of U.S. companies admitted to have failed to exploit their international business interests due to a lack of internationally competent personnel. And as advanced as they are technologically, the United States and Japan are the main culprits when it comes to the failure to groom leaders who can manage divisions that might cross regions or continents. It's an unfortunate state of affairs, since even lower-level IT jobs can be enriched by staff with "transcultural" employees who can function effectively as they serve business units that cross nationalities and cultures. The challenges that multinational companies face include not only acquiring and keeping skilled IT resources, but also ensuring global continuity in their hiring, management, and reward policies.

As the dozens of leaders interviewed for this book confirmed, finding good technical talent has become a competitive sport. And as Western education institutions fail to produce qualified STEM skills, the jobs will increasingly be filled by people from around the globe. While this diversity isn't necessarily bad for business, it's expensive to sustain. And for the economies of western nations watching their GDPs plummet, it's simply dangerous.

Same to Different

Admonishments to build a more diverse workforce often belie the behaviors of hiring managers who, studies show, hire people like themselves. Research has proven that diverse teams make better decisions, are more productive, and are more effective at driving change.

In their book *Gender Intelligence*, authors Barbara Annis and Keith Merron advocate a "strength through differences" model, arguing that businesses that ignore diversity, those that fail to understand and appreciate what different genders bring to the table, will find themselves competitively inferior to companies that prioritize it. Yet a 2014 report by the Center for Talent Innovation found that of women working in high tech, 45 percent were more likely than their male peers to leave the industry within a year.

So much for leaning in.

As leaders begin considering different genders, races, cultures, and belief systems, they expose both their direct teams and their companies to broader experiences, fresher ideas, and even newer technologies. What previously would have been seen as incompatibilities will actually result in more creative teams, driving a higher degree of innovation.

Some would argue that demographic shifts make workplace diversity inevitable. But why wait?

Side note: Embracing diverse work cultures might be one area where established companies have the upper hand over newer startups. Mature HR departments and policies can be advantageous when it comes to embracing diversity and treating people fairly.

According to the *New York Times*, 70 percent of employees at Apple, Google, and Twitter are male.[3] "Tech luminaries make sexist comments so often that it has ceased to be news when they do," wrote Farhad Manjoo in the *New York Times* piece. As recent discrimination allegations at Silicon Valley companies including GitHub, Mozilla, Tinder, and Yahoo have shown, being born digital is no defense against bad behavior.

Thinking to Execution

Every company needs people who can think. But that's increasingly foundational in today's competitive environment, where execution capabilities are at a premium. Traditionally, larger companies promote putative fast-trackers every two years, often before they've had a chance to see their work come to fruition. Now in management positions, these same leaders promote people like themselves who may fit their image of what a leader looks like but who nevertheless haven't delivered anything.

Definitions of success are changing. Promotion no longer hinges on intellectual prowess, how closely you resemble your boss, the number of weekends you work, or whether higher-ups consider you management material. Companies are increasingly measuring people by the value they create.

As we outlined in Chapter 5, IT portfolio management is an effective means of delineating and prioritizing projects. When a new project is approved, a team is assembled to deliver it. When the project has been completed, the team is disbanded and assigned to new projects. The diverse skill sets of the team members ensures that this practice is effective and sustainable (see "Depth to Reach" below). This method of allocating resources not only maximizes staff engagement and utilization but it also keeps the company agile.

An IT portfolio driven by strategy ensures that the connection between performance and reward is all about contribution to a company's future direction and priorities. Strategy provides the focus. That focus guides execution.

Depth to Reach

If senior managers are indeed letting their corporate futures lead them, they need to hire employees who are not only diverse but also multitalented and flexible. This means that employees no longer do the same work day after day, defining themselves narrowly based on the job they were hired to do. HR departments are increasingly searching for the "T-shaped employee"—grounded in expertise but broad in perspective—in order to satisfy this need.

The popular buzzword *intrapreneurial* has as much to do with redeploying employees to various meaningful projects, each serving a common purpose, as it does about creative funding schemes and mold-breaking ideation. These days, an employee's skill set should scale beyond a central work effort or team. Her skill set should apply to important projects, here and there, present and future.

"We're a nonprofit organization," says Larry Bonfante, CIO of the United States Tennis Association (USTA) based in White Plains, New York, and best known for running the U.S. Open. "I can throw a rock from my office and hit PepsiCo, ITT, and Avon."

So how does USTA keep good people? "Our people don't come here for the money," he says. "Most of them could get a job anywhere. But there's a camaraderie, an esprit de corps here. We let people take risks. And we let them learn things that might be outside their core skill sets. We have a very, very low attrition rate here—I've lost two key people in the last 10 years."

The winner of a CIO 100 award, Bonfante is circumspect about his contribution to the talent culture at USTA. "When people Google us, they see we've been recognized as leaders, and they view us as an attractive employer. This isn't just my success—it's the organization's."

Bureaucracy to Holocracy

Many executives feel the change coming: the days of the top-down, operational, internally focused IT model are coming to an end. The term *holocracy* refers to work that is purpose driven and delivery focused, with minimized chain-of-command and hierarchical structures.

As younger workers expect to migrate laterally both within and outside their companies, organizational influence often cedes to the ability of individuals or small groups to determine their own direction. They are guided by the overall mission of the company, not by middle managers monitoring staff utilization against project codes, and they collaborate via a lean and flexible network of peers.

In 2014, Zappos CEO Tony Hsieh, the poster child of the new holocracy, announced his plans to eliminate job titles and managers, making Zappos business operations more "self-governing." Hsieh promised to work toward an organization that was at once flatter and more collaborative.

Holocracy doesn't mean lack of authority. Instead, it relies on a pervasive understanding of the company's or team's overarching objectives, and it rewards people for delivering against those objectives. Mike Curtis, VP of engineering at Airbnb, explained it this way: "Fundamentally, we believe that engineers having more control over what they work on is more motivating and leads to higher-quality results."[4]

IQ to EQ to SI

Everyone wants to hire smart people. Academics John Mayer and Peter Salovey were the first to coin the term "emotional intelligence" to indicate not only newly identified qualities for professional success but also a general excellence in life. Inspired by Mayer and Salovey, Daniel Goleman wrote the book *Emotional Intelligence: Why It Can Matter More Than IQ*, which became a fixture on management reading lists. Since then, tools to measure emotional intelligence have proliferated, and companies like Johnson & Johnson have found that candidates with a higher emotional intelligence have more leadership potential than their high-IQ peers.

Another emerging trend gaining ground is the principle of *spiritual intelligence*. At first glance, this has little to do with hiring talent, but a growing number of managers would argue that in today's economic and political climate, spiritual intelligence has everything to do with hiring—or at least it should. In his 2014 book *Conscious Capitalism*, Whole Foods founder John Mackey argues that business leaders should be mindful of their purpose and "overall impact on the world," extending an ethics and spiritual-based business philosophy to shareholders, customers, and employees.

"Conscious capitalism," Mackey explains, "requires that good deeds also advance the company's core purpose and create value for the whole system."[5]

The Leader's Hiring Cheat Sheet

If you're a leader on either the IT or the business side, it's likely you've made your share of hiring mistakes. It's also likely that you've made some slam-dunk hires—people you're proud of, whom you've nurtured or even groomed to take on more responsibility. All in all, most of the executives I talk to admit that if they had to do it over again, they would have been much more selective in their hiring decisions.

A lot of us won't admit that we hire people because we like them. We see their untapped potential. They're hungry. At best, we're confident enough in our leadership skills that we think we can train the candidate in the job, rounding out her sunny disposition and earnestly presented work samples with some well-honed skills. At worst, we hire for personality and looks and hope for the best.

Of course, this isn't fair to our current staff, who must often spend their time training, mentoring, or covering for the new hire. And it's not fair to our company, whose investment in recruiting, onboarding, salaries, benefit plans, training, equipment, overtime, and personal time off is substantial. When the wrong hire leaves the company—or worse, job shops within the company, never landing in one place long enough to create value—the company's investment is lost. One study estimated that the time it took for a company to recoup the hiring cost of a midlevel manager was 6.2 months.[6]

The reality is that executives who hire well use a more complex blend of intuition and hard evaluation metrics, plus a keen awareness of their current team's strengths and weaknesses, all within the context of their company's short- and long-term objectives. Depending on the need, the priorities of these items will differ, and they will change over time. Figure 9.4 shows the areas that executives who hire well take most seriously.

Savvy managers are, of course, applying fresh interview techniques along with this rigor. Some audition applicants, asking them to take a crack at existing technical or business problems. Others conduct probing assessments, forsaking casual Q&A in favor of *behavior event interviews* in which candidates are asked to tell stories of experiences they faced in real life similar to ones they'll face on the job. Trite questions about where the candidate wants to be in five years are replaced by dialogues about delivery capabilities, existing skill sets, and learning styles. Indeed, changing entrenched interview habits may be the most intense stretch assignment many executives have had in a long, long time.

The fact is that the best job candidates, the ones with specialized skill sets who will thrive in the knowledge-based economy, have choices. They know their worth, they're well connected, and they have a low tolerance for boredom. These are the candidates you need to work the hardest to hire. They're worth your time.

Chinese philosopher Confucius said, "Choose a job you love and you will never have to work a day in your life." Irrespective of age, race, or gender, everyone wants meaningful work that fulfills them. Hire the people whose goals meet yours and who can deliver what your strategy demands. They'll be an asset to your company—and to you.

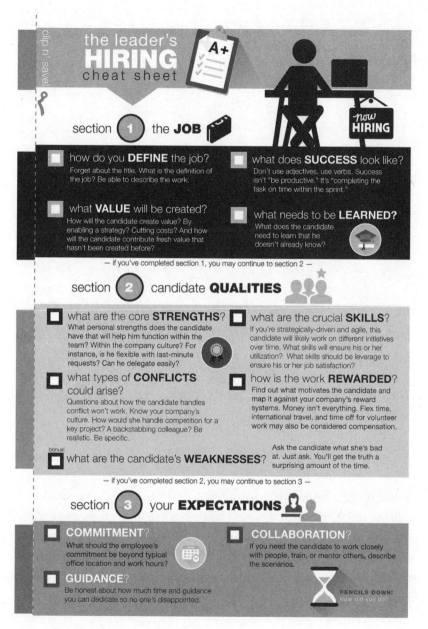

Figure 9.4 **The Leader's Hiring Cheat Sheet**

CHAPTER SUMMARY

Key Takeaways

- Hiring and retention philosophies are changing as companies compete for top talent. But simply adding workplace perks and paying lip service to diversity belie the real changes needed in hiring behaviors.

- Like most assets, employees should be hired and retained based on their ability to help achieve business goals. Simply hiring a bunch of millennials, PhDs, or data scientists won't give your company a leg up. Aligning talent to your business priorities will.

- Just as hiring philosophies are changing, so are hiring priorities. Managers who hire the most capable people and succeed in keeping them use some type of abbreviated formula or cheat sheet to assess whether the job candidates will add value and balance the existing team.

- Optimize your talent pool. The phrase "Hire slow and fire fast" has never been more important.

Note to the CEO

A lot has been written on how to hire, retain, and reward talent. But the volumes explaining why senior executives should keep talent management at the top of their priority lists are much slimmer. CEOs emphasize the importance of people as pillars of corporate success and competitive advantage, while at the same time, they pull funding from HR and slash headcount from critical projects in an effort to reduce costs. And more often than not, IT is a victim of these cuts.

CEOs distracted away from talent management will wind up supporting what becomes little more than HR bureaucracy. These same CEOs will watch their growth wane and their corporate reputation suffer. Good people aren't just your vehicles for profitability—they're your brand ambassadors.

It's a continuous struggle for executives: finding ways to close the distance between themselves and the people they lead. Leaders who are justifiably more intimate with company direction and investment potential need to get out in front of staff hiring, management, and retention. This is not just about having enough people to keep the plates spinning. It's about your company's capacity to deliver products and services.

For example, a U.K. consulting firm was awarded a significant outsourcing contract with a bank that would mean $100 million over three years. The firm's partners discovered that the principals they had in mind to oversee this highly profitable effort were already assigned to multiple projects. The company had failed to hire proactively and to groom other consultants to assume high-priority client work.

Perhaps the best way to close this chapter is with a quote from Mike Rowe, host of the Discovery Channel show *Dirty Jobs*. "The single biggest challenge facing everybody I met," Rowe said of his time hosting the show, "was finding people who were willing to retool, retrain, learn a truly useful skill. And then work their butt off."[7]

Getting and Keeping a Seat at the Table

If I leave here tomorrow
Would you still remember me?

—Lynyrd Skynrd, "Freebird" (1973)

On a recent episode of *The Daily Show*, host Jon Stewart interviewed author Peter Schuck about his new book, *Why Government Fails So Often*. Stewart asked Schuck why conversations about government are so often focused on conflicts within institutions rather than on the business of governing.

Good natured and earnest, Schuck explained that government institutions simply weren't, as a practice, measured for delivering value. "People would rather talk about what they wish would happen, how the world should be rather than the way it actually is," he said, adding that oversight agencies performed periodic assessments "only when Congress asks them to do that. And they have a variety of methodologies—cost effectiveness being the major criterion."

Stewart prodded Schuck on why government leaders struggled to institute lasting improvements and get meaningful work done.

"People who support these programs can find lots of reasons to think they're succeeding," Schuck responded dryly.[1]

As I watched Schuck answer Stewart's questions, it struck me that he could have been talking about the way companies work (or don't) and he would have been just as accurate. He illustrated the transcendent point that the dysfunctions of any kind of institution can actually be traced back to the failures of its leaders.

We've all known people in leadership positions who thought they were succeeding when in fact they were failing. And we've worked with leaders who, full of hubris, hide behind the greater failings of the corporate bureaucracy as a pretext for their own shortcomings. These managers spurn measurement and obfuscate facts with finger-pointing, and they are intent at all costs to preserve the status quo. Say what you want about government institutions, their leaders are a lot like our leaders, and that's not a compliment.

Even well-meaning IT executives lurch toward leadership in fits and starts. They don't have a concise career plan. How could they amid constantly shifting corporate priorities, reactive regulatory maneuvering, all-hands emergencies, and feuding in the C suite?

This chapter isn't about how to be a better leader. There are plenty of books on that topic already. They offer advice for operational management, effective team building, developing listening skills, clear communications, and maintaining an active professional network. They're already on your bookshelf.

Instead, we'll talk about how technology managers can do a better job—indeed, how they can earn the right—to get their ideas heard, their problems fixed, and their visions taken seriously.

Enough About Governance Already!

"Show me a successful IT organization, and I'll show you good IT governance," said a principal consultant with a major systems integrator. Of course, he'd seen a lot of beleaguered IT departments, and most of them had no governance at all. But when I pressed him on how he had managed to convince leadership teams to support and fund IT governance, he couldn't call up a coherent argument. In fact, the examples he did share weren't really about IT governance at all. They were examples of effective prioritization processes, organizations structured around key competency areas, and efforts to modernize and innovate. (See Chapters 5, 6, and 7.)

The problem with IT governance is that C-level executives don't want to hear about IT governance. At many companies, governance has become a four-letter word. "Could we not call it 'governance'?" an applications development director politely asked as we set about establishing processes for managing IT assets and projects at the brokerage firm where he worked. "It makes us sound like a state-funded public agency." Until we came up with a euphemism, we temporarily called it "the G word."

The mistake leaders make is announcing a new governance effort, enlisting often-reluctant participants, and convening meetings in which decisions are made without rigor or context. Governance is oftentimes a Trojan horse, hiding other bigger problems like lack of accountability, inadequate strategic focus, or autonomous silos.

"We're going to cement financial metrics to apply to individual projects!" IT promises. Executives send delegates to meetings, then fewer people show up. IT governance becomes a big bouillabaisse of measurements, behaviors, organizational structures—if a competency center is going to be suggested, it will be suggested in a governance meeting—and processes.

This is heresy in many IT circles, but here goes: I'm a fan of bottom-up governance. The process used by CheckFree and described in Chapter 5 is an example of bottom-up governance, where IT projects were prioritized and rules of engagement emerged as a result of strategic objectives, past successes, established cultural norms, and specific delivery goals. It was a process that was applied to a specific area—enterprise business analytics—and then replicated across other IT efforts effectively. It had to be proven in order to get adopted.

One problem with most governance efforts is that leaders expect their constituents to adopt untried behaviors on faith. "We are launching formal IT governance," they announce. The implication is that resistance is futile. The other problem is that squishy philosophical pronouncements—my favorite: "Technology at the speed of business, at the enterprise, on the desktop, going mobile"—do nothing to quell suspicions that management can't get out of its own way and needs to use pithy missions and aphorisms to reassure employees that a plan is forthcoming. When the plan arrives, it's replete with upgrade targets and platform consolidation projects that never materialize.

Irrespective of its varied definitions, the end result of effective IT governance is a set of tactical checks and balances whose purpose is to ensure that IT isn't a barrier to progress as it has so often been labeled. But many of the problems that governance intends to address could be solved with better accountability and clearer executive communication. It's astonishing how many companies have these problems and use the G-word as a pretext for solving them.

Considering that 70 percent of change efforts fail, what makes change stick? Effective IT change is driven not from detached committees instituting cumbersome top-down processes but from addressing a real-life business problem and scaling outward. Consider the conundrum of a European IT executive, flummoxed at how to make his CEO's priority into a reality.

Earning C-Level Authority: A True Story

There's a lot of advice out there about raising awareness of IT's potential as a value creator. Certainly the executives profiled throughout this book personify the business transformation that took place in their companies courtesy of technology. Here's a story of one executive who, rather than bemoaning the fact that he was always behind the scenes, seized an opportunity.

Werner, a director of IT operations at a European insurance company, had just been asked by his boss, the CIO, to examine how the company could adopt a digital strategy. The CEO wondered why the company was being left behind in the realm of digital. He wanted a thoughtful analysis of digital opportunities that could help the company reach customers anywhere, through their preferred channels, with more relevant messaging, at any time.

The CEO had asked the CIO for a recommendation. Trouble was, embattled by lumbering claims systems, higher churn rates, and too much data, neither Werner nor his boss knew what to do next. Both understood that new technologies would be needed. Both understood that their analytics capabilities would play a role in the company's digital future. But how? And in what order?

When Werner approached me, I asked him to forget about digital for a minute and tell me what the insurer already had in the way of analytics to support customer outreach. That's when he pulled out the pyramid.

A little backstory here: Back in the era of ecommerce, circa 2000, I wrote a book called *e-Data*. The book used the dot-com frenzy to warn executives that their newly minted ecommerce platforms, CRM systems, and multi-channel outreach plans would only take them so far. The book warned that in order to truly harness the benefits of these and other Internet-enabled developments, executives needed to start taking business intelligence and data warehousing seriously. It offered a taxonomy in the form of a pyramid, shown in Figure 10.1, to explain the evolution of business analytics.

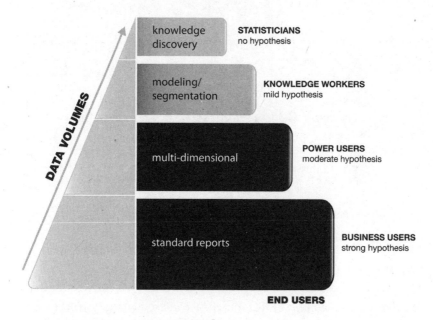

Figure 10.1 **The e-Data Analytics Pyramid**

Flash forward to today. Though the job roles may have changed somewhat—you could argue that the data scientist has taken over the top two tiers—the structure itself represents a solid taxonomy of analytics stages that are, in fact, easier to reach today than they were when I first designated them. The pyramid has been adapted by hundreds of consultants and vendors since that time, and despite the inevitable customizations, it still holds up.

The pyramid had made the rounds at Werner's company, and I was surprised to see it displayed in its original form on his tablet computer. He and the CIO had been using it to explain the evolution of their enterprise analytics program to the CEO. They had been advocating centralization of all the company's data silos. Werner figured that would be Step 1. Step 2, which would begin after the summer break, would be to get the senior leadership team in a room and define what the word *digital* meant.

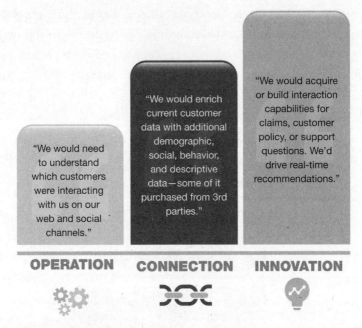

Figure 10.2 **Digital Capabilities by Category**

I realized I had to have the "don't go into the light" conversation with Werner. I explained to him that rather than consolidating systems and debating definitions, he needed to demarcate an initial action plan that would help the insurer deliver digital capabilities. We talked a bit more about integrating all the company's data silos and why that felt important. Werner mentioned the frustration businesspeople felt at having to go find data and the time it took to access that data from various systems. It was giving the CIO a black eye.

I then brought up the three factors mentioned in Chapter 1: operation, connection, and innovation. I asked what it would take in each of these three areas to enable digital marketing. What operational improvements would need to be made to support digital? The company had multiple systems duplicating different versions of customer data, and some of them were in dire need of modernization. What connections would need to be made? Multiple CRM systems in different departments often meant the insurer was *overcommunicating* with its customers, confusing them with different messages and offers. Likewise, data needed to be integrated from the growing list of new customer data sources.

What innovation opportunities would there be? IT had a laundry list of possible digital technologies, but they had created the list independent of any specific business need. Likewise, several people had come forward with new ideas based on mobile and GPS technologies, but there was no way to keep track.

It was a rudimentary conversation, but it got Werner thinking in terms of the three different areas and the role each played in a set of digital functions. He bucketed some nascent digital marketing capabilities as illustrated in Figure 10.2.

Werner, like most executives, was overwhelmed with systems, design, data, and organizational what-ifs that were impeding him from working toward the initial plan that the CEO had requested. While he realized that digital meant changing fundamental assumptions about business processes, he had no idea what that looked like. The prospect of architecting a major enterprise transformation had rendered him inert.

As we pored over the three categories and discussed the insurer's maturity with each one, Werner realized that being a digital business and being information driven went hand-in-hand. We decided that the operation,

STEP 3
determine digital business processes and deploy them.

STEP 2
integrate data and platforms to inform systems of reference for digital data.

STEP 1
determine initial digital customer communities.

OPERATION   CONNECTION   INNOVATION

Figure 10.3 **Steps to Digital Delivery**

connection, and innovation categories could, in fact, represent separate stages in digital delivery, as shown in Figure 10.3.

Steps 1 and 2 represented the steps the insurer would need to take before digital communications could be deployed and digital offers could be made. Werner began to see the role that analytics and data would have in contributing to the company's digital strategy. He intuitively knew that being information driven was no longer a luxury. The company couldn't decouple digital from the data analysis that would be necessary for its success. In looking at the three steps, we realized that each could be supported by increasingly sophisticated analytics as represented by the pyramid.

So we overlaid the pyramid with the digital delivery steps, as shown in Figure 10.4.

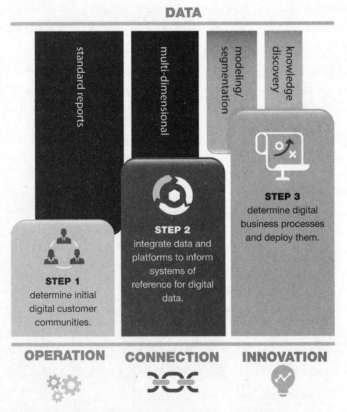

Figure 10.4 **Blending the Analytics Evolution with the Digital Plan**

Applying the pyramid to the three digital delivery stages provided Werner with a construct he could use to communicate more clearly to the

CEO. They could share it in order to level set, manage expectations with other leaders, and engage in initial planning discussions beyond just defining terminology and bemoaning their competitive handicaps. They could experiment, touching their customers through digital channels instead of trying to define digital absent any context.

Besides, Werner had already socialized the pyramid, so he didn't need to start from scratch. He would be communicating new concepts with an already-socialized paradigm. There would be context. He was visibly relieved.

"But this is a specific answer to a specific problem," you're thinking. Nevertheless, it represents a problem that IT executives face daily: cutting loose from thinking, talking, and meeting and moving toward scoping a unit of work that is the beginning of a larger set of capabilities. Blame the well-meaning manager's willingness to satisfy the organization's perceived need for consensus. Werner felt he needed to get everyone at the table to define *digital*. He intuitively knew that defining the term *digital* using group-think would be a protracted process, if not a doomed one.

Though this example is specific to one company's digital strategy, a similar process can be applied to just about any modernization initiative involving big data, mobile reporting, the cloud, social media, enterprise security planning, or other technology enhancements.

Our exercise released Werner from the systems thinking that preoccupies many IT professionals and becomes the implied excuse for inaction. "We can't [fill in the blank] until we fix/integrate/sunset/upgrade the [fill in the blank]." Boom! The deluge of budgeting, vendor engagements, requests for proposals, system decommissioning planning, and resource allocation begins. Again. In the meantime, someone starts a skunk works project and solves the problem (if only temporarily).

When I talked to Werner a few months later, he was rolling out the company's new digital initiative, code-named MobileFirst! His data scientists were using analytics to derive microsegments of customers likely to adopt mobile premium payments. Days before the CEO had promoted Werner to the role of chief digital officer. He knew the effect the promotion would have on his internal influence with senior leadership, not to mention on his external brand. He was already getting calls from recruiters.

As Walt Disney once said, "The way to get started is to quit talking and begin doing."

EXECUTIVE PROFILE

Dave Delafield, Swedish Medical Group

He has a professional pedigree that includes leadership roles at Microsoft and Deloitte, not to mention a handful of technology consulting stints, so you'd be forgiven if you didn't immediately pin Dave Delafield down as a chief financial officer in healthcare. But Delafield's experience has given him a business perspective that he might not have gotten any other way.

As CFO of Swedish Medical Group, which is part of a nonprofit health system based in Seattle with over 10,000 employees across a range of hospitals and clinics, Dave Delafield joined the company as a healthcare neophyte.

"When I got to Swedish, I didn't have a whole lot of healthcare background," he explains, adding, "and that's turned out to be a good thing. Healthcare companies are facing the same types of pressures as other industries. They're collecting more data about patients, locations, geography, and pricing. The challenge is the same challenge that other businesses face: How do you take all that data and prevent it from strangling your operations as you're continuing to make capital investments?"

Making Things Simpler

Every healthcare provider lays claim to some version of the promise to ensure quality, consistency, and continuity of care across its network, often adding a focus on patients and staff as a guiding principle. Facing disruptive competition and evolving government regulations, healthcare providers are under mounting financial and regulatory pressures. In an industry known for investing in packaged applications and funneling IT budgets into electronic medical records, the phrase "evidence-based medicine" has morphed from fuzzy vision to a complex delivery framework.

As Delafield began managing Swedish Medical Group's financials, he began noticing that the business challenges had little to do with technology.

"We literally had thousands of reports being used across the organization," he says. "We needed to break things down into logical areas: How do we want to view our physicians? What are the important areas in surgery? In patient care? For patient satisfaction?"

Working with physicians and administrative leaders to isolate the highest-profile opportunities, Delafield's team eventually distilled the thousands of reports across the Swedish system down to 37 or fewer common reports. The entire company has established a single direction around this consolidated reporting. And in the spirit of paring things down, Delafield and his leadership team delivered these results with a small team of specialists. (Six, to be exact.)

But what about adoption? Heck, what about politics?

"We didn't force anyone to do anything," Delafield explains. "The organization minimized current and any future investment in other analytics solutions. We've been able to sunset applications. And we did it with a relatively small team and a minimal investment in technology."

Delafield was never asked directly to cut costs or drive operational efficiencies. For him, and for Swedish, these are the happy benefits of simplification. "There will always be people who want more," he says. "But the idea is to shrink the footprint of the people and capital necessary to solve real business problems. That way, we're not only effective but we're also fast."

Fostering Relationships

Author and management guru Roger Martin coined the term "integrative thinkers" to describe leaders who seek out less obvious but nevertheless relevant issues during decision making and who perceive problems "as a whole, examining how the parts fit together, and how decisions affect one another."[2]

For Delafield, collaboration with other organizations was one of those relevant issues. Streamlining data-driven decision making at Swedish meant not only doing the missionary work of educating

(continues)

different lines of business about the value of rationalized enterprise reporting but also collaborating with executive leadership and peers around a common vision for success. Delafield works closely with both his chief medical information officer and CIO counterparts, both of whom were involved in helping approve his team's direction.

Delafield's team was equipped to execute on the vision. They maintain the company's data warehouse and business intelligence tool sets. They worked with physicians and administrative leaders to isolate the biggest opportunities and to deploy solutions quickly.

The team avoids functionality in a vacuum, instead ensuring that individual reports ultimately have a broader reach. "What's important is how this fits into the larger fabric at Swedish," Delafield explains. "So if one group wants to measure quality and outcomes in the cardiac area, we need to also deliver those capabilities to oncology. So it's not about building one-off reports. It's about working cross-functionally to support strategic levers."

And wherefore shadow IT? Delafield reiterates the specialized skills of his team. "Almost everyone who builds a report has been moved into my group, which has been a big benefit," he says. "We're using intakes from across the organization to support the requirements of the larger organization."

Delivering Value

Delafield's gamble ended up being about more than just consolidating enterprise reports. Simplifying the technology helped align the company around a common set of measures, with a focus on delivery.

"We could have solved the problem with 20 different technologies. It really didn't matter," he says. "The whole idea was to shrink the footprint of the necessary people and capital. This entire effort helped simplify and align the organization, which is the goal of any large company."

He pauses, then adds, "Improving a small number of levers can redirect an entire business."

Six Ways IT Leaders Sabotage Themselves

You're probably thinking that this chapter should have been subtitled the "Jill Spanks CIOs and Sends Them to Bed Without Their Suppers." But really my intention—as it has been with the rest of the book—is to promote the kind of thoughtful approaches that drive improvement in real life.

Except for this section. Now it's time to call out the behaviors of well-intentioned (mostly) IT executives who have jeopardized their reputations and those of their departments through bad behavior or poor choices. These aren't mere personality quirks. Everyone has those. These are behaviors that can ultimately ruin IT's reputation. Here are the biggest missteps they make.

Misstep 1. Overrelying on Consensus

During my consulting career, I worked with a Japanese car company that was renowned for its culture of consensus. In senior staff meetings, people were loathe to disagree with one another. Affirmative head nodding was practically a sport. "In meetings here," someone joked, "9 to 1 is a tie."

Of course, most of us would love to work at a company where everyone is unified around a common vision or idea. After all, it's so much easier to move forward when everyone agrees.

Work is just harder when opinions aren't unanimous. Rather than cultivate agreement or engage people in alternatives, executives will marginalize detractors or, worse, use them as excuses for not executing a key project or idea. Every leader has experienced the discomfort of calling someone aside, asking him to explain his problem, and either arguing with him or moving forward despite his misgivings.

Many executives use a disagreement as their tacit excuse for inertia. To quote corporate culture observer Seth Godin: "Nothing is what happens when everyone has to agree."

We can all point to a particular meeting or conference call where a good plan went bad. And most can name at least a few individuals who routinely raise doubts about new ideas or publicly call out colleagues' motives, without being accountable for their concerns or proposing alternatives.

IT leaders need to balance soliciting opinions with making decisions that will inevitably be unpopular with a portion of constituents. The leader's responsibility isn't only to reward good ideas, as we discussed in Chapter 7. It's to penalize passive-aggressive behavior and the all-too-familiar backdoor sabotage that can occur when someone has an agenda that's in jeopardy. Problem with the new mobile initiative? You're not on the project. Consistently late to the staff meeting? You're disinvited. Complaining about a colleague? Congratulations, you're her new mentor! (Microsoft founder Bill Gates famously put people who were against a particular idea in charge of executing it.)

Some CIOs can trace IT's poor reputation to the culture's mandate for consensus and to the resulting inertia when it's missing. But through a combination of greater decisiveness, tiebreaking metrics, and good old-fashioned coaching, they can reverse their overreliance on consensus and start getting things done again.

Misstep 2. Not Delegating Enough

Soccer legend Pelé once said, "I had to tell [my teammates]: 'Don't give every ball to me. We have to play as a team.'"

Sure, you got to where you are because you're good. But you're not that good. You can't possibly play every position on the field. That's what the talent on your team is for. A single, earnest brain puzzling its way out of its own organizational dramas is no match for a collection of smart minds working both separately and together toward action.

This is one of the more obvious items on the list. After all, how many leadership best practices don't mention delegation skills? However, many leaders don't recognize this as a failing. After all, our people are really busy. They probably can't even handle more work. But most of our team members can do more than what we're giving them, and the exceptional *want* to do more. Let's give them that opportunity. In so doing, we're setting a precedent for their colleagues to step up their games too.

Misstep 3. Abusing External Relationships

I remember the phone conversation very clearly. "This place is so messed up," said the vice president at a regional U.S. bank. "I can't get budget.

[nervous laugh] So I'm thinking we'll just do the initial discovery ourselves. [awkward silence] But I'll call you if I hear anything, okay?"

Huh?

The discussion occurred after my firm had flown to New York for a bidder's meeting, constructed a comprehensive custom proposal outlining our approach, conducted half a dozen "educational" webcasts at the client's request, and then traveled again for a "shortlister summit" to walk through our process for tackling the company's new marketing automation initiative. Now the vice president who had initially engaged us was coming clean: he didn't have the organizational authority to move forward with the project.

Sure, I should have heeded the warnings: Other VPs not acknowledging his comments in our preliminary meeting. Apparent confusion about their own internal decision processes. Urgency with no projected start dates. His asking a bit too earnestly for soft copies of our PowerPoint deck. It was clear this manager was using us, and perhaps several other firms, to learn enough to deliver the project himself.

My bad. But then—and this has happened to you—I ran into him a few years later at another company. He invited me to come in and pitch my services. I steered clear. Recently, I heard he was looking for work.

The lesson here is that he could have been honest with us, and we might have helped him, providing some initial coaching and some low-cost injections of expertise along the way. But, absent money and clout, the vice president misrepresented the opportunity and used the exhaust to try and save some cash. The hoped-for halo effect didn't happen. And he underestimated how many paths cross in the miniscule world that is information technology. People talk, and they have. About him. Unkindly.

Be honest with your business partners about your weaknesses, as well as your strengths. A little vulnerability goes a long way. And remember: the IT industry has a short attention span, but it has a very long memory.

Misstep 4. Overexplaining

In their exuberance about cool new technologies, many IT professionals overexplain. This is particularly true when it comes to how things work. You've heard it. It usually begins with something akin to, "First there was the world, and it was round . . ." Other people, perhaps unaccustomed to being understood, tend to talk too much about a particular point of detail, losing most of their audience in the process. (The scene in the movie *Airplane!* where the talkative guy's seatmate hangs himself comes to mind.)

Effective IT leaders understand that businesspeople don't care about the "how" as much as they do about the "what" and the "when." Whether or not IT decides to use MapReduce or Apache Spark to accelerate Hadoop processing is much less interesting to a marketing manager than when customers' social influence scores are appended to their profiles to drive campaign response uplift and—not to put too fine a point on it—drive profitability.

"We just need to stop talking about technology outside of a business context, period," says Rahoul Ghose, CIO and vice president of Lifetouch. "There's a tendency within our function to use technical knowledge as our primary show of competency. Coming from a CIO, this can project an image of grandstanding, without the necessary connection to solving actual business problems. Any time an IT leader veers in this direction, he or she loses goodwill."

The problem is that these types of conversations, like other behaviors, marginalize IT as focused on platforms and shiny toys, not on enabling business goals. The CIO of a consumer packaged goods company wrote his organization an all-hands memo giving everyone the leeway to abruptly leave any meeting if, after 10 minutes, there was no reference to a business initiative or to a customer. Every time an IT person gets excited about a new technical capability, celebrating its genius and marveling at its design without coupling it to a business need, an outside systems integrator gets a new pair of wings.

Ghose suggests that IT executives learn how to change the conversation. "I find the use of analogies to be very powerful in making the technology-to-business connection" he says. "Personally, I like the house building analogy since it's so close in context to IT. If a house is falling down, it may need to be rebuilt, not just remodeled. Systems likewise may need to be replaced, not just upgraded. Analogies make the complex simple, and one of the best things an IT executive can do on behalf of the business is to make the complex simple."

Misstep 5. Tinkering with Organizational Charts

I once asked my veterinarian whether it was okay to occasionally give my dog a bone to chew. In response, my vet explained the theory that when dogs chew bones (ideally real beef bones), their primitive dog brains kick in, and they feel as if they're doing their jobs. A dog chewing a bone, ostensibly fresh from the kill, is doing its dog thing. (Never mind that its pack leader bought the bone shrink-wrapped at Whole Foods.)

The same thing is true with managers and organizational charts. By moving tiny boxes and lines around a page, managers feel as if they're accomplishing something. Creating something. Driving change. Doing their leadership thing. They have something tangible to show for their efforts. Never mind that the org chart was redesigned based on personalities and cultural fit, and not clear business planning or strategic transparency. And never mind that it's the third one in as many years, igniting ownership battles that exacerbate politics and staff turnover.

I've referred to this phenomenon several times in the book because organizational redesign has become nothing short of a management panacea. Some leaders use organizational misalignment as an excuse for poor execution. Others use it to showcase their fearlessness, reassigning staff members into other roles, disrupting teams, and delaying delivery. Indeed frequent and cavalier organizational changes are the main culprit behind the legendary Peter Principle.

Of course, if you've been reading this book, you know that I come down squarely on the side of letting strategy drive organizational structure. For one, strategy sheds light on corporate priorities and investments that can, in turn, focus teams and individuals. Ideally, it informs how those people and teams are measured and rewarded. And a clear strategy will inform new structures that can set the company apart competitively. As W. Chan Kim and Renée Mauborgne, authors of *Blue Ocean Strategy*, have said, "The economic challenges organizations face today only underscore the importance of understanding how strategy can shape structure."[3]

The ripple effect of misdirected organizational change can cost a company millions of dollars and hundreds or even thousands of employees. At the end of the day, people don't quit their jobs; they quit their leadership. Or the lack of it.

Misstep 6. Waiting to Get Invited

You've met that virtuoso leader who does everything right. He communicates clearly, he inspires his team, and he's earned the trust of his business colleagues. He might have an MBA or other advanced degree. Neverthe-less, his talents belie his job title. You've watched as less talented leaders are routinely invited to board meetings, leadership offsites, and golf outings.

Why not him? The short answer is simple: it's because he hasn't asked to be included.

As simplistic as this sounds, many senior leadership teams are too busy with their workaday concerns and daily routines to notice that a talented manager might have earned the right to join their ranks. The talented leader may be seething, but he doesn't say he's angry. He might have some new ideas, but he might not be sharing them. He might have a job offer from a com-petitor that he's considering because he feels like a commodity. The offer is so good that when he leaves, half his team will follow him out the door.

The leader's superiors are, of course, responsible for checking in on him. Is he happy? Does he feel he can contribute? Is he driving value? Does he have more to offer? They may never know because they never asked. But neither did he.

Pull Up a Chair

If you want a seat at the table, first determine what that means to you. Does it mean a C-level title? Does it mean participating in senior leader-ship meetings? Contributing to corporate strategy? Shedding operational responsibilities to someone else? All of the above? Know three things:

1. **You need to show senior leadership what getting a seat at the ta-ble looks like.** Be specific about what you want—and what you don't want. For instance, one director of application development applied for the outgoing CIO's job by explaining that he would morph the role into the chief insight officer position, guarantee strategic alignment in 90 days, and launch a design and innovation lab to accelerate the firm's mobile delivery capabilities. In turn, he expected to attend the CEO's management meetings and annual planning sessions to stay on top of corporate direction. He got the job, and he was empowered in the bargain.

2. **You have to do something new.** You can't just fight for a bigger ti-tle and more organizational authority and do the same thing you're doing. That puts leaders in the position of justifying why they never

included you in the first place. Better to propose some new areas of responsibility and delivery. Yes, it's a negotiation, and you have to sweeten the deal.

3. **You need to continue to sharpen the sword.** You're still learning. Everyone is. Be honest about that, and be an example to colleagues both above and below you in the hierarchy. Learn new things and apply them.

James Dallas, CIO emeritus of Medtronic, who was profiled in Chapter 4, explains how he built learning into his job. "As a CIO, I knew I had to drive value. I had to think with both sides of my brain. So I went from being a project manager to a change manager. From being a speaker to a communicator. From managing risk to thinking critically. But these skills didn't come naturally. So I started learning.

"I took classes. Sure, I'd already taken classes on how to deliver a good PowerPoint presentation. But if people are watching your PowerPoint slides, they're probably not listening to you—I don't care how many spinning globes or dancing babies you have. I took media training. I even took an assessment, and then I took a class on how to become a better listener."

As Simon Sinek says in his inspiring TED Talk, "People don't buy what you do. They buy why you do it."[4] If the perception is that you're leading a technology organization because you used to write code and still dabble in the occasional Perl script, then by all means code away! But if the perception is that you're leading IT because you want to contribute to the company's direction in a more transcendent way, enhancing competitive advantage through automation and innovation, then say so. They'll not only invite you to the table but they'll also pull up a chair.

Getting to CEO

You asked for an hour to brief the board on your IT roadmap. They gave you 20 minutes. On Friday. After lunch. This means they don't see IT as strategic. Or, worse, they see you as the Techie Who Made Good.

You can count the number of CIOs who've scaled the invisible hurdle to CEO in the past year on one hand. You may have even memorized their names. While it might seem like an impossible feat, it's not. The problem is that the talents of IT leaders are as diverse as corporate cultures. IT executives don't come from predictable career backgrounds, and their career trajectories, strengths, and successes run the gamut.

But a handful of IT leaders have actually risen through the ranks to become CEOs. What does it take to make the leap?

"When the board promoted me from CIO to general manager of automobile insurance, it was because they knew that I understood how the company worked from the inside out," explains Dr. Rafael González Añorve, former CEO and general manager of Serfin Seguros, one of Mexico's largest insurers.

González Añorve says that being a CIO gave him unique insight into the "plumbing" of insurance companies, and that insight was the reason he was subsequently recruited to be CEO at Serfin. "As a CIO, I already had a detailed knowledge of how the company worked operationally," he says. "But being CIO also allowed me to work across business functions. That gave me the vocabulary to manage the strategic aspect of the company. It was the ideal training ground."

Under González Añorve's guidance, Serafin rose from the forty-second to one of the top 10 insurance companies in Mexico.

Besides a broad understanding of company operations, what other unique IT leadership traits up the odds for other offices in the C suite? Here are some other qualities of IT leaders who get rewarded and promoted into more senior leadership roles.

They Tell Their Stories

Every executive (heck, everybody) has a personal narrative about how she got where she is. And in everyone's story, there's some sort of tangent, a counterintuitive event that set her on a different path than the one she had envisioned.

I was an English lit major who began my undergraduate thesis on Milton's pastoral poems, went to work for a pioneering database vendor, subsequently cofounded a high tech consulting firm, lived for two years in Paris, got acquired, and became an executive at the world's largest privately held software company. (And that's the short version.) Sure, other people are more successful than I am. But not in exactly the same way.

What's your story? Michael Dell starting his company in a dorm room and Jeff Bezos writing a business plan on a road trip from New York to Seattle are compelling stories to be sure. But the less linear and predictable the story, the more captivating it is. People are actually interested in hearing where you've come from. Your personal narrative not only colors in some of your habits and strengths but it also humanizes you. Tell it. We're listening.

They Manage Down, Then Earn the Right to Communicate Up

We've all known an executive who manages up, spending more time with people senior to her than managing her team. She runs from one urgent meeting to the next one, name-dropping as she sucks down her macchiato, never really paying much attention to the people who work for her until there's a crisis or until someone quits and she's forced to do damage control.

Earning the right to communicate up doesn't mean spending all your time upstairs in the C suite. It means having the organizational authority because you manage down so effectively. Your staff and peers listen to you. Your team implemented a new business continuity plan, and so far it's been bulletproof. Your mobile strategy has resulted in a 34 percent uplift in field service productivity. And you just won an industry best-practices award for connecting your big data platform to your legacy data warehouse.

You've improved the company's bottom line and burnished its brand. You're not just invited to the table. Your executive superiors and the board of directors want to hear what you have to say. And like most effective executives, you credit your team every step of the way.

They Display Mastery of Non-IT Issues

Any IT leader can show an architecture diagram that illustrates how the company's information systems are interconnected. He can even explain how hard the company is working to modernize those systems. But show me an IT leader who can explain how those systems support upstream customer-facing business processes to personalize customer interactions, or how they integrate product sales and online surveys to optimize inventory forecasts that drive cost savings, and I'll show you an IT organization that's delivering business value.

Larry Bonfante, CIO at the USTA, executive coach, and author of *Lessons in IT Transformation*, cites three capabilities of IT leaders:

1. They deliver IT services and projects.

2. They understand how technology can drive business value.

3. They master competencies of human dynamics.

Bonfante explains that all CIOs typically master Number 1. He goes on to admit that most are also relatively competent at Number 2. But Number 3, he insists, remains a challenge for many career CIOs who continue to wonder why they don't have a seat at the executive table.

"CIOs need to look at things from a business perspective," he says. "If technology is an investment, how should we use it to differentiate ourselves in the marketplace? Granted, there's an operational component to IT, and it's not going away. But if that's *all* you do, then you'll never have the level of influence you could have."

They Have the Support of Their Peers

I'm always amazed at how few senior leaders are willing to upset their direct reports by choosing a leader from among them. Conflict averse, they don't want to suffer the backlash of indignant managers who thought the role should have been theirs. So the leaders hire from outside the company, or worse, they choose the least controversial, not the most talented, candidate.

CEO-class IT leaders get the support, albeit sometimes grudgingly, of their peers. Their business prowess and collaboration skills have been proven and are thus inarguable. When chosen, they return the favor, bringing the senior team members who produced under their purview along with them. Merit-based promotion has a ripple effect.

They Resist the Pull of the Past

You could accuse many executives of looking too far forward and not learning from their mistakes. But most IT leaders are guilty of what I call "stressing to their comfort zones." In other words, they fall back on what they're good at, despite the reality that it's not what the company needs. Put another way, if you always do what you've always done, you'll always get what you always got. (I'll credit Weight Watchers with that one.)

This tendency is the reason I've emphasized corporate strategy so heavily in this book. Strategy alignment invites, yea forces, IT executives to constantly scan the horizon for fresh business imperatives to support and new innovations to conceive.

Now go reread Chapter 4. I'll wait.

CHAPTER SUMMARY

Key Takeaways

- An institution's dysfunctions can usually be traced either directly or indirectly to the skills of its leaders.

- Many IT executives vainly use IT governance as a pretext for fixing problems that are in reality more fundamental. Governance is often a knee-jerk response to a set of root-cause problems that leaders in both IT and business units should be addressing more directly.

- Executives who reach the inner sanctum of senior leadership typically do so not by politicking or using PowerPoint presentations, but through some sort of breakthrough execution. Tying an overarching corporate strategy to a tactical plan with executable steps gets noticed. And why wouldn't it? So few executives can do it!

- IT leaders seeking to get ahead in their organizations are often their own worst enemies. Common behaviors such as overexplaining cryptic technical concepts or misrepresenting authority to outsiders only result in the leader being more marginalized by his or her constituents.

- Conversely, there are habits that IT leaders practice that not only get them noticed but also get them invited to participate in higher-level leadership activities. This type of invitation is the doorway into which smart executives enter, with existing skills, new ideas, and a greater sense of purpose.

Note to the CEO

Your CIO doesn't just want to be at the center of your business. She wants to be at the edges, advancing strategic efforts and guiding innovation. She can't do that if you and the board make it tough for her to transcend the workaday operational details of running computers.

So give her a shot. Put her in stretch situations in which she'll be responsible for setting direction at a more macro level, creating marketplaces that might upend existing hierarchies, building innovation cells that empower high-producing renegades, or establishing internal and external partnership networks that propel you toward your desired-state IT archetype. In short, let her lead.

In his book *Management Challenges for the 21st Century*, Peter Drucker wrote the following:

> One cannot manage change. One can only be ahead of it. . . . In a period of upheavals, such as the one we are living in, change is the norm. To be sure, it is painful and risky, and above all it requires a great deal of very hard work. But unless it is seen as the task of the organization to lead change, the organization—whether business, university, hospital, and so on—will not survive.[5]

Obviously this isn't exclusive to your CIO. There are other serious players on your management staff who can lead change. But why not give yourself a stretch assignment and do something different? Why not start with IT for a change?

. . . .

Self-Assessment Three: Your Leadership Alignment

Who bears the blame for IT's problems isn't the question. You know as well as I do that won't stop the finger-pointing that happens as people shrink from accountability. The question is whether or not you're willing to speak the truth, and maybe even schedule a one-on-one with the CEO to lay out the issues and explore ways to fix them.

Bring the results of this final self-assessment with you to that meeting. It will let you pinpoint some of the more systemic problems and suggest ways to turn things around. In addition to a final score for this assessment, you'll be adding the scores from the other two self-assessments in Chapters 3 and 8, giving you a list of suggestions for where to begin.

Take the Assessment

As with the prior assessments, answer the questions in Table 11.1. For each question, you'll give yourself a score of 1 to 9 by measuring the degree to which the answer is positive or negative. The descriptions in the three columns will help guide you toward the best score.

You'll notice that the questions in this assessment aren't just about the current situation at your company. They're also about you and your ability to lead. To the extent that you're able, abandon your biases. There's a lot to learn from how well you and your colleagues are guiding IT into its—and your—next stage.

TABLE 11.1: Self-Assessment Three: Your Leadership Alignment

Question	Scoring Spectrum									Your Score
	1	2	3	4	5	6	7	8	9	
Work environment. How would you characterize your and your employees' work environment?	Our work environment is a holdover from the company's beginnings. The company doesn't spend money on workspace design or meeting-friendly spaces. People regularly describe the offices and common areas as "retro." The term "cell" has been used to describe someone's office or meeting room.			The company is investing in improvements to the buildings' interiors and exteriors. The company has made an effort to design and decorate offices and common areas. Workplace modernization plans are in the works.			The company has a recognizable aesthetic. Work areas are designed with employee work habits in mind. There are open spaces and plenty of meeting rooms, and there is access to private work spaces. The company offers recreation and fitness facilities. Employees can conduct personal business (for example, dry cleaning, child care) without leaving company premises.			
Skills delineation. How well does the company cultivate the individual skill sets of employees?	The company doesn't distinguish skills among individuals. It's more about hiring smart people. Everyone's replaceable. When people leave the company, HR gets into gear. Performance reviews are up to the employee's manager. There are no standards.			The company encourages skills or strengths assessments such as the Myers-Briggs Type Indicator or Gallup StrengthsFinder. Comprehensive job descriptions outline the ideal candidate's qualities and skills. We make sure that the interview and performance review processes include colleagues, not just the manager. This cements the team's charter and fosters unity.			The company mixes formal talent management processes with culture- and team-specific criteria. Interview and review processes encourage both hard and soft skills. Atypical qualities like curiosity and "willingness to fail" are considered. When people leave, their comments are heeded, and changes are routinely made to job descriptions, management policies, or measurement criteria.			

Question	Scoring Spectrum									Your Score
	1	2	3	4	5	6	7	8	9	
Diversity. Describe the company's emphasis on diversity.	We're not diverse, and behind closed doors, people sneer at the term. I've been told we don't need to worry about diversity because [insert the reason here]. Our diversity is manifested in the hiring habits of our senior leaders. Those habits trickle down. Enough said.			Executives have begun emphasizing the importance of diversity. We've just expanded internationally, so diversity is our new reality, whether we like it or not. A high-profile company just got into trouble for bad behavior, and our executives noticed. More attention to diversity is inevitable.			Diversity isn't just an HR priority. It's an executive priority. Diversity is visible at all levels of the corporate hierarchy. Our company mandates diversity training at the beginning and throughout an employee's tenure.			
Staffing. Are decisions about what work staff members take on deliberate and goal driven?	We don't qualify who works on what project. It's more about who's not busy. The most politically-savvy people tend to get the most interesting work. No one moves around here. You work on the project you were hired for.			There are identified talent pools for certain skills. People here call on the members of other teams for help based on the work they need done. The managers with the most successful projects tend to keep their staffs.			Business strategy informs each project, which in turn informs team members. Staff members are measured according to both company and discrete team goals. Improvement ideas during projects are encouraged, and improvement is rewarded.			

(continues)

TABLE 11.1: Self-Assessment Three: Your Leadership Alignment *(continued)*

Question	Scoring Spectrum			Your Score
	1 2 3	**4 5 6**	**7 8 9**	
Leadership and collaboration. What's your perception of how business and IT leaders are collaborating with respect to IT effectiveness and engagement?	Most people on the business side work around IT, and their management does little to discourage this. IT is still considered a cost center. Messaging from IT management perpetuates this reputation. Politics and turf wars have made everyone cynical.	Business unit heads are encouraging partnerships with IT on targeted projects. The CIO or CTO has just launched an initiative, lab, or other strategic project that is demonstrating IT's value. IT hiring has focused on more well-rounded workers, giving its reputation a shot in the arm.	IT leaders have recently presented compelling work that has led to measurable improvements both internally and externally. The CIO has presented a refreshing new model for IT and a plan for how to realize it. The CEO has recently encouraged support for key IT programs or restructuring.	
Bureaucracy. What's the perception of how smoothly technology is delivered? How easy is it to get things done?	No one really knows how to formally engage IT for new solutions or for technical help. Getting into IT's pipeline is cumbersome and often deemed not worth the effort. There's no transparency or collaboration. IT is considered a black hole.	The business units that work with IT have their own individual ways of engaging. How easy it is to work with IT comes down to the individual team and its members. IT is easy to work with if the business sponsor is strong and provides clarity.	IT has a lightweight and formal engagement process. IT is transparent and proactive. There is an Internet portal or social media community that makes it easy to view progress and ask questions. The CEO or board regularly publishes IT successes and measurements in their internal communications.	

Question	Scoring Spectrum			Your Score
	1 2 3	4 5 6	7 8 9	
Governance. How is IT governed, and is that oversight considered a competency or a barrier?	The company culture is averse to any type of formal governance. The word "governance" is received with humor at best, skepticism at worst. If there is any governance, no one outside of IT knows about it.	IT governance has begun, but its value is still in question. There are "pockets of governance" within IT, with reliable oversight processes in place. Governance is being rolled out based on the company culture's acceptable rate of change.	IT leaders are transparent about how they prioritize activities, select and procure technologies, and measure results. Senior executives participate in IT steering committees and funding decisions. Governance has been linked to strategic enablement or competitive advantage.	
Leadership involvement. How active are IT executives in senior management? How involved are they in strategic, financial, competitive, or customer-focused conversations?	IT management is completely marginalized here. They're not seen as leaders; they're techies. The CIO or CTO are called upstairs only when something breaks.	IT leadership participates in senior management meetings when IT status updates are requested. IT leaders and key managers are called on when strategic initiatives are understood to require new technology. The CIO has strong relationships with some—but not all—business leaders.	The CIO is an active member of the management team. The CIO has successfully delegated key operational functions, thus ensuring time for more strategic and competitive involvement. The CIO is externally visible, ensuring that the company is acknowledged in the marketplace for technology innovation.	
			Total Score	

What Your Score Means

- **A score of 8 to 24.** A low score suggests that leadership has a credibility problem or that key decisions don't have teeth. Check your workplace. It's likely that employees aren't accountable for collaborating, nor are they measured on their support of executive mandates. It's likely that there are no visible rewards for taking risks and driving toward more diversity or working within new organizational structures. And equally, there might not be penalties for sticking with the status quo. Meanwhile, CIOs and business leaders jut against one another like tectonic plates, and the resulting movement is not so much an organizational earthquake as it is a series of destabilizing temblors. This lack of strong leadership might result from the aforementioned phenomenon of IT being the organization of "No," particularly when nobody loses anything by avoiding collaboration, rejecting new ideas, or hunkering down to avoid any type of change. Employees and managers who experiment with new ways of working and who support one another's big ideas do so without sanctions from leadership, suggesting institutional ambivalence about people's value.

- **A score of 25 to 48.** If you scored in the middle, it might mean that leadership is situational at your company and relying on human relationships and rule breaking are the best ways to get things done. While the well-meaning leaders who take these routes do so in order to accomplish often-important tasks, the "Ask for forgiveness, not permission" tactic is only as effective as the leaders who share the zeitgeist. It's not scalable, and it's not sustainable. Having so-called pockets of competence might work when it comes to fulfilling operational goals, but over the long term, they never get enough traction to be truly strategic.

- **A score of 49 to 72.** A score of 49 or higher means that executive leaders are getting it. They are fostering a culture of transparency by making their goals clear, and they are holding people accountable for their contributions to those goals. They are also cultivating an awareness that the company is changing in order to meet market demands for skilled staff members, a broader perspective, and a renewed role for technology as strategic. It's also likely that they're modifying their own behaviors in order to reach this new frontier.

Okay, So Now What?

Using Table 11.2, let's calculate your "what to do next" score by bringing in the scores from the book's prior two self-assessments.

TABLE 11.2: Calculating Your "What to Do Next" Score

Self-Assessment	Your Score
1. The Scope of the Problem	
2. Your Transformation Readiness	
3. Your Leadership Alignment	
Total Score	

If Your Total Score Is 24 to 72

I'll reiterate the point made in the earlier assessments that scoring in this tier indicates the need for change, if not wholesale modernization. Or perhaps a leadership shakeup.

This isn't to say that your IT department isn't delivering on its objectives or that there isn't strong leadership. The question that needs to be asked is this: "Are we doing enough to stay at parity or better with our competitors?"

If you're a leader in IT, this might present nothing short of a metaphysical reckoning since it's likely that you could be contributing much more than you are. Think about it. You're getting the message from your boss and peers to keep your nose to the grindstone. ("Just keep doing what you're doing" is the clarion call of the ordinary leader.)

Sure, you might have scored higher on specific assessment questions. There are pockets of competence at every company. You can try to drive small, incremental change in the interest of seeding improvements. If you need to, reread Chapter 2 to reconfirm your as-is and to-be IT archetypes. Then craft your pitch for an evolution, putting some pieces in place to cultivate a more robust partner network, shedding commodity technologies to the cloud, or inspiring business and IT colleagues to begin a healthier and more regular dialogue.

On the other hand, you might know in your gut that it's time for you to make a move. Your company isn't going to innovate anytime soon. Its vision statement sounds like a game of Mad Libs, complete with absurd exhortations and buzzwords. Heretofore strategic projects disappear from the radar with no explanation. Executives mumble opaque references to unanticipated market forces and budget constraints. Booking a meeting room with a projector takes an act of Congress. People who stick their necks out are sidelined. Closed-door chatter about transfers of power amounts to nothing. No one knows where the company is headed, but everyone continues to hang on for dear life.

Is this a company that deserves you? Can you honestly say you're doing your best work? Or are you waiting for some career deus ex machina to provide the answer?

So I'll ask the same question I asked my client Mike at the beginning of Chapter 1: "Who do you want to be?" If your answer isn't "Me right now, contributing, learning, and making a difference," then start working your network.

If Your Total Score Is 73 to 144

Change is afoot, and it's had a ripple effect. Some of that change has already affected the way IT works, and that's largely good news. Sure, there are the naysayers and saboteurs, but mostly everyone's on board and supporting evolving strategies, new delivery processes, and an increasingly technology-savvy business community.

If your total score falls in this category, it's likely that senior-level managers are saying and doing the right things, for the most part. They might have issues with execution. This is particularly true as new strategies beget new delivery mechanisms (think digital and big data). The adoption of emerging technologies by nontraditional constituents introduces additional risks, including slower time to market, higher initial costs, and ownership boundaries that have been upended as the lines blur between technologies, people, and accountability.

Admit it. There's still a play-it-safe mentality at your company. As a leader, you can push against it. Be on the side of experimentation and discovery, advocating a shift toward trial and error and original thinking. Bang the drum on behalf of your employees and peers for measurement and new reward systems, as well as a more friendly and flexible work environment. In addition to helping your company, this will (as good as you are) stretch your own skills. Your company deserves the intervention, and you deserve the newfound wisdom you'll get by going there. Now go.

If Your Total Score Is 145 to 216

Sure, you've earned that swagger. Your leadership has not only encouraged changes from the top down but it has also nurtured new thinking from the bottom up. People aren't only saying but doing the right things. As we've shown through the profiles of exemplary leaders, IT maturity is ultimately achieved through delivery.

You're not off the hook. Figure out where you might have scored in the assessment's middle or bottom tiers, and understand the root causes behind why. Are remedies being tried? Is there an individual to blame for the status quo? If you're an IT leader, find out how IT can help.

Indeed, bringing lines of business closer to IT, fueling new ways to connect and collaborate, can actually inspire team unity in other areas of the company. "I call it 'convening the core,'" a CEO told me. "I don't do a lot of the off-site recreational activities, like swinging from trees. This is more about getting people together to go on record with the what-ifs. I ask everyone to explain their best- and worst-case scenarios. It usually comes down to giving up control. But it's my job to show them that prestige and promotions don't come from control. They come from participation."

Leaders like this—and perhaps, like you—do more than simply inspire their teams. They encourage new attitudes and belief systems from the bottom up. This isn't management by finger wagging. These leaders walk the talk, changing their own behaviors in order to model the desired state. (Intel's Andy Grove, former New York mayor Michael Bloomberg, and Meg Whitman when she led eBay famously worked among their staffs in cubicles.)

Don't pave over those executive parking spaces just yet. Focus on fostering the trust necessary to incent influential employees to follow your lead. Being ambitious on behalf of your company can help you realize your own ambitions. The point is to lead by example and toward desired behaviors.

Examine your desired-state IT archetype. Are you and your team modeling the behaviors that will help you get there? Is your CEO?

NOTE TO THE CEO

Total digitization. The cloud. Advanced analytics. Big and bigger data. Agile anything. Robotics. The Internet of everything. The impact of these and other high-tech developments will hinge on the ability of leaders in both business and IT to drive transformative change, to be more nimble in their delivery, and to fulfill corporate objectives.

You have a choice. You can sit back and watch as your personality-driven culture rewards its squeaky wheels and penalizes thoughtfulness, failing to recognize improvements and to formalize processes that produced them.

Or you can begin seeding change, recognizing the role that technology can play in your company's future, rewarding the agents who deliver it, and renewing the role of the IT group, whatever its ideal archetype might be.

And someday in the not-too-distant future, you'll be in a meeting, and it will dawn on you that these changes are making a difference at your company and that something you did, some series of decisions—perhaps inspired by a discussion in this book—made things a little better than they were.

Coda

In keeping with the book's rock and roll references, I felt that some sort of culminating anthem was in order to set you on your path to IT transformation. I walked around singing various Nirvana, AC/DC, and Led Zeppelin lyrics quietly to myself (an act of discipline, for sure) in hopes of stumbling upon some transcendent inspiration.

I finally settled not on a lyric, but on a passage from a book. After all, who better to inspire than Keith Richards? In his memoir, *Life*, the legendary Rolling Stones guitarist describes his longtime collaboration with Mick Jagger. He remembers their early partnership this way:

> First off, we never had to question the aim. We were unerring in where we wanted to go, what it should sound like, so we didn't have to discuss it, just figure a way to do it. We didn't have to talk about the target, we knew what it was. It was basically just to be able to make records. The targets get bigger as things happen.[1]

Notes

Chapter 1

1. Paul Babiak and Robert D. Hare, *Snakes in Suits: When Psychopaths Go to Work* (New York: HarperBusiness, 2007).
2. Bill Inmon, "Big Data: Who's Leading the Charge?" *B-eye-Network* blog, January 9, 2014, http://www.b-eye-network.com/view/16942.
3. Jim Stikeleather, "The IT Conversation We Should Be Having," HBR blog network, April 25, 2013, http://blogs.hbr.org/cs/2013/04/corporate_it_and_the_conversat.html.
4. Nicco Mele, *The End of Big: How the Internet Makes David the New Goliath* (New York: St. Martin's Press, 2013), p. 225.
5. "State of the CIO 2013: Elevating Your Game," *CIO Magazine*, January 1, 2013, p. 36.

Chapter 2

1. From a PowerPoint presentation shown at the Gartner Symposium/ITxpo 2014, October 5–9, 2014, Orlando, Florida, https://twitter.com/hashtag/GartnerSYM.
2. Bob Ronan, "Is Your IT Shop a Scrambler or a Leader?" *CIO Magazine*, February 26, 2014, http://www.cio.com/article/748481/Is_Your_IT_Shop_a_Scrambler_or_a_Leader.html.

Chapter 3

1. "2014 State of the CIO," *CIO Magazine*, January 2, 2014.
2. Gordon Barnett, "IT's Business Capability Map Guides IT Evolution," Forrester Research, July 24, 2013, www.forrester.com.

Chapter 4

1. A 2013 Bain & Company Management Tools & Trends survey of 1,208 global executives found that strategic planning was the tool that executives considered to be the most important in their leadership functions. See Figure 8: http://www.bain.com/publications/articles/management-tools-and-trends-2013.aspx.
2. Chris Heivly, "The One Word That Will Crash Your New Consulting Business," *Inc.*, July 17, 2014, http://www.inc.com/chris-heivly/the-one-word-that-will-crash-your-new-consulting-business.html.
3. Richard P. Rumelt, *Good Strategy, Bad Strategy* (New York: Crown Business, 2011), p. 66.

4. Robert S. Kaplan and David P. Norton, *The Execution Premium: Linking Strategy to Operations for Competitive Advantage* (Boston: Harvard Business Review Press, 2008).
5. Naufal Khan and Johnson Sikes, "IT Under Pressure: McKinsey Global Survey Results," Insights & Publications, McKinsey & Company, March 2014, http://www.mckinsey .com/insights/business_technology/it_under_pressure_mckinsey_global_survey_results.

Chapter 5

1. See Robert Plant, "A Kodak Moment to Reconsider the Value of IT," *Harvard Business Review* blog, October 12, 2011, http://blogs.hbr.org/2011/10/a-kodak-moment-to -reconsider-t/.
2. CheckFree was acquired by Fiserv Corporation in 2007, http://www.checkfreecorp .fiserv.com/cda/corp/.
3. Build Network Staff, "Every Misaligned Team Is Misaligned in Its Own Way," published in *Build Quarterly*, October 2, 2013, and in *Inc.* as a Navigator Survey, December 20, 2013.
4. CEB report, *The Rise of the Network Leader*, http://www.executiveboard.com/exbd/executive -guidance/2014/annual/index.page?path=phero&cid=701800000018liH.
5. Nicolai Wadstrom, "Reinventing IT: Clayton M. Christensen at Gartner Symposium 2011," October 19, 2011, http://nicolaiwadstrom.com/blog/2011/12/05/reinventing -it-clayton-m-christensen-gartner-symposium-2011/.

Chapter 6

1. Dan Munro, "The Big Disruption That Isn't Happening in Healthcare," Forbes.com, September 6, 2013, http://www.forbes.com/sites/danmunro/2013/09/06/the-big -disruption-that-isnt-happening-in-healthcare/.
2. See Phil Thames, "Can the Cloud, ITIL, and ITSM Coexist?" *Leverhawk* blog, September 25, 2013, http://leverhawk.com/can-cloud-itil-itsm-coexist-20130925462.
3. Laura McLellan, research vice president, Gartner, "By 2017 the CMO Will Spend More on IT Than the CIO," webinar, January 3, 2012. See www.gartner.com.
4. Peter Weill and Jeanne Ross, *IT Savvy: What Top Executives Must Know to Go from Pain to Gain* (Boston: Harvard Business School Press, 2009).

Chapter 7

1. "Harvey Nash CIO Survey of 3,211 IT Leaders in over 30 Countries," April 2014, http://www.harveynash.com/ciosurvey/.
2. Torben Schubert, Peter Neuhauseler, Rainer Frietsch, Christian Rammer, and Hugo Hollanders, *Innovation Indicator: Methodology Report*, October 2011, http://www .innovationsindikator.de/fileadmin/user_upload/Dokumente/Innovationsindikator _methodology_report.pdf. This paper describes indicators of economic innovations used by Deutsche Telekom in conjunction with other business partners.
3. Janaki Akella, Sam Marwaha, and Johnson Sikes, *How CIOs Can Lead Their Company's [sic] Information Business*, McKinsey & Company Business Technology Office report, May 2014.
4. Accenture Survey of 1,041 C-Level Executives in 20 Countries, January 2014.
5. Roger L. Martin, "Rethinking the Decision Factory," *Harvard Business Review*, October 2013.

6. Gavin Newsom and Lisa Dickey, *Citizenville: How to Take the Town Square Digital and Reinvent Government* (New York: Penguin Press, 2013), p. 204.
7. "Harvey Nash CIO Survey."
8. Joanna Barsh, "Innovative Management: A Conversation with Gary Hamel and Lowell Bryan," *McKinsey Quarterly* 2008, no. 1, p. 54.
9. Rob Petersen, "21 Companies Use Gamification to Get Better Business Results," BarnRaisers .com blog, March 30, 2013.

Chapter 8

1. "Harvey Nash CIO Survey of 3,211 IT Leaders in over 30 Countries," April 2014, http://www.harveynash.com/ciosurvey/.

Chapter 9

1. See Computerworld Salary Survey 2014: http://www.computerworld.com/s/article /9246878/IT_Salary_Survey_2014.
2. Peter Cappelli, "Talent Management for the Twenty-First Century," *Harvard Business Review*, March 2008.
3. Farhad Manjoo, "Exposing Hidden Bias at Google," *New York Times*, September 24, 2014, http://www.nytimes.com/2014/09/25/technology/exposing-hidden-biases -at-google-to-improve-diversity.html?_r=0.
4. Owen Thomas, "How Airbnb Manages Not to Manage Engineers," readwrite.com, June 5, 2014, http://readwrite.com/2014/06/05/airbnb-engineering-management-mike-curtis -interview#awesm=~oGmD3FnvPScxFY.
5. John Mackey and Rajendra Sisodia, *Conscious Capitalism* (Boston: Harvard Business School Publishing, 2014). See also the Conscious Capitalism website, www.conscious capitalism.org.
6. See Michael Watkins, *The First 90 Days* (Boston: Harvard Business School Publishing, 2003).
7. *Mike Rowe Suggests a Solution for the Skills Gap*, Learning Series Channel, engineering.com, http://www.engineering.com/Videos/LearningSeriesChannel/VideoId/3360/Mike -Rowe-Suggests-A-Solution-For-The-Skills-Gap.aspx#.U4oKpu7WrqQ.twitter.

Chapter 10

1. Jon Stewart interview with Peter Schuck, *The Daily Show with Jon Stewart*, Comedy Central, aired on May 6, 2014.
2. Roger Martin, "How Successful Leaders Think," *Harvard Business Review*, June 2007.
3. W. Chan Kim and Renée Mauborgne, "How Strategy Shapes Structure," *Harvard Business Review*, September 2009.
4. Simon Sinek, "How Great Leaders Inspire Action," TEDxPugetSound, September 2009, http://www.ted.com/talks/simon_sinek_how_great_leaders_inspire_action.
5. Peter F. Drucker, *Management Challenges for the 21st Century* (New York: HarperCollins, 1999).

Coda

1. Keith Richards, *Life* (New York: Little, Brown & Company, 2010).

Song Lyrics Credits

Chapter 1
"Century City"
Words and Music by Tom Petty
Copyright © 1979 TARKA MUSIC
All Rights Administered by ALMO MUSIC CORP.
All Rights Reserved. Used by Permission.
Reprinted by Permission of Hal Leonard Corporation

Chapter 2
"Glycerine"
Words and Music by Gavin Rossdale
Copyright © 1994 BMG Rights Management (UK) Ltd (PRS)
All Rights Administered by BMG Rights Management (US) LLC
International Copyright Secured. All Rights Reserved.
Reprinted by Permission of Hal Leonard Corporation

Chapter 4
"Don't Look Back"
Words and Music by Tom Scholz
Copyright © 1978 Pure Songs
All Rights Administered by Next Decade Entertainment, Inc.
All Rights Reserved. Used by Permission.
Reprinted by Permission of Hal Leonard Corporation

Chapter 5
"Paranoid"
Words and Music by Anthony Iommi, John Osbourne, William Ward, and Terence Butler
© Copyright 1970 (Renewed) Westminster Music Ltd., London, England
TRO–Essex Music International, Inc., New York, controls all publication rights for the
 U.S.A. and Canada.
Used by Permission.

Chapter 6
"Fell on Black Days"
Words and Music by Chris Cornell
Copyright © 1994 You Make Me Sick I Make Music
All Rights Administered by BMG Rights Management (US) LLC
International Copyright Secured. All Rights Reserved.
Reprinted by Permission of Hal Leonard Corporation

Chapter 9
"You've Got Another Thing Comin'"
Written by Glenn Raymond Tipton, Kenneth Downing, and Robert Halford
Copyright © 1982 EMI April Music Inc., Crewglen Ltd., Geargate Ltd., Ebonytree Ltd.
All Rights Administered by Sony/ATV Music Publishing LLC, 424 Church Street, Nash-
ville, TN 37219
All Rights Reserved. Used by Permission.

Chapter 10
Free Bird
Words and Music by Allen Collins and Ronnie Van Zant
Copyright © 1973, 1975 Songs of Universal, Inc. in the United States and Canada and Duchess
Music Corporation elsewhere throughout the world.
Copyrights Renewed.
All rights for Duchess Music Corporation administered by Universal/MCA Music Limited.
All Rights Reserved. Used by Permission.
Reprinted by Permission of Hal Leonard Corporation and Music Sales Limited.

Index

About the Author

 **Jill Dyché**—frank, funny, and full of great stories—has been thinking, writing, and speaking about business-IT alignment for over two decades. In her career as a consultant and advisor to executives across industries, she's seen technology organizations deliver strategic change, and she has worked with managers across IT and business functions to make it stick.

Jill has lived in far-flung locales including Paris, London, and Sydney, lecturing at industry conferences, tech events, and leading business schools, and blogging on the topic of why corporate technologies are—or, at least *should be*—business driven. She is the author of *e-Data* (Addison-Wesley, 2000), *The CRM Handbook* (Addison-Wesley, 2002), and with coauthor Evan Levy, *Customer Data Integration* (Wiley, 2007). Her work has been featured in numerous magazines and journals including Newsweek.com, HBR.org, *Information Week*, *Computerworld*, and Forbes.com.

Jill was the cofounder of Baseline Consulting, a management consulting firm that was acquired by SAS in 2011. She lives in Los Angeles, where she samples fringe Cabernets, rescues shelter dogs, and writes the occasional haiku. Reach her at jill.dyche@sas.com.